MANAGING
WEB PROJECTS

ESI International Project Management Series

Series Editor
J. LeRoy Ward, Executive Vice President
ESI International
Arlington, Virginia

Managing Web Projects
Edward B. Farkas
1-4398-0495-7

Project Management Recipes for Success
Guy L. De Furia
1-4200-7824-4

Building a Project Work Breakdown Structure: Visualizing Objectives, Deliverables, Activities, and Schedules
Dennis P. Miller
1-4200-6969-3

A Standard for Enterprise Project Management
Michael S. Zambruski
1-4200-7245-5

Determining Project Requirements
Hans Jonasson
1-4200-4502-4

The Complete Project Management Office Handbook, Second Edition
Gerard M. Hill
1-4200-4680-2

Practical Guide to Project Planning
Ricardo Viana Vargas
1-4200-4504-0

Other ESI International Titles Available from
Auerbach Publications, Taylor & Francis Group

PMP® Challenge! Fourth Edition
J. LeRoy Ward and Ginger Levin
ISBN: 1-8903-6740-0

PMP® Exam: Practice Test and Study Guide, Seventh Edition
J. LeRoy Ward
ISBN: 1-8903-6741-9

The Project Management Drill Book: A Self-Study Guide
Carl L. Pritchard
ISBN: 1-8903-6734-6

Project Management Terms: A Working Glossary, Second Edition
J. LeRoy Ward
ISBN: 1-8903-6725-7

Project Management Tools CD, Version 4.3
ESI International
ISBN: 1-8903-6736-2

MANAGING WEB PROJECTS

EDWARD B. FARKAS

CRC Press
Taylor & Francis Group
Boca Raton London New York

CRC Press is an imprint of the
Taylor & Francis Group, an **informa** business

CRC Press
Taylor & Francis Group
6000 Broken Sound Parkway NW, Suite 300
Boca Raton, FL 33487-2742

First issued in paperback 2017

© 2010 by Taylor and Francis Group, LLC
CRC Press is an imprint of Taylor & Francis Group, an Informa business

No claim to original U.S. Government works

ISBN-13: 978-1-4398-0495-7 (hbk)
ISBN-13: 978-1-138-11602-3 (pbk)

Library of Congress Cataloging-in-Publication Data

Farkas, Edward B.
    Managing web projects / author, Edward B. Farkas.
        p. cm. -- (ESI international project management series)
    "A CRC title."
    Includes index.
    ISBN 978-1-4398-0495-7 (hardcover : alk. paper)
    1. Web site development. 2. Project management. I. Title. II. Series.

    TK5105.888.F368 2010
    006.7--dc22   2009030586

Visit the Taylor & Francis Web site at
http://www.taylorandfrancis.com

and the CRC Press Web site at
http://www.crcpress.com

Contents

Web Download

Checklists, forms, and templates listed in Chapter 6 may be downloaded from:

www.crcpress.com/product/isbn/9781439804957

Preface

How to Use This Book

The book is divided into four parts: a step-by-step guide to managing Web projects; instructions for creating a quality system that will continually improve your project management methodology; reproducible tools and templates, and wraps up with technical and project management glossaries with associated formulas. Throughout, you will find many useful hints and insights.

The flow of the step-by-step guide is synchronized with a typical Internet project life cycle. At the end of each project phase you will find a "What do I do now?" box containing practical tips.

The book includes a tools suite with a proven track record of success, containing—

- Project initiation tools
- Project planning tools
- Project execution tools
- Project control tools
- Project close-out tools

The book, additionally, includes Work Instructions that can be used to develop a formal quality management system specific to a project management organization. If you seek ISO 9001 certification, the Work Instructions will be invaluable. The Work Instructions can also be leveraged in either a TQM (Total Quality Management) or a Six Sigma environment. While they are not specific to the CMMi (Capability Maturity Model) or ITIL (Information Technology Infrastructure Library) frameworks, they are compatible with the planning and deployment elements or processes. The glossary portion of the book contains the following useful sections:

- A project management acronym table
- An Internet project management glossary
- A technical Internetworking glossary

The methodology defined in this book is applicable for the implementation of most Internetworking projects and Internet Service Provider (ISP) offers, including:

- Managed Web hosting
- Collocation Web hosting
- Application loading and testing
- Web site security products
- Web site load (stress) tests
- Web site load balancing
- Virtual Private Network (VPN)
- Voice-over-IP (VoIP)
- Disaster Recovery

Introduction

This book has been designed for project managers in the Internetworking industry, which includes everything from Web developers to Internet Service Providers (ISPs). It will walk you through a typical project life cycle, and provide you with a comprehensive set of practical tools.

Project Management is a profession based on a body of knowledge and internationally accepted standards codified in the Guide to the Project Management Body of Knowledge (PMBOK®) and a group of Practice Standards focused on specific elements of importance to the practice of project and program management. University-level certificate and master's degree programs, as well as most professional project management training and certification programs, are based on the PMBOK® and the related Practice Standards. The Project Management Institute (PMI) helped develop the PMBOK®. Additionally, the Project Management Institute manages an internationally recognized certification program. Project managers can become Certified Associate Project Managers (CAPM®) or Project Management Professionals (PMP®). A number of the Project Management Institute's standards have been adopted by other professional organizations such as the Institute of Electrical and Electronics Engineers, Inc. (IEEE), the International Standards Organization (ISO), and the American National Standards Institute (ANSI).

The PMBOK® includes the following nine knowledge areas:

1. Project Integration Management
2. Project Scope Management
3. Project Time Management
4. Project Human Resource Management
5. Project Cost Management
6. Project Risk Management

7. Project Quality Management
8. Project Procurement Management
9. Project Communications Management

In addition to the nine knowledge areas the PMBOK® includes five major processes:

1. Initiation
2. Planning
3. Executing
4. Controlling
5. Closing

This book will focus on those areas of the PMBOK® that correspond to Internetworking project management. In other words, the book will show you *how* to get the projects done! You will learn how to go from an architecture diagram to the deployment of sites on the World Wide Web.

The tools, methods, and techniques in the book can also be used for managing programs, Program Offices, or ongoing support functions. The book will help you lead project teams and manage your customers' expectations.

Checklists, forms, and templates from Chapter 6 may be downloaded from:

www.crcpress.com/product/isbn/9781439804957

They are in Word or Excel formats and may be customized.

About the Author

Edward B. Farkas, CFC, CHS, MIEEE, PMP, has worked as a project and program manager in the public and private sectors. During his career he has managed over $6 billion of aviation, construction, engineering, ecommerce, information technology, public safety, and telecommunication projects in Argentina, Colombia, China, England, Hong Kong, Saudi Arabia, and the United States, and has firmly established his reputation as an expert in program project management services all over the world. He is a published author and frequent guest speaker at distinguished educational institutions and professional organizations such as the Project Management Institute and the New York Software Industry Association. Mr. Farkas' undergraduate degrees are in engineering and management; he is a certified Project Management Professional, certified Lead ISO (Quality Management Systems) Auditor, Certified Forensic Consultant, and Certified in Homeland Security—Level III. He is currently a program director for a major government agency and, time permitting, teaches project management for the City University of New York.

Chapter 1

The Project Life Cycle

Project Integration

Understanding project integration requires viewing where and how the project manager fits into the project life cycle. To do this, we first need to examine a typical Internet project life-cycle methodology.

This is a high-level view of the key processes and the project manager's role in them. Subsequent parts of the book will further define the terms and related mechanisms.

In many companies, a typical project life cycle contains phases such as Concept, Development, Execution, and Termination. Another example is Concept, Requirements Definition, Development, Testing, and Close-Out. In an Information Technology Infrastructure Library (ITIL) framework organization, you might have Service Strategy, Service Design, Service Transition, Service Operations, and Continual Service Improvement.

In an Internet methodology, there typically are seven phases in the project life cycle:

Phase 1: Presales
Phase 2: Project Planning
Phase 3: Provisioning
Phase 4: Acceptance Testing
Phase 5: Site Launch Support or going live
Phase 6: Quality Assurance
Phase 7: Ongoing Support

Presales

The Presales phase includes solution design and proposal development. The sales team provides the scope definition of the work by identifying the technical, business, and customer requirements for a solution. Key deliverables in this phase are the development of a quotation, offer, or statement of work (SOW), and in many cases a design document or drawing.

The project manager reviews the design documents, which typically include an architecture. The project manager should make sure that the bill of materials (BOM) is complete. The BOM should list all the hardware components and all the software elements shown or implied in the architectural drawing. A complete BOM will result in better cost estimates. Another benefit of a complete BOM is avoiding delays due to incomplete purchasing or shipping.

Beyond ensuring the integrity of the BOM, with the assistance of the project team's architect, the project manager performs a scope analysis by reviewing the scope documents to identify the following.

1. Project stakeholders
2. Project constraints
3. Project dependencies
   a. Customer
   b. Third parties
   c. Internet service providers (ISPs)
4. Assumptions that may become risk issues or are dependencies.
5. Initial project risks. A more detailed risk analysis is completed during the project planning phase, employing tools that will be described later.
6. Deliverables

The scope analysis will yield critical inputs to the project planning effort. For example, knowing the stakeholders helps determine the project's organization breakdown structure (OBS) as well as the Project Communications Plan. The identified constraints, for example, may influence the schedule's end date or be managed as a potential project risk. The Tools and Templates section in Chapter 6 includes a scope review guide that will facilitate a detailed scope analysis.

Table 1.1 shows how the scope analysis yields critical information needed to develop a project plan.

Tip: *When you read the scope documents highlight, in different colors, text that describes stakeholders, constraints, dependencies, assumptions, and risks. When you go back to the scope documents to develop the project plan the highlighting will save you a lot of time.*

An alternative tool, Table 1.2, is displayed in the following text; this can be in either MS Word or Excel.

Table 1.1 Results of Scope Analysis

Element	Leads to	Drives
Project Stakeholders	Responsibility Assignment Matrix, Communications Plan	Resource Management, Expectations Management
Project Constraints	Potential risks, possible milestones, potential end dates	Project Schedule
Project dependencies	Potential risks	Risk Management Plan, Project Schedule
Assumptions	Potential risks or dependencies	Schedule or Risk Management Plan
Project Risks	Risk Management Plan	Resources, Project Schedule
Deliverables	Work breakdown structure	Work packages—levels of effort, Project Quality Plan

Table 1.2 Scope Analysis Table

Scope Analysis					
Stakeholder	Deliverable	Dependency	Assumption	Risk	Constraint

Additionally, for complex projects, the project manager decomposes the scope of work by developing a work breakdown structure (WBS). Later, we give a step-by-step guide to help you create a WBS. One of the many WBS outputs is an understanding of the project manager's level of effort (LOE), which helps determine the labor hours you will need to manage the project. The LOE output will also determine the labor hours the project team will need to complete the project. The project manager is responsible for evaluating the scope of work.

Ideally, the project manager should be sufficiently empowered to withhold approval from project scope documents when the scope analysis indicates constraints, dependencies, and risks will jeopardize the project's success. When the project manager is not sufficiently empowered, the concerns from the scope analysis should be well documented and shared with the project team.

This phase ends after the opportunity has been approved.

Project Planning

Upon the project manager's approval of the scope of work, and in many cases the cost, defined in the quotation, SOW, or contract, the project manager proceeds with the development of a project plan. The project plan, at minimum includes a Project Scope Analysis, Risk Breakdown Structure, Risk Management Plan, and a Project Schedule. The project plan may be expanded to include a baseline WBS, Escalation Matrix, Communications Plan, Responsibilities Assignment Matrix, Resource Management Plan, Roles and Responsibilities Chart, Organization Breakdown Structure, and other plan elements described in greater detail in the following text.

The number of project plan elements is a function of the project's complexity. A listing of the plan elements is displayed in Table 1.3.

The project manager chairs the internal kick-off meeting with all the internal stakeholders. The internal kick-off meeting is designed to ensure that the deliverables and project plan are finalized and agreed upon. The internal kick-off meeting facilitates the project team's buy-in and resource commitments. This meeting may include subcontractors and in some cases suppliers as well.

Prior to the external (customer facing) kick-off meeting, the project manager should develop a communications plan for the meeting. This will determine who presents the plan, responds to questions, and manages expectations.

After the internal meeting, the project manager runs the external (customer-facing) kick-off meeting to obtain customer sign-off on the deliverables and the project plan. The next phase begins upon the completion of the external kick-off meeting.

The external kick-off meeting is an invaluable opportunity to manage the customer's expectations! If, for example, an external risk has been identified along with a plan to manage it, the external kick-off meeting may be the best time to secure the customer's buy-in of the proposed risk response. Candid communication at this point will go a long way to avoiding "surprises" that internal and external managers do not wish to have.

Refer to the Tools section to access the Project Kick-Off template that can be used to manage the kick-off meeting.

Table 1.3   Project Plan Elements

Project Plan Element	Why and What the Element Represents
Activity Sequence Diagram	Helps determine the critical path; can be used to calculate project level start and end dates (backward and forward pass techniques); provides a foundation for the project
(Network)	Schedule.
Communications Plan	Determines content and frequency of reports; defines who can discuss issues with the customer.
Escalation Matrix	(This may be part of the Communications Plan) Defines how and within what time frame issues are escalated—and to whom.
Organization Breakdown Structure	Similar to an Org Chart; clarifies the working relationships associated with the project. (In many cases, this will translate to a project team matrix.)
Project Schedule	Defines the tasks and subtasks of project activities; typically determines which resources will be applied to the task and subtasks; provides specific time frames for completion of activities and milestones.
Responsibilities Assignment Matrix	Determines what each member of the project team is responsible for. (For example, who approves scope changes.)
Risk Breakdown Structure	This can help define the risks associated with the project.
Risk Management Plan	Identifies risk issues by root cause and indicates how each risk issue will be managed.
Roles and Responsibilities Chart	This can indicate who does what and when.
Work Breakdown Structure	Helps break down the project deliverable which, in turn, facilitates definition of work packages that simplify level of effort calculations.

Additional planning tools that are available in the Tools section include the following:

1. Scope review guide (also used during the Presales Phase)
2. Risk management checklists
3. Project schedule templates, offering various levels of complexity

Tip: *If you define successful project completion as part of the external kick-off meeting, you can avoid problems later on. Gain buy-in from internal and external stakeholders, and document your common understanding of the goals of the project. For example, Success might be a dedicated server, with a certain amount of memory, and an architecture that will back up files every night. If this is documented as the measure of successful project completion, then there should be no misunderstandings later on regarding the frequency of data backups or the fact that automatic virus protection and root access are not part of the scope. Service level agreements (SLAs) are often used to define ISP responsibilities such as maximum percentage of server down time, site access time, time frames for problem resolution, and more.*

Provisioning

Most ISPs use the term *provisioning* to describe the physical installation of hardware and software. For Web hosting projects, this term also covers the associated order management activities. For nonhosting projects, *circuit provisioning* and *provisioning* are common terms.

Other corporations may use equivalent terms such as *construction, deployment,* and *installation* to describe an implementation. During this phase, the project manager tracks the tasks; monitors the milestones, dependencies, risks; and communicates status information to internal and external stakeholders, as needed. The Tools section has tools, such as the Progress Meeting template, to facilitate the management of this phase.

Project managers can control the labor hours charged to the project employing earned value management (EVM) formulas that will be detailed later.

Tip: *Checking the status of intermediate milestones can provide early warnings of potential schedule delays.*

Acceptance Testing

Upon completion of the provisioning of at least one unit or server, a unit acceptance test (UAT) is conducted and the Acceptance Testing phase begins. Project managers ensure that UAT has been completed and that all the units have passed the test.

The *unit* in UAT refers to a server. Depending on the ISP procedures, UAT has different meanings. For some ISPs, UAT is no more than proving a communication link from the operations group or operations center to the server in the data center. For other ISPs, UAT includes verification that the server's operating system (OS) has been loaded. In application development, UAT is used to refer to customer testing from a usability perspective.

For further details on acceptance testing, see the "Work Instruction— Acceptance Testing" in Chapter 5. Note that this phase does not include the validation of acceptance testing by the customer, only UAT testing.

If the ISP has the technical capacity, it is advisable to request a test of the entire architecture. The architecture test, sometimes known as a *systems test*, should include key functions such as data backup and recovery. The systems test includes all hardware components, such as routers, not just the servers.

The object of this phase is to ensure that the ISP has provided the customer all contractual deliverables in working order. This assurance will aid in managing, and meeting, the customer's expectations.

Tip: *Well-thought-out testing protocols can mitigate risk issues. For example, if the customer is providing applications, UAT and system testing prior to loading the software will eliminate finger pointing if the loaded application is not working correctly. By eliminating the server or architecture as a possible cause, the customer and the project team know that the problem resides in the customer-provided software.*

Site Launch Support

Let's begin by defining the term *launch support*. This phase begins after the servers or system is handed off to the customer. It concludes when the applications (software) the server will run have been installed. The contract determines which party is responsible for loading and testing the applications.

The timing for the beginning of this phase will vary, especially for those projects that include a phased implementation whereby completed components and servers are incrementally handed off to the customer. This phase is best described as proactively planning the "hands-on" post-provisioning customer support needs. Customer support is most critical if, based on the contract, customers begin installing their own content and applications in preparation for launching their Web site on the new servers.

Chapter 5 contains suggested procedures that can be used to manage the Launch Support phase.

Quality Assurance

When the implementation is complete, the project manager requests the customer to complete your organization's customer satisfaction survey (sample survey is shown in the Tools section) to capture the customer's feedback on the implementation. This feedback is an invaluable input to your company's quality management system.

It is highly recommended that post-project reviews be completed to evaluate the project processes and project team, and to provide feedback to the project manager's organization. An essential component of continuous improvement, post-project reviews enable team members to identify lessons learned from a project (so that we do not repeat the same mistakes) and best practices (so that we continue to use processes that work). This phase is referred to as the Quality Assurance phase.

Chapter 6 contains customer survey question samples.

A well-designed quality assurance program is continuously evolving; thus, the related work instruction the book contains will change over time.

Ongoing Support

Certain customers may meet the engagement criteria for ongoing support services of the ISP and include these services as part of their contract. The Ongoing Support phase begins once the project is complete: The customer has accepted the deliverables, and a closure letter has been sent. At this point, designated staff supporting the account take over as primary point of contact (PPOC) responsible for coordinating all communications between the customer and the ISP. If ongoing support is included in the contract, the ongoing support PPOC is included at the external kick-off meeting to introduce him or her to the customer. At the conclusion of the project, the project manager works with the ongoing support PPOC to ensure a smooth transfer of the customer. The ongoing support PPOC should be responsible for creating an account or account transition plan.

The PPOC is defined as the individual authorized to discuss and approve project scope cost or schedule changes. The PPOC is usually the project manager throughout the project life cycle. The post-project, ongoing support, or account manager becomes the PPOC. Why is the PPOC designation important? It is not unusual for members of the project team, with the best of intentions, to inadvertently change the scope in meetings with the customer. An example of this would be the customer discussing new functionality, and the technical team member indicating that the new functionality is doable. That conversation may be misinterpreted to mean that the technical team member will, in fact, add the new functionality. The identification and communication of who the PPOC is will help prevent scope creep.

The account plan should include a copy of the installed architecture along with a complete BOM that includes all the applications loaded on the servers. The plan should list all the daily, weekly, and monthly maintenance items such as virus checks. The plan should include mechanisms to measure the ISP's SLA performance.

The Tools section of the book contains templates such as a deliverables acceptance form, closure letter, and account transition plan.

Each phase of the project life cycle, as depicted in Figure 1.1, may be viewed as a subproject within the overall project. The project manager must have a clear idea of all tasks, when each must be completed, and who is responsible for each.

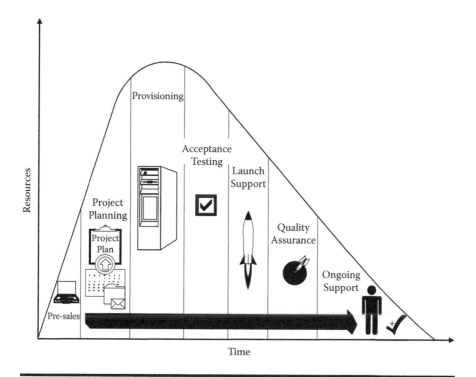

Figure 1.1   The project life cycle.

In PMBOK® parlance, this would be a Responsibility Assignment Matrix. We will discuss schedule development later.

Tip: *The project life cycle is part of a larger customer life cycle. The customer life cycle begins with initial contact and may end at either accounts receivable or a post-project/post-service quality survey.*

Chapter 2

From Scope to Schedule

In this chapter, we will move from scope definition to the process of developing a schedule. This can be done by an individual project manager alone, within the context of a quality management system as described in Chapter 5 or as part of a Project Management Office (PMO). Before drilling down into the steps that take us from scope to schedule, we will take a moment to define the PMO.

The Project or Program Management Office

Now that we have a conceptual understanding of the project life cycle and the elements that the project manager manages, we need to take the next step. It is recommended that Internet companies, such as Internet service providers (ISPs), and Web design and application development companies, have a Program or Project Management Office (PMO). A typical PMO provides functional contributions as outlined here:

- Develops and deploys project management methodologies. The project life cycle for each product may be customized.
- Coordinates process improvements and initiatives that include project management activities.
- Creates project and program management standards and tools. For example, one standard might be that all projects must have a risk management plan.
- An associated tool might be a risk checklist, customized by product line.

- Standardization facilitates consistency and repeatability. The challenge is to develop standards that empower the project manager. Samples of empowering standards are contained in the Work Instructions section of the book (Chapter 5).
- Facilitates focus groups, composed of project managers, to evaluate methodology, standards, or tools changes prior to release.
- Analyzes needs for communication mechanisms, such as an internal Web site, and implements solutions that meet requirements.
- Provides specialized human resource training, coaching, and development.
- Captures and disseminates best practices and lessons learned.
- Provides strategic, financial planning, and budgeting services to executive management.
- Enables a project management organization to be its own cost center. This, in turn, can lead to a billable project management group.
- Collects and analyzes key performance indicators and recommends corrective or preventative methodology or tool improvements.
- Provides portfolio management advisory guidance to executive management.
- Ensures quality through internal quality assurance reviews. Such reviews can be based on the standards, processes, tools, and work instructions developed by the PMO.

A well-thought-out PMO serves as the Project Center of Excellence.

To be successful, the project manager must be able to identify project stakeholders and must know how to manage them as resources. It is the norm rather than the exception that project managers direct "virtual" staffs that change as projects move into different phases.

Managing and coordinating the activities of staff who are not direct reports can be done employing the techniques in this book that speak to human resource management.

Tip: *Leadership is an act of self-empowerment.*

Stakeholders may be defined as those individuals who have a vested interest in either the project activities or the project outcome. By project activities, we mean the tasks and subtasks identified in the project's schedule. Project outcome refers to the direct and indirect results of the project as a whole.

It is noteworthy that good project managers begin by identifying the important internal and external stakeholders. Important stakeholders are individuals having the ability to affect the project's success, that is, individuals who can affect the scope, schedule, or budget.

External stakeholders may include vendors, subcontractors, and third parties. Earned value management formulas that provide objective data points for resource management are given in the appendix titled "Project Management and Internetworking Glossaries and Formulas."

At this point, we will drill down and describe the elements to be considered when moving from scope to schedule.

The stakeholder identification component of the project scope analysis facilitates the development of a project communications plan. A later section will cover the details of project communications management.

The world of project integration also includes the relationship between the project manager, project sponsors, and the PMO. This book views the customer as the sponsor.

Triangle of Truth

To help place scope, time, and cost in perspective, we will take a moment to review how these elements relate to each other.

The Triangle of Truth: The Big Three Known as the Triple Constraints

Figures 2.1 and 2.2 illustrate the Triangle of Truth, also known as the *triple constraints*. Figure 2.1 depicts how the triangle is incomplete if we think of one item without the other two. In Figure 2.2, we see a triangle in which each side represents one side of the triple constraint, and if we change the lengths of one side, the lengths of the other two sides are impacted.

Tip: *The key lesson is that a project manager must always view events affecting the project within the context of the Triangle of Truth. In other words, assume that any change in one element will somehow affect the other two, unless proved otherwise. The three key elements are scope, schedule/time, and cost.*

If you are responsible for the management of a project, you will discover that you have to manage the project's scope, schedule/time, and cost. A common mistake that new project managers make is that they do not realize the critical

Figure 2.1   Triangle of truth.

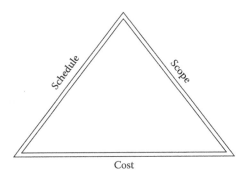

Figure 2.2 Triple constraints.

relationship among these three elements. This book will present simple ways to manage each element. As we move forward, it is important to remember the Triangle of Truth.

The price of forgetting the Triangle of Truth can be high: budget overruns, late schedules, and a scope that has gone out of control. This truth cannot be over-emphasized. Any change in scope that includes changes to deliverables must affect cost. It is impossible to modify the architecture to include more servers without increasing the cost. Deliverables are either procured or produced and, as a rule of thumb, if items are added it will take more time, thus changing the schedule.

Project Scope Management

The Project Management Institute (PMI) and the Project Management Body of Knowledge (PMBOK®) define scope management as the ongoing process of ensuring that the project includes the deliverables, *and only those deliverables* agreed upon in the contractual documents.

Scope creep occurs when we do not understand the scope of work, forget the phrase "and only those deliverables," or do not remember the Triangle of Truth. Another cause of scope creep is the lack of a well-designed change management process. We will address change management processes later.

Project scope is usually articulated in a group of documents. At an ISP or a development firm, these documents may include a Master Agreement, a Service Quotation, a Deliverables Document, and an Architectural Diagram that includes a Bill of Materials (BOM).

If the documents defining the project scope conflict with one another, the project manager defaults to the *controlling* document. In most companies, the Master Agreement is a controlling document for terms and conditions, and the Service

Quotation controls the architectural drawing. It is useful to remember that regardless of the written scope of work, the customer's expectations may not be stated in those documents. A good project manager *continually manages expectations.* Those who don't may complete the project scope on time and within budget and still have an unhappy customer. (Typically, the controlling document is specified in the contract.)

Another document that is related to scope is the "Charter," and selected lines of business within ISPs may use a "Statement of Work" or SOW. Some basic information regarding both documents is given in the following sections.

Charter

A direct way of viewing the charter is to see it as a sort of passport-to-proceed. The key elements of a charter include the following:

- **It should formally recognize that the project exists.**
  Why? This will legitimize the project. It will force other departments in the organization to acknowledge the project and allow the project team to process project actions such as purchasing, obtaining materials, and setting up accounting codes, etc.
- **It should state the individual who is charged with managing the project.**
  Why? This provides the project manager the authority needed to implement the project. This, in some companies, indicates "signature authority" to approve project team activities. It will help the project manager in obtaining accurate information from other departments to track and manage the project's progress, and allows the project manager to directly interact with entities internal and external to the company.
- **It should give the project manager the explicit authority to either obtain or negotiate the human and material resources needed to implement the project.**
  Why? Project teams rarely have permanent team employees. Usually, a team is developed based on the nature and needs of the project. This element empowers the project manager to obtain team members.
- **It should indicate how the project links to the organization's business plan, mission statement, or strategic vision.**
  Why? Higher-level executives are the ones who develop these items. More importantly, they themselves are judged by how effectively they actually implement these items. Bluntly put, it may become difficult for an executive to not support a corporate activity that ties to one of these key documents.
- **It should briefly describe the project in nontechnical terms.**
  Why? This closes the loop by stating what the project manager will implement. In a way, this provides a framework on which to move forward.

Statement of Work (SOW)

An SOW is a description of what the project is in plain English. It may be supplemented by other, more technical, documents such as drawings, specifications, catalog cuts, etc. This book contains an SOW template in the Tools and Templates section in Chapter 6. The SOW actually describes what the project manager has to implement. It should be clear and concise, and must include the items detailed in the following subsections.

General Scope of Work—Include Goals and Related Background

Why? This allows the reader to understand, without jargon, what actual work the project team will perform. It places work in a larger context. In other words, it explains why the project exists.

Contractor Deliverables

Why? This element clarifies the specific end-products that have to be produced or "delivered." The term *deliverable* refers to the product or service the customer pays for. Deliverables can be anything from a set of drawings to a truck filled with tomatoes. Sometimes, when dealing with electronic files or written reports, the deliverable may be referred to as an *intellectual product* or *property*.

This element of the SOW facilitates the development of agreements and contracts with consultants, contractors, and subcontractors. Finally, it's important because this element effectively defines who is responsible for what, and it may contain milestone dates.

The term *milestone* can refer to the completion of an activity or task that marks the initiation or completion of a project phase. Milestones can also represent the completion of significant deliverables. Finally, milestones can be decision points or stage gates.

Contract End Items and Performance Requirements

Why? The listing of contract end items helps define project completion. An example of this would be the submission of a system operating manual and final drawings after the installation. For example, in ISPs or software development projects, the final deliverables may be source code documentation and user manuals. The end items in this subsection are deliverables. Beyond deliverables, contract end items may be related to specific performance criteria, such as throughput.

Studies, Documentation, and Related Specifications

Why? By referencing the document, the studies, documentation, and related specifications become part of the scope of work. It's important to make sure that the documents don't conflict. If there is the possibility of a document conflict, indicate which are the controlling documents.

Data Requirements

Why? If the project manager or the client is expecting deliverables, such as a final report or the results of an acceptance test, it should be explicitly stated. If statistics or data, such as Web site hits, need to be obtained or analyzed, they should also be indicated.

Equipment and Materials for Contract End Items

Why? Contract end items may include available spare parts, additional documentation, and related equipment.

Customer-Furnished Property, Facilities, Equipment, and Services

Why? This item will reduce the project's cost. This section is particularly important for PMOs, and refers to the customer providing items such as office space, office equipment, hardware, or associated infrastructure.

Documentation Provided by the Customer

Why? This may be essential for the project team. Customer-furnished documentation can be anything from a telephone directory to a set of Web site documents. It is recommended that receipts of such items be flagged in the project schedule. Customer-provided documentation is an excellent example of a dependency.

General Schedule of Performance

Why? This section identifies the milestones (e.g., the project start date, completion of a study, approval of a quotation, definition of the project team members, and project completion). It's a double-edged sword because on the one hand it creates targets and may even provide needed internal pressure to obtain resources, but on the other hand if the dates are not realistic you have committed yourself to a certain problem. It is critical that all stakeholders agree to any milestone-level dates included in the project schedule.

Tip: *For customer-facing meetings, a milestone-level schedule is suggested. This will prevent possible micromanagement of the project schedule.*

Exhibits, Attachments, and Appendices

Why? This is required to ensure that the scope is understood in its entirety. Basically, this item refers to additional documentation supplementing the SOW. It's particularly important if the charter or SOW reference an exhibit, attachment, or section.

Clear Definitions

The SOW should, as discussed earlier, be worded in a nontechnical way. It is a document employed to secure buy-in from all the project customers, both internal and external. The higher up the organization the stakeholders are, the simpler the document must be. High-level executives simply do not have the time to read documents requiring interpretation. Additionally, your customer may not have the technical expertise to understand a document full of specialized terminology.

Finally, the SOW serves as a kind of road map for the project team. It provides direction, which allows the team members to quickly match their work product with the intended scope.

Different people can interpret certain words in many ways if they're not explicitly clarified, for example, "the system should always be available." What does "available" mean? Are we saying 24 hours a day, 7 days a week, or just during business hours? What is meant by the "system"? Does this imply the customer's right to go into an ISP data center? A well-drafted SOW can help manage customer expectations and provide a framework for the development of a project plan. Clarity in language also reduces project risk.

Managing Scope Changes

Though scope may, at times, appear to be "dynamic," project managers want to keep the scope well defined and as static as possible though there may be occasions when scope changes are advised. When changes must be made, project managers must manage them and take into account the way in which such changes affect the project.

Tip: *Remember the Triangle of Truth. Scope/cost/schedule: Change in one usually means change in the other two.*

Scope change is not a brand new project. If the scope revision is so radical as to effectively redefine the initial service quotation (SOW or charter), it is known as a *cardinal change*. A cardinal change may well invalidate the contract. If the change is so monumental as to fundamentally alter the original project and it can't be rejected, it's best to stop, close out the original project, and start afresh.

Tip: *Scope changes are not inherently bad. An example of a good scope change is one that results from an up-sell or improved quality.*

Scope change management is the process by which scope changes are handled. A few quick pointers on scope change management are listed as follows:

1. Document the change.
2. Determine whether the change will create a risk issue.
3. Document the effect of the change on the schedule.
4. Evaluate the budgetary impact of the change.
5. Secure and document stakeholders' buy-in to your decision regarding the proposed change.
6. Ensure that the decision is effectively communicated to all the affected members of the project team.
7. Reissue either the schedule or the budget, or both, if affected, to all concerned parties. The reissued documents become the new baselines.

In the Tools section, you will find template tools that will help you manage scope changes.

The scope change management process should be part of a larger integrated change management process. An integrated, project-level process helps manage changes affecting project plan elements such as cost control, resource management, schedule, and potentially other project plan elements as well. If the project has a defined governance structure, the process should integrate with that as well. The related scope change management tools suite shown later (Chapter 6) addresses all the elements we have described.

Table 2.1 summarizes typical ISP and application development company documents that are associated with project scope and any subsequent changes.

What do I do now?
See Figure 2.3.

Having reviewed the scope and developed a framework for managing changes to it, we move on to refining our understanding of the scope's deliverables through the use of work breakdown structures (WBSs).

Work Breakdown Structures and Project Planning Sessions

Note that while the WBS is essentially a deliverables-driven document, it can be used, as is the case here, to go beyond the standard to facilitate the development of an integrated project plan. In other words, we may deviate from how some

Table 2.1 Scope-Related Documents

Document	Author	Content	Comment
Master Agreement	Legal department	Terms and conditions	Signed by customer, and processed by the sales team.
Task Statement	Sales or account manager	Form of contract with pricing	Can serve as an amendment to the Master Agreement.
Service Quotation	Account manager or sales	Form of contract with pricing	The project manager reviews the scope of this document and provides approval.
Architectural Drawing	Engineer or technician	Representative diagram of hardware configuration	This may be attached to the Service Quotation or contract. Must include Bill of Materials (BOM).
External Kick-off and Launch Support Meeting Minutes	Project manager	Contain commitments and any identified scope changes and risks	The project manager submits minutes and action items from these meetings to the project team and the customer.
Project Plan	Project manager	Includes the project schedule, risk assessment, and any other scope management documentation	Project schedules are sent to the customer, and Tiers 2 and 3 after the first baseline as well as any subsequent changes.
Risk Assessment	Project manager	Includes risks identified at both the external and launch support meetings	The project manager completes the risk checklist and reports on the status of risks in ongoing customer status meetings.
Scope Review Guide	Project manager	Scope analysis/review	This is a tool used by the project manager.
Statement of Work	Sales and project manager	Scope identification	The project manager reviews and approves the SOW.

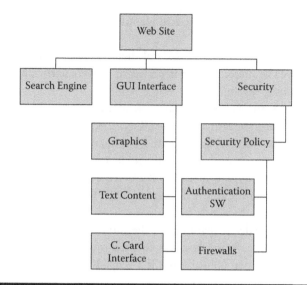

Figure 2.3 Partial work breakdown structure.

practitioners interpret the PMI practice standard a tad to extract more detailed planning information.

A well-managed WBS-based planning session with the project team can result in the following:

- Understanding the project's deliverables
- Defining work packages and associated levels of effort
- Defining the activities and tasks required for each deliverable
- Clarifying activity relationships
- Aiding the development of a project budget
- Determining how the activities and tasks are related
- Clarifying possible dependencies, inputs, and outputs of activities
- Understanding what resources are needed for each activity and task
- Uncovering hidden risk issues

This, in turn, drives the development of the following:

- A plan to provide the deliverables and other contractual obligations
- A detailed project schedule
- Strategy for managing customer and stakeholder expectations
- Understanding the root cause of risk issues
- Definition of what is needed to mitigate risk issues
- Estimate of the project's material and human resource needs
- Estimate of total project costs

Prerequisites for a successful WBS-based planning session are as follows:

- Early identification of principal stakeholders. Each principal stakeholder should have the subject matter expertise to actively participate in the WBS-based planning session.
- The project manager should make attendance in this meeting mandatory. The idea is not necessarily to invite all the stakeholders; rather, it is to invite the stakeholders who will do or manage the actual work.
- Premeeting between internal stakeholders when the customer or third parties will participate in the WBS-based planning session. (This is to address how confidential information will be handled during the planning session.)
- Internal stakeholder preparation in the form of reading and fully comprehending the scope documents. It is essential that the session members understand the contractual obligations. (The Scope Review Checklist tool given in Chapter 6 can help the participants.)
- Focused facilitation of the planning session by asking the right questions to prompt participation and information exchange.

Preparing for the WBS-Based Planning Session

The project manager must perform a detailed project scope analysis. As the scope documents are reviewed, he or she must have a blank sheet of paper with the following columns:

1. Stakeholders
2. Deliverables
3. Dependencies
4. Assumptions
5. Risks
6. Constraints

During the review, note the contract item and contract section number in the appropriate columns. The item and section numbers will help the participants locate the exact verbiage in the contract during the session.

Table 2.2 (containing the aforementioned six columns) will help you facilitate the dialogue during the WBS session. It's preferable that the participants raise these items during the session. If, however, important items are not mentioned, use the information in Table 2.2 to bring them up.

With the six-column table, you are in a position to *ask the right questions that will get the discussion going.* The following are some sample leading questions that can help define necessary project activities and uncover missing deliverables or tasks:

Table 2.2 Scope Analysis Tool

Scope Analysis					
Stakeholder	*Deliverable*	*Dependency*	*Assumption*	*Risk*	*Constraint*

- Do we need anything (advance notice, time, deliverables, etc.) to complete this deliverable? *The answer is Finish-to-Start (FS) tasks.*
- Can this task or activity be done at the same time as …? *The answer is Start-to-Start (SS) tasks.*
- Are we required to do this? *This question helps to manage scope creep, but it should be phrased carefully if external stakeholders participate.*
- Does this task or activity contain any assumptions? *This question helps identify risk issues.*

When we explore schedule development, also known as project time management, we will review the four types of task relationships (FS, Start-to-Finish [SF], Finish-to-Finish [FF], and SS).

For example, if an identified task is to "Load Monitoring Scripts," assumptions may be as follows:

1. We know exactly what we want to monitor.
2. We have the ability to monitor.
3. We have the expertise to write the test script.
4. We have addressed the potential impact of the failure of monitoring.

This type of facilitated discussion helps identify issues or risks that have to be addressed in the project plan.

Managing the Actual WBS-Based Planning Session

Find a large blank wall space to begin arranging project deliverables, recognizing that you will need room for new tasks as they are identified.

Tip: *Bring different colored Post-it® notes. Color them by department or resource. Leave enough space to add notes and draw lines between Post-it notes. At the very end, you can draw lines (e.g., → FS) between the Post-it notes, indicating relationships. This will facilitate activity sequencing and schedule development. Leave room on each Post-it note to include the associated resource and his or her level of effort (LEO).*

■ Begin by posting the major deliverables across the top (level 1 or 2, as column headers); then, using Table 2.2 and prompting questions developed earlier, break down each deliverable into subdeliverables (levels 3 and 4) down to work packages which will contain activities.

■ The Post-it notes are placed on the board to determine, within the group, whether they have any dependencies, and if so add them to the board.

■ As each Post-it note is placed on the board, work with the stakeholders to identify the associated resource.

■ After the resource has been identified, determine the LEO (LEO represents labor hours).

■ After the deliverables, activities, and tasks are posted (or as you post them), review them to determine possible risk issues.

■ If risk issues are identified, discuss the possible ways to respond to them and add the corresponding Post-it notes. In Chapter 3, we will discuss the risk management process in greater detail.

■ As immediate action items develop, define the action owner, set a due date, and agree to a communication mechanism (to close the loop). Add a Post-it note for each activity of the action item.

■ Add Post-it notes for activities associated with project meeting (kick-off, progress, and closure).

■ Add Post-it notes for internal deliverables such as reports.

■ After all the Post-it notes are in place, draw arrows between them to show their relationships (FF, SS, FS, and SF).

■ With MS Project or some other project management software, enter each Post-it note by simply typing each one, column by column, as displayed on the board. Each Post-it will be typed into the Task Name field.

■ The top Post-it note of each column (the major deliverable) will become the Summary Task in the Task Name field.

■ For each task, type in the Predecessor field and the task relationship as FS, SF, SS, or FF.

■ Indicate the resource for each task in the Resource field.

■ Prepare a Working Schedule in the software for each resource type.

■ Add, for each task, the estimated duration in the Duration field. Remember to differentiate LEO from duration. This will result in more accurate resource histograms (e.g., the activity is painting a wall: the LEO to paint might be 8 h, and the duration may be 20 h because it will take 12 h for the paint to fully dry.) If the electronic schedule is created during the WBS-based planning session, it will highlight the following:

  – Resource over and under allocations

  – Tasks that are not in the critical path and may actually not even be needed

  – Time-compressed sections of the schedule that need resource leveling

Once these project issues are uncovered, they may be addressed in real time during the session.

Tip: *Many project management software packages contain a "Resource leveling" function. The function is designed to address resource constraints. Be careful, however, because in most cases this will significantly extend the project end date.*

Figure 2.3 displays a partial WBS. The top level represents major deliverables. Each level breaks down the deliverable into smaller components.

What do I do now?

1. Review the scope documentation provided by the sales team using the Scope Review Checklist (Chapter 6).

2. Complete the risk checklist (Risk Management Checklist) found in Chapter 6. Identify any new risks that may come up in the external kick-off and launch support meetings. A hard copy of this tool may be viewed in the Tools section of the book.

3. Document scope changes and customer changes, and adjust the project schedule as needed.

4. Set up a project folder as indicated in work instruction on documentation mentioned in Chapter 5.

Figure 2.4   Scope planning steps.

Chapter 3

Developing the Plan

At this point we understand the scope of work, a work breakdown structure (WBS) has been developed, and we have the foundation for a schedule. We still need, however, other elements to complete the Project Management Plan. What follows are the components recommended for a robust plan.

Risk Management

All projects contain elements of risk. Risk refers to a positive or negative uncertainty.

The possibility that a given task is completed ahead of schedule is an example of positive risk. The possibility that a vendor will not deliver the hardware on time is an example of negative risk. Risk is a factor that impacts the Triangle of Truth: Scope, Schedule, and Cost.

The risk management process contains the following elements.

1. Risk identification: Define the risk issue by root cause
2. Risk qualification: The high, medium, or low impact it can have on the project
3. Risk quantification: The probability, schedule, and cost impact
4. Risk response: Strategy and activities to manage the risk
5. Risk control: How the responses will be monitored and controlled

As a number of risk issues are identified, qualified, and quantified in the course of the WBS-based planning session (Chapter 2), we will go directly to the risk response.

The project manager begins by identifying the risk elements in the project plan. Once the risk elements have been identified, the project manager determines how to *avoid, mitigate, transfer,* or *accept* the risk.

> *Avoidance* refers to a strategy that will allow the project to prevent the risk from occurring. For example, if the risk is that new code may prove to be unstable, we may avoid the risk by leveraging proven code (perhaps with less functionality) that has greater stability.
>
> *Mitigate* refers to actions that may be taken to minimize a risk. If long lead times are a potential risk issue, they can be partially mitigated by adding longer lead times when scheduling these items.
>
> *Transferring* risk implies assigning it to another party. For example, if you have the customer sign a waiver, you have effectively transferred the risk. Car insurance is a good example of risk transfer. This may be referred to as *deflection*.
>
> *Accepting* the risk implies that no mitigating or transferring action is possible.

The Tools and Templates section of Chapter 6 contains Risk Management Checklists to help identify the risk issues.

The checklist is a tool. No checklist can predict every possible situation, so the project manager complements the Risk Management Checklist with his or her own assessment.

After the assessment has been completed, the project manager must document the result of this analysis and have an action plan to address it. The documentation of the analysis and the associated response may be in the form of an e-mail to File with a copy to the business team manager and the associated salesperson. The action plan may include schedule changes, budget revisions, or new tasks to mitigate or transfer the risk.

Imagine another case in which the customer supplies an application to be installed on the Web server. The project manager could mitigate the risk associated with this unknown variable by doing acceptance testing in stages, having the customer first sign off on the server itself, and then the server with the application installed. This tactic mitigates the risk that the software does not work on the server by first proving that the server works.

Personal risk mitigation for the project manager takes the form of solid and comprehensive documentation. Note that it is not possible to overdocument. In the world of project management, documentation is critical. Ideally, the project management group uses a document management system. There are software applications that can automate document management.

The Risk Management Checklist should be completed before finalizing the schedule and, when appropriate, the budget.

Tip: *Use the WBS to uncover risk issues. For example, taking the WBS created earlier, probing questions can be asked.*

What do I do now?
For each item on the WBS, ask these questions (Figure 3.1):

■ What do I need for this activity/deliverable? *Dependency Risks*
■ Is what I need available (When I need it)?
 – Human resources?
 – Documentation?
 – Hardware?
 – Approvals?
 – Funding?
■ Does this activity/deliverable assume anything? *Assumption Risks*
■ Are the assumptions valid?
■ Does this activity/deliverable have constraints? *Constraint Risks*
 Can it be done within the constraints?

Figure 3.1 Probing risk quesitons.

The following are formulas that address risks associated with the project's activity network diagram.

O = Optimistic, M = Most Likely, P = Pessimistic

■ $(O + 4M + P)/6$ is *PERT* (Program Evaluation and Review Technique)
■ $(P - O)/6$ is *Standard Deviation*
■ $[(P - O)/6]^2$ is *Task Variance*
■ $\Sigma[(P - O)/6]^2$ is *Project Variance* (sum of the task variances)

Risk calculation is the product of two variables:

■ **Risk Event Probability**:
 – An estimate of the probability that a given risk event will occur

■ **Risk Event Value**:
 – An estimate of the gain or loss that will be incurred if the risk event does occur

{Probability of Impact × Dollar Value = Event Monetary Value: $(P)\$ = EMV$}

What do I do now?

---

1. Complete the Risk Management Checklist in the Tools section.
2. Ensure that mitigating, acceptance, or transfer actions are taken as indicated on the Checklist.
3. Whenever possible add the risk mitigation tasks to the project schedule.
4. Supplement the checklist with any commonsense- or experience-based concerns.
5. Identify Site Launch Support Phase risks as early as possible.
6. Determine the need, if any, to modify the scope documents in light of your risk analysis.
7. Identify if scope changes were due to a customer request or due to an ISP constraint or requirement (*see* the Work Instruction on Scope Change Management).
8. Check internally for any best practices or lessons learned in Risk Management.

(*Note:* The Risk Checklist is a living document that should be reviewed and updated on a regular basis. For most projects, the Progress Report Template in the Tools Appendix will aid this process.)

Project Time Management

In the project management context, time management refers to developing a project schedule and managing its changes.

In ISPs, Schedule Templates (see sample in Chapter 6) should be made available to expedite the development of project schedules. The project manager modifies the template to match the project scope and customer expectations. If a template is not available, the suggested way to develop a schedule is by first completing a WBS. The WBS helps define the deliverables and work packages that help determine activity relationships. The WBS helps drive the schedule. The activities in the schedule are meant to produce the deliverables in the most efficient way. Microsoft Project is a tool that may be used to develop a schedule. Fluency in Microsoft Project is, by itself, not project management!

There are a number of techniques and tools to develop a schedule. For your information, we'll list a few, bearing in mind that they are not universally employed in ISPs, development, and Web content firms:

1. PDM: Precedence Diagramming Method
2. AON: Activity On Node Method
3. ADM: Arrow Diagramming Method
4. CDM: Conditional Diagramming Method
5. CPM: Critical Path Methodology
6. CCM: Critical Chain Methodology
7. NLD: Network Logic Diagrams
8. Flow Charts/ Process Maps/Logic Diagrams
9. Monte Carlo Task Calculation/Simulation/ Analysis
10. PERT: Program Evaluation and Review Technique

Road Map to Developing a Project Schedule

At this point we will provide a simplified road map for developing a schedule. Some of the following topics may be addressed later in the book. (Note: Items may be intentionally repeated.)

Project managers working on complex projects develop a WBS *prior* to beginning working on the project schedule. Before you work on developing an MS Project schedule make sure you have included, at minimum, the following elements. Please review the checklist on the following page.

Scheduling Elements Checklist

- Internal kick-off meeting
- External (customer-facing) kick-off meeting
- Progress meetings
- Provisioning tasks
- Site launch support meeting, if applicable
- Risk mitigation tasks
- Third party deliverables
- Customer dependencies
- Acceptance testing tasks
- Launch support tasks
- Confirmation that all contractual deliverables have been provided to the customer
- Quality assurance tasks, if applicable
- Project closure or disengagement
- Identify "summary" tasks such as policy issues, provisioning issues, resource issues, risk issues, and administrative and financial issues.

List the tasks in a logical order by asking yourself simple questions:

- Can this task start before another is completed?
- Can I start this task at the same time as other tasks?
- Does this task have to be completed before another task starts?
- Should this task be tackled before another?
- Does any task depend on another?
- Are any tasks time sensitive?
- Do any "summary" tasks have subtasks?
- Have the activities needed to produce the deliverables been indicated?

Remember the four task relationships shown clockwise in the diagram that follows beginning with "finish" to "start":

- *Finish To Start:* "From" finishes before "to" starts
- *Start To Start:* "From" starts before "to" starts
- *Start To Finish:* "From" starts before "to" finishes
- *Finish To Finish:* "From" finishes before "to" finishes

Tasks relationships are shown visually in Figure 3.2. Prompting questions to help determine network logic and uncover risk issues are included as well.

SS, FF, SF Diagram

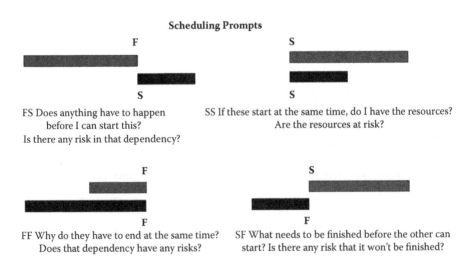

Figure 3.2 Task relationships.

After all the task relationships have been addressed:

1. Determine task durations.
2. Identify time-sensitive tasks.
3. Identify scope constraints (such as committed milestones).
4. Identify lead time tasks.
5. Correlate to labor plan (matrix resources/project team).
6. Assign resources to tasks.
   - Assign persons for each task.
   - Assign corresponding materials.
   - Assign matrix (subcontract/vendor) resource.

The results of the scheduling road map should be entered into a Microsoft Project schedule. It's helpful to use the percent complete progress bar to visually track task status. If you wish, you might format the task bars to highlight important tasks; for example, risk-related tasks might be formatted red, and so on.

Tip: *After the project plan schedule is finalized, using most project management applications, save it as Baseline or Original. As the project progresses, use the Track Gantt view to compare Actual versus Baseline. This will visually demonstrate your progress to date.*

As a side note, it is possible to construct a WBS from the Gantt chart by clicking on the Task ID numbers and noting the WBS codes. Microsoft Partner software packages that link to Microsoft Project's menu bar are available to create a WBS pictorially or to calculate task risk employing statistical algorithms. Bear in mind, though, that this is not the best way to construct a WBS.

A (partial) typical Gantt chart is partially shown in Figure 3.3.

What do I do now?

Here are the steps, at a high level, to get from a scope of work to a schedule (Figure 3.4).

Customer Program Management Offices (PMOs) and Program Schedules

A Program Management Office or Program Schedule includes discrete projects and ongoing activities in support of a single customer, department, or business unit.

The Program-Level Schedule includes the following activities (use them as is or create a table):

1. Elements needed to create an organizational breakdown structure (OBS).
2. Tasks required to set up a program office at a customer site.

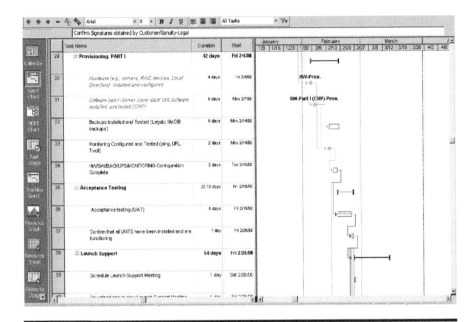

Figure 3.3 Typical Gantt chart: partial view.

3. Activities to manage cash flow.
4. Elements that can be used for event and site change management.
5. Tasks for meetings and reports.
6. Items for upselling additional ISP, or development company products and services.

A program-level (partial) Gantt chart can be seen in Figure 3.5.

What do I do now?
See Figure 3.6.

Human Resource Management

There are various types of organizational structures in corporations. The two most common are known as the *pyramid* and the *matrix*.

In the pyramid, we have well-defined vertical reporting relationships. For example, in a pyramid organization, technicians report to engineers, engineers report to task or team leaders, task leaders report to a project manager, project managers report to senior project managers, senior project managers report to a program or operations manager, program managers report to a principal project manager, principal project managers report to a director, directors report to a vice

1. Scope analysis.
2. Extract deliverables from scope analysis.
3. Develop WBS.
4. Ensure this includes project plan or subplan deliverables.
5. Decompose WBS to work package level.
6. Define the activities within work package.
7. Determine the duration and level of effort of the activities.
8. Determine the applicable resources.
9. Activities, with time data, are inputs to activity network diagram (AND).
10. Define and/or optimize the critical path within the AND.
11. Employing either a forward pass or backward pass, determine the start and finish dates of the AND nodes.
12. Input this information into a scheduling application.
13. As project proceeds, what-if scenarios and changes or re-baselines may impact schedule using either hard or preferential logic.
14. Review time constraints.
15. Apply resources to scheduling application.
16. Fix working calendars within scheduling application.
17. Baseline, interim baseline, or re-baseline as appropriate.

Figure 3.4   Steps to develop and maintain a schedule.

ID	Task Name	1st Quarter Qtr 1	2nd Quarter Qtr 2	3rd Quarter Qtr 3	4th Quarter Qtr 4	1st Quarter Qtr 1
1	(CPO) Work Breakdown Structure					
2	Project Management Organization					
29	Meetings					
37	Genuity-CPO Operations Manual					
100	Financials					
144	Quality Assurance					
153	Statements of Work					
180	Subcontracts					
189	On-Going Support					
195	Upsell Strategy Development					
199	Potential P&P Revenue Upsell (Vendor Neutral)					
364	Potential Upsell Opportunity: (Benchmarking)					
379	Potential Upsell Opportunity (Training)					
401	Potential Upsell: Security					
484	Potential Upsell Opportunities (Reports)					
510	(template-future use) Complex Hosting Project w/Sub.					

Figure 3.5   Program-level schedule.

1. Read work instruction on Project Schedules (in the Work Instructions section).
2. Make sure that all your scope management documents are complete.
3. Review the completed Risk Management Checklist.

Figure 3.6   Program level schedule tips.

president, vice presidents report to a president. The chain of command is vertical, and each employee has a reporting relationship with another specific individual and no other.

In the matrix structure, reporting relationships are vertical and direct, horizontal and indirect. Typically, matrix organizations are composed of two different types of departments or business units: line and staff. Line departments usually have direct external customer interaction or are units that directly generate revenue. Staff departments support the line departments and, typically, internal customers; from an accounting perspective, staff departments are expenses to the corporation's balance sheet. Examples of a line department include a LOB, or line of business, such as a Sales unit. Examples of staff departments include Human Resources, Purchasing, and Legal.

In a matrix organization, staff may have direct or indirect reporting relationships. The direct reporting relationship is usually within the line or staff department that the employee is in. For the readers of this book, the indirect reporting relationship is any project-related relationship that the project manager has with anyone not in his or her department.

Many ISPs, Web content firms, and development companies have matrix organizations. Project managers may be part of a line department, and the members of the project manager's team are indirect reports with staff from other (both line and staff) departments. It's quite possible that all the project team members have an indirect reporting relationship with the project manager.

The policy regarding communications on a project is driven by the organizational structure. In a pyramid, the direct supervisor is almost always sent a copy of all communications sent to his or her direct reports. In the Project Communications management, we will explore the unique aspects of communicating in a matrix environment.

Leading by example is the foundation for team building. Team building is reinforced when communication is open, accomplishments are recognized, and all the stakeholders feel that they are part of the decision making process.

Kick-off and progress meetings facilitate team building. This is supplemented by clear objectives and well-defined policies. An example of the former is completing the software configuration as scheduled, and an example of the latter is

1. Read work instruction on Communications.
2. Review escalation paths with the project team and customer.
3. Review the Event Management Escalation Matrix your Internet-related company or ISP may have.

Figure 3.7   Project communications tips.

clarifying a rule of engagement that ensures the project manager is the primary ISP point of contact during implementation.

The PPOC may change after the project is completed.

Tip: *The work instruction on Communications contains valuable insights that can be applied when managing meetings.*

The key points are summarized as follows:

■ Conflicts happen.
■ Avoid conflicts by gaining stakeholder buy-in early on.
■ Mitigate conflicts through effective project management.
■ If required, escalate.
■ Provide leadership.
■ Leadership tactics should be supported by comprehensive documentation.

What do I do now?
See Figure 3.7.

Communications Management

Project communications management is one of the basic elements of the Project Management Body of Knowledge. Communications comprise all interactions with internal and external stakeholders, including meetings, telephone conversations, and correspondence.

To adequately manage communications for a project, managers must be familiar with all forms of communication, when each should be used, and to whom one should communicate. Electronic mail has become a primary mode of communication in many companies.

Electronic mail has benefits and drawbacks. On the pro side: e-mail is easy to use, manage, track, and document. On the con side: e-mail can reach unintended recipients, and contents can be altered or data corrupted during transmission.

It's important to recognize that the reader of a message is limited to the displayed text. When speaking, your voice, its tone, and inflection help convey the intention behind the words. Depending on tone of voice, words may be perceived as humorous or critical. Electronic mail does not allow for these variations, and the typed words are often taken in their most literal context. A useful rule of thumb with e-mail is to never write anything that would be misunderstood if it landed on the company president's desk.

Routine notices and reminders may be e-mailed to your customer electronically. Beyond routine transmittals, communication should always be in the form of a letter (with or without attachments) unless the customer has explicitly requested otherwise.

All written forms of communication, letter or e-mail, should be logged in into the project's file.

Communications, particularly written communications, are subject to legal discovery. In other words, don't commit, request, or imply anything that is not consistent with the project scope and plan.

Project-related conversations or meetings, whether in person or by telephone, should be documented as well. The former is limited to conversations that include deliverables definition or commitments.

Tip: *Minutes are easier to record if an agenda is prepared in advance and followed. In the same way that e-mail may reach unintended recipients, conference calls may be broadcast to unknown parties. It is recommended to have teleconference participants overtly log in and indicate if guests are present.*

Be aware that voicemail can also be relayed to third parties in and out of your company. This form of communication should be short and clear, and if critical remarks are included (try to avoid this), be prepared to substantiate the comment with documentation.

The copy or cc line of correspondence is important. When deciding whom to list on the copy line, bear in mind that this may be an opportunity for an indirect escalation or a mechanism to keep stakeholders informed. An example of indirect escalation is placing the name of someone's supervisor on the copy line. A copy line that includes all the key stakeholders is a way to keep people informed. In both cases, the names on the copy line determine the nature of the correspondence.

An important option that the project manager manages in a matrix environment is escalation. When and how an issue escalates determines, in large measure, on the extent to which the project manager is self-empowered.

If, as a last resort, issues need to be escalated, the following guidelines can be helpful.

Guidelines for escalation should, at minimum, include the following:

Calls or e-mails should be supported by existing documentation such as:

1. Project plans signed by internal stakeholders
2. Internal kick-off meeting minutes
3. External kick-off meeting minutes
4. Prior e-mail commitments
5. Written confirmation of telephone commitments
6. Existing policy memos that include time commitments

The initial escalation step should be in e-mail *and* voicemail to the individual's direct supervisor (first line manager) with e-mail copies to your manager and the Program Management Office manager—when the ISP has a PMO. The subject line of the e-mails should indicate the escalation level (i.e., "Escalation Attempt #X").

The second escalation step should be in e-mail *and* voicemail to the individual's second line manager (i.e., director) with e-mail copies to your manager and the Program Management Office manager.

The third escalation step should be directly to your manager for direct involvement in escalating the issue to the individual's third line manager (i.e., vice president) with e-mail copies to the director, the Program Management Office manager, and the project manager.

The fourth escalation step should be initiated by your manager in e-mail *and* voicemail to the director for further escalation and resolution with copies to all parties engaged up to this point. The director may elect to initiate a project recovery effort if necessary. When an ISP or other Internet-related company has a PMO, it should have the ability to lead project recoveries.

It is possible to preclude situations requiring escalation by clearly identifying all the people who have a vested interest in the project's success prior to developing a project plan. These individuals are known as the *project stakeholders*. Include their concerns in the plan. The project plan should include activities designed to achieve buy-in for the stakeholders as early on as possible. This will often prevent issues from getting out of hand. Examples of this would include having matrix resources physically sign off on the project schedule defined during the internal kick-off meeting.

In direct reporting relationships, "authority" like that of a subordinate to a supervisor is a major factor. In indirect reporting relationships, "power" is a key element. Power is not given; it is assumed. Technical experts, for example, have power because of their subject matter knowledge. Project managers assume power through their professionalism, discipline, and ability to maintain the focus on the customer. Do not underestimate the power of a project manager with a plan and the discipline to follow through!

Self-empowerment, escalation when justified, and early stakeholder buy-in are all elements that help avoid conflicts and escalations. Conflicts may, nevertheless, surface during implementation. Managing them requires understanding the underlying cause. In the project management context, conflicts are usually associated with mismatched expectations. The customer's scheduling expectations may be unrealistic. Our expectation of a project team member's capability may not have been based on his actual skill set or authority level. Virtual team member agendas may not match the objectives of the project plan.

Project managers work with their teams as leaders. Leaders are distinguished by their ability to motivate. In the context of this book, motivation occurs when the project manager gets the project team members to internalize the need to fulfill the agreed-upon tasks and activities.

The leadership skills that facilitate implementation include the following:

1. Knowing when and how to communicate information
2. Leading by example
3. Managing the project with a "can do" approach

Information on progress or scope changes should be communicated promptly, confirmed in writing, and placed in the project file. Leading by example means creating clear documentation such as meeting agendas and minutes, maintaining a project schedule, managing internal and external expectations, promptly responding to customer inquiries, and seeking creative solutions when problems arise.

Primary points of contact (PPOC) coordinate communications. Others on the project team may communicate with the customer *after* they have advised the PPOC and with the understanding that the results will be relayed to the PPOC. The PPOC function is designed to avoid duplication, as may happen, for example, if various team members ask the same set of questions to the same customer. The PPOC function helps project managers manage the customer's expectations by ensuring that all commitments and delivery dates are consistent with both the scope and schedule. To a certain extent, the PPOC function is similar to the Single Point of Contact concept in the ITIL framework.

What do I do now?
See Figure 3.8.

Quality Management

Ensuring that the focus is on the customer is good business practice.

> *It is the totality of characteristics of an entity that bears on its ability to satisfy stated or implied needs. A critical aspect of quality management in*

1. Document and log any telephone conversations that include a discussion of deliverables or schedules.
2. Electronic mail and voicemail should be transmitted bearing in mind that it may be heard or read by an unintended recipient. Copy lines may be used to either inform or indirectly escalate.
3. The project manager or program manager (Phases 2–6) and program or service manager (in Phase 7) are primary points of contact (PPOCs). If the company has no designated program or service manager, the function reverts to the project manager. PPOCs coordinate communication to avoid duplication and manage expectations.
4. See the External Kick-Off Meeting Template and Launch Support Meeting Template in the Tools Section.

Note: Don't forget to archive key communications as described in greater detail in the work instruction on documentation.

Figure 3.8   Communications management tips.

> *the project context is the necessity to turn implied needs into stated needs through project scope management. PMBOK®, 1996, Chapter 8*

It is interesting to note that the preceding Guide to the PMBOK® quotation speaks directly to the issue of managing customer expectations in a quality context. The project manager may provide all the contractual deliverables on time and still have an unhappy customer if expectations are ignored. Customer satisfaction begins during presales and continues through support. Quality and customer satisfaction can be measured. Metrics, however, are only useful if they facilitate improvement.

Deming's principles based on Plan–Do–Check–Act, ISO, and TQM each approach quality management in different ways. There are, however, key concepts that are common to all systems:

1. Quality is conformance to requirements.
2. Quality systems are preventative.
3. Quality standards are based on zero defects.
4. Quality implies continuous improvement.

Work instructions, written procedures, and metrics are all part of the quality assurance effort. These key concepts imply processes to manage quality:

1. Quality planning
2. Quality assurance
3. Quality control

Customer satisfaction is achieved when we provide the deliverables, meeting all requirements, on time. Quality systems are absolute in that the end result either conforms to requirements or does not.

The project manager has to make sure that the project's scope is understood, in the same way, by all stakeholders. The scope must be consistent with the customer's requirements *and* expectations.

In practical terms, the hardware, software, and services provided must perform as specified. Further, delivery must be completed within the time frames agreed to at the external kick-off meeting or as appropriately re-baselined.

This book, along with its work instructions, represents tools your company can leverage to develop a formal system of quality assurance.

The quality management system (QMS) discussed in this book can be customized by your company to achieve ISO 9001:2000 certification. The work instructions provide a strong foundation for quality. A well-designed QMS contains the following elements:

1. Quality manual
2. Work instructions
3. Tools and templates as referenced in either the quality manual or work instructions
4. A project and program audit review program
5. A preventative and corrective actions program
6. A training program to support the promulgation of new QMS elements
7. The analysis of key performance Indicators
8. A tools review focus group that test-drives new tools
9. An ISO focus group representing staff not in management
10. The ISO management review team
11. External ISO registrar field audits
12. Formal document control process for reviewing, approving, and managing the version of all QMS documents

More detailed information on the creation of a project-centric quality system will be discussed, in detail, later.

Tip: *If your organization is committed to quality, including but not limited to ISO certification, the work instructions, tools, and project management methodology can save you years of work. Chapters 5 and 6 contain the framework needed to buiild a methodology and quality system that in some organizations takes years to develop. This book can save you significant time.*

What do I do now?
See Figure 3.9.

1. Read work instruction on Customer Satisfaction Survey.
2. Read work instruction on Quality Assurance Review.
3. (Recommended) Complete a Post-Project Review.
4. Direct the customer to take the Customer Satisfaction Survey.
5. Complete a closure letter (project completion notification letter) upon successful completion and acceptance of the solution.
6. If ongoing support will be provided post-implementation, schedule a meeting with the ongoing support PPOC to review the account details.

Figure 3.9   Quality management tips.

The Project Plan Elements in Table 3.1 summarize the key components of the Project Management Plan.

Table 3.1   Description of Project Plan Elements

Project Plan Element	Purpose and What the Element Represents
Activity Sequence Diagram	Helps determine the critical path, can be used to calculate project level start and end dates (backward and forward pass techniques). Provides a foundation for the project.
(Network)	Schedule.
Communications Plan	Determines content and frequency of reports, defines who can discuss issues with the customer.
Escalation Matrix	(This may be part of the Communications Plan.) Defines how and within what time frame issues are escalated, and to whom.
Organization Breakdown Structure	Similar to an org chart; clarifies the working relationships associated with the project. (In many cases this will translate to a project team matrix.)
Project Schedule	Defines the tasks and subtasks of project activities; typically determines which resources will be applied to the task and subtasks. Provides specific time frames for completion of activities and milestones.
Responsibilities Assignment Matrix	Determines what each member of the project team is responsible for. (For example, who approves scope changes.)
Risk Breakdown Structure	This can help define the risks associated with the project.
Risk Management Plan	Identifies risk issues by root cause and indicates how each risk issue will be managed.
Roles and Responsibilities Chart	This can indicate who does what and when.
Work Breakdown Structure	Helps break down the project deliverable, which in turn facilitates definition of work packages that simplify level of effort calculations.

Chapter 4

Implementing a Quality Management System

How to Implement a Quality Management System

Tip: *What follows can be applied within a Total Quality Management (TQM) or Six Sigma environment. It, additionally, provides a comprehensive framework for an ISO: 9001:2000 certification.*

The steps outlined in this chapter for the creation and management of a quality management system (QMS) are based on the following framework:

1. The project management methodology should be based on the Project Management Body of Knowledge (PMBOK®) and be consistent with Project Management Institute (PMI) standards.
2. The QMS must be measurably responsive to customers.
3. The QMS must be measurably responsive to the experience of the project and program managers in the field.
4. The project management methodology should be aligned with the company's strategic objectives.
5. The stakeholders should be encouraged to achieve professional certification. In the case of project managers, there are certifications such as CAPM® (Certified Associate Project Manager) or the more advanced certification of PMP® (Project Management Professional).
6. The project management methodology and associated QMS should yield measurable operational efficiencies.

Finally, the creation of the QMS should be managed similar to any other project, employing the same methodology, tools, processes, and techniques. This approach can validate the implementing organization's standards, tools, and methodology.

Defining the Project Life Cycle: Step 1

Definition of the project life cycle is the starting point. Although this may sound easy, it requires complex process mapping including all key stakeholders. Use standard TQM techniques; begin with a macromap (entire project life-cycle map) and drill down into discrete phases. The process maps should have swim lanes and a time line to better identify who does what, and when. Within the Internet service provider (ISP), be sure to identify the correct stakeholders.

While mapping the process, expect gaps and white spaces to appear and leverage this opportunity to improve processes. Pay special attention to process inputs and outputs. Finally, internal and external measurement points can be identified for future use.

Translate the Project Life Cycle into a Formal Methodology: Step 2

After identifying the project phases during macroprocess mapping, drill down to the next level and determine the following:

1. What activities or milestones determine the beginning and end of each phase within the project life cycle?
2. What are the roles and responsibilities of stakeholders in each phase of the project life cycle (create a Roles and Responsibilities Matrix)?
3. Which corporate policies or standards are in force and should be viewed as methodology constraints?

After these three elements are defined, translate the project life cycle, phase by phase, into a methodology document. The processes mapped earlier will facilitate this translation.

Develop Standards to Provide a Consistent Methodology: Step 3

Having defined the project life cycle and the associated roles and responsibilities, the next step is fostering consistency. This is where "how projects are implemented" gets defined and documented. You also need to define the minimum standards that will provide quality and repeatability.

When developing the standards, called *work instructions,* find the balance between the minimum amount of direction and overstandardization. The design criteria should take the following into consideration:

1. The standards should create a model of empowerment. The project and other managers should have latitude and real decision-making authority.
2. The standards should facilitate the capture of key performance indicators.
3. The standards should provide for roll-up management reports.
4. The standards should facilitate enterprisewide reporting and information sharing.
5. The standards should be designed so that it is possible to verify and analyze the results of conformance to the standards.

The recommended set of work instructions for an ISP, Web content management, or development firms are shown here. The standards cover activities within each phase of the project life cycle. This model includes a Project Management Office (PMO). If your organization is too small for a PMO, its functions can be assigned to a project manager.

The methodology standards, when completed, should be posted and should become part of a document management system. A template to format work instructions is included in the Tools and Templates section in Chapter 6 of the book.

Note that while work instructions and other elements of the QMS indicate "ISO," the designation can be changed for your organization's quality assurance plan. The standards are listed in Table 4.1.

Standards such as Quality Assurance Reviews and Post-Project Reviews have the additional benefit of extracting best practices and lessons learned, both of which should be made available to all project teams.

Drilling down a bit, we can see in Table 4.2 the *why* behind the standards.

Develop Tools to Support Standards: Step 4

You now need to develop tools that will support the standards developed earlier. It is strongly suggested that a cross section of the staff subject to the quality management system be formed to test the proposed new tools. This focus group will provide invaluable feedback.

The basic guidelines for developing tools are listed as follows:

1. Tools should be intuitive and user friendly.
2. Ensure the tools' compatibility with the PMBOK®.
3. Whenever possible, leverage the organization's intranet or enterprise project management software. Tools, whenever possible, should have automated features, such as e-mail triggers.

Table 4.1   Work Instruction Standards

Work Instruction	Standard Name
1	Project Documentation
2	Risk Management
3	Project Schedules
4	Quality Assurance Reviews
5	Escalation
6	Project Tracking
7	Communications
8	Infrastructure Support
9	Customer Acceptance
10	Transferring Accounts or Projects
11	Customer Satisfaction Surveys
12	Document Control Process
13	ISO Document Review Process
14	Post-Project Reviews
15	Scope Change Management
16	Presales Process
17	Preventative and Corrective Actions
18	Tools Development and Review Procedure
19	Training Procedure
20	Program Resource Management
21	Master Records Procedure
22	Management Review Meetings Procedure
23	Project and Program Progress Reporting

Table 4.2   Standards Rationale Table

Standard Name	Standard Objectives
Project Documentation	Provide accessible project documentation, with a consistent directory structure.
Risk Management	Identify risk issues during the project-planning phase, and determine how they will be managed.
Project Schedules	Standardize the use of minimum milestones for roll-up reporting and nationwide use of the application. It should have a consistent look and feel for all customers.
Quality Assurance Reviews	Observe the results of standards and tools. Verify conformance to standards. Extract best practices and lessons learned.
Escalation	Empower project managers, and standardize the escalation chain and process.
Project Tracking	To facilitate capturing, on an enterprise level, business metrics.
Communications	Define the manager's role as primary point of contact.
Infrastructure Support	Internal corporate process.
Acceptance Testing	Validate that all promised deliverables are provided to the customer in good working order, and secure customer validation.
Transferring Accounts or Projects	Process to foster continuity between staff, regardless of job function.
Customer Satisfaction Surveys	To measure the effectiveness of the project management methodology and secure input for improvements.
Document Control Process	To comply with basic ISO element.
ISO Document Review Process	To provide management buy-in of policies and procedures. Basic ISO element.
Post-Project Reviews	To determine what is working and what requires improvement.

(continued on next page)

Table 4.2 (continued)   Standards Rationale Table

Standard Name	Standard Objectives
Scope Change Management	To standardize change management in a way that addresses customer expectations, cost, and schedule.
Presales Process	Internal corporate procedure. Initial point at which the project manager evaluates scope documents.
Preventative and Corrective Actions	Create a mechanism to address the observations gleaned from project reviews and audits.
Tools Development and Review Procedure	Develop a process that allows for staff input when developing new tools.
Training Procedure	Schedule staff training prior to promulgating a new standard, process, policy, or tool.
Program Resource Management	Provide guidelines that empower project managers when securing and managing matrix resources.
Master Records Procedure	Basic ISO element.
Management Review Meetings Procedure	Create a mechanism that continually evaluates the system effectiveness.
Project and Program Progress Reporting	To foster consistency and look and feel when reporting project progress to the customer.

4. Tools should have a professional look and feel so that they can be used without modification by customers.
5. Tools should have, when appropriate, mechanisms for roll-up reporting.
6. Tools should facilitate documentation and follow up issues identified in the project plan.
7. Remember to reference the tools in their corresponding work instructions.

Tip: *Add a column (next to the task description) to your scheduling software, such as MS Project, to type in hyperlinks or URLs that will point to the tool required to complete the task.*

Provide Standards and Tools Training: Step 5

From a QMS perspective, within an ISO 9000 series context (or any other quality system), confirming that staff are qualified and trained is essential.

This element of the standards starts with a clear definition of the organization's structure and reporting relationships, and clarifies roles, responsibilities, and job descriptions. Within the QMS, the following should be addressed:

1. Creation of a training and certification database
2. Management interview guides
3. Staff competency assessment tools
4. Documented job descriptions
5. New hire checklist
6. Introductory, intermediate, and advance training paths
7. Training seminars scheduled to coincide with project or program audits
8. A standard, with mechanisms, to confirm that prior to the issuance of a new standard, policy, procedure, or tool, staff has been properly trained

Tip: *Remember that most of the referenced standards are mentioned in this book and can be used by your organization. The Tools section contains many templates that can be used to create the QMS.*

There are many organizations that provide training, based on the PMBOK®, for PMI certification. Many of these organizations can provide training on both project management and some of the associated soft skills. For project management training, use firms that are Registered Education Providers (REPs) certified by the PMI.

Promulgation, Documentation, and Version Control of Standards and Tools: Step 6

The PMO or assigned project manager should be charged with ensuring that staff (in the organization seeking certification) is fully aware of the system and is trained on the project management methodology, standards, tools, processes, and policies.

The PMO should develop training material to cover the following areas, specific to your company's quality system:

1. What a QMS is
2. What the organization's quality policy is
3. What the organization's business objectives are

4. How the project management methodology synchronizes with the elements of the quality assurance system

At this point, you have to form a management review committee charged with ensuring the integrity of the quality system. This committee also reviews and approves new quality standards. The committee, additionally, evaluates and analyzes internal and external customer satisfaction data.

Feedback from the tools focus group and the management review committee should become the mandatory inputs of a documented quality improvement process.

Internal Audit Program to Measure Effectiveness: Step 7

An internal audit program to foster standards conformance is typically a part of an ISO 9000 series quality management system. The program objectives should include the following:

Tip: *Audits are designed to evaluate processes and tools, not individual staff members. If this is not fully understood, replace the word audit with review.*

1. Evaluate projects in real time to determine the effectiveness of the methodology.
2. Observe the tools in action to identify areas for improvement.
3. Validate the accuracy of the key performance indicators rolled up from individual projects and programs.
4. Verify conformance with the standards within the QMS.
5. Proactively gauge the health of active projects.
6. Observe the presence of performance trends that may point to root-cause issues in how the work is being performed.
7. Provide feedback on best practices and lessons learned.
8. Develop an objective and verifiable audit protocol and checklist.

To maintain audit objectivity, the PMO's internal auditors should have substantial experience in managing projects and, ideally, should be trained in QMS. Project reviews can become opportunities for coaching and mentoring.

Preventative and Corrective Actions to Improve System Effectiveness: Step 8

Feedback, observations, and findings may be generated from, and directed to, multiple sources. This may be graphically represented as displayed in Figure 4.1.

The acronym QAR in the process map indicates Quality Assurance Review (Audit). cSat is an acronym for customer satisfaction.

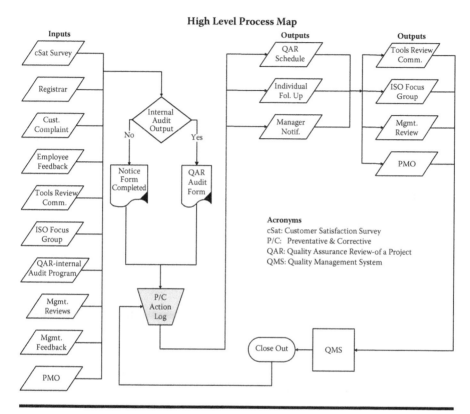

Figure 4.1   Quality system feedback loops.

Feedback, observations, suggestions, and findings should be tracked in a database. This database ought to be structured to facilitate data analysis and trending. For example, you may wish to track issues by specific standards.

Staff and Management Review: Step 9

The management review committee should be regularly convened to assess the proposed standards, project management methodology, analysis of key performance indicators, and results of the preventative and corrective actions process. In some cases, the proposed complex tools should be brought to this committee. The term *complex* can be based on an estimated level of effort threshold required for use.

The meeting schedule should be designed so that prior to management review committee meetings, staff and focus group feedback is solicited. In this way, the PMO will be aware of staff concerns and issues prior to potential management intervention. The entire PMO should be prepared for these sessions to ensure the inclusion of the following items:

1. Staff training and professional development
2. Project management methodology definition and improvement
3. Process and tools development
4. Business analysis and metrics
5. Internal and external satisfaction survey data
6. Project audits

The meetings should be documented and progress on resulting action items reported at subsequent meetings.

Quality Manual—QMS: Step 10

The PMO must have a location or Web site that project team members can access. This location should contain version-controlled copies of the standards and tools upon which the project management methodology is based. Tools, best practices, and lessons learned can be posted as well.

You may wish to use this location to keep track of labor hours of each project team member. Finally, this location or Web site may be leveraged to secure data for roll-up reports. The quality manual (QM), at a high level, outlines the logic behind the QMS and is a primary mechanism to administratively link tools and standards to the implementation methodology.

The QM begins by defining the project management organization and its quality policy and objectives, and methodically correlates virtually every standard, process, and tool to specific ISO (or QMS) elements.

The Certification Process

The PMO should begin by developing a formal Project Charter and securing executive sponsorship. The Project Charter can be the starting point for the development of a work breakdown structure. Risk issues as well as mitigation strategies ought to be identified. Associated tasks for mitigating risk should be included in the project schedule. Project team member roles must be well defined. In other words, develop a project plan based on the standards of the proposed implementation methodology and quality system.

The milestones required for certification by an ISO registrar are as follows:

1. Finalization of the delivery methodology.
2. Definition of the QM.
3. Completion of the system standards.
4. Review of QM and QMS documents.
5. Incorporation of QM review comments.

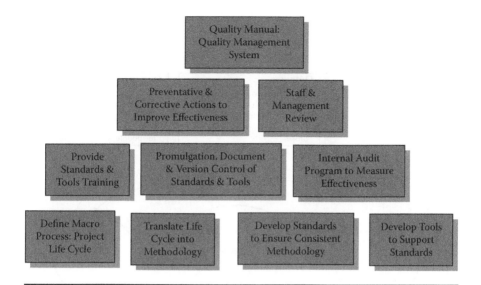

Figure 4.2 Ten building block steps for a formal quality management system (QMS).

6. Resubmission of QM and QMS documentation.
7. ISO Awareness and System Training.
8. Mock ISO audits.
9. ISO Assessment Audit by registrar.
10. Management of comments generated during the Assessment Audit.
11. ISO Registration Audit.
12. Management of nonconformities observed during ISO Registration Audit.
13. Furnish evidence that Registration Audit findings have been addressed.
14. Registrar's auditor submits certification recommendation, with associated checklists and documentation, to registrar's internal review committee.
15. Registrar determines that ISO certification is warranted.

The exhibit in Figure 4.2 summarizes the 10 steps needed to create a formal QMS.

A Systems View of the QMS Inputs and Outputs

A perspective of the quality system building block inputs and outputs and their relationships are depicted in Figure 4.3. Figure 4.4 shows how the major components integrate.

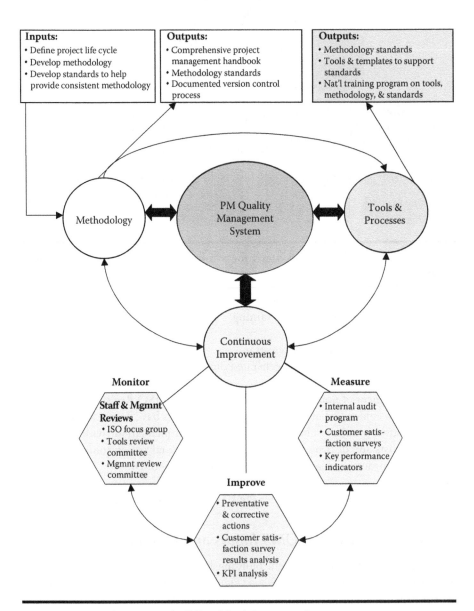

Inputs:
* Define project life cycle
* Develop methodology
* Develop standards to help provide consistent methodology

Outputs:
* Comprehensive project management handbook
* Methodology standards
* Documented version control process

Outputs:
* Methodology standards
* Tools & templates to support standards
* Nat'l training program on tools, methodology, & standards

Methodology

PM Quality Management System

Tools & Processes

Continuous Improvement

Monitor

Staff & Mgmnt Reviews
* ISO focus group
* Tools review committee
* Mgmnt review committee

Measure
* Internal audit program
* Customer satis-faction surveys
* Key performance indicators

Improve
* Preventative & corrective actions
* Customer satis-faction survey results analysis
* KPI analysis

Figure 4.3 Quality system building block inputs and outputs.

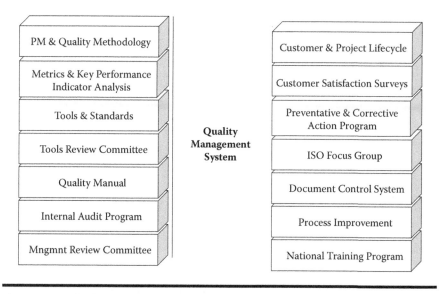

Figure 4.4   The integration of the major components of a QMS.

Chapter 5

Work Instructions

Internetworking as an industry may be viewed as a convergence of multiple industries and disciplines: computer science, information technology, software, and telephony. Many of these industries output products based on national and international standards. Project managers, who have to coordinate the activities of staff from all these industries, did not always have a robust set of standards to guide the development of their work products. Today, the project management discipline is guided by a set of practice standards, many of which have been accepted or are being accepted by organizations such as the Project Management Institute, the American National Standards Institute, and International Standards Organization.

Beyond individual practice standards, entire Program or Project Management Offices can operate within the guidelines of these standards and become third party certified by managing within the context of a quality management system.

With time, different quality systems and orientations become more popular than others. Through the years we have seen Total Quality Management, Deming, Business Process Management, Six Sigma, Information Technology Infrastructure Library, Maturity Models; the list goes on. The framework of the International Standards Organization has withstood the test of time. Importantly, the latter framework is compatible with many others. As the International Standards Organization framework has withstood the test of time, is compatible with other models, and is consistent with existing project management practice standards, we have selected it as a way of formalizing the methodology described earlier in the book. What follows are the artifacts needed to create a strong foundation for formal certification within this framework, with or without a third party. The framework that follows may reference or speak to different tools or templates; by and large, they can be found in Chapter 6.

Key Quality Management System Elements

The next section of the book contains a set of work instructions that form a coherent quality management system based on ISO 9001 standards. The elements that are *not* included here but would have to be part of a certifiable system are as follows:

- A document management system that provides, at minimum, for the following:
  - Version control
    - Ideally showing what changes have been made between versions
  - A record of who reviewed the document
  - A record of who approved the document
- A system that will only allow the retrieval of the most current version
- A database or spreadsheet that includes the following items:
  - A listing of all work instructions
  - A listing of all tool templates
  - A listing of all record types
  - A listing of all process documents
    - The database should indicate the location and document owner for each of the above categories.
- A database or spreadsheet that lists all the employees subject to the quality management system with the following elements:
  - Name
  - Job title
  - Job description
  - Education and certifications
  - Training received
- A training program with a corresponding database or spreadsheet
- Training on the quality management system
- Training on the embedded project management methodology
- A document that explains or shows the organization chart:
  - Include job titles
  - Include the employee names

■ A quality manual that includes the following elements:
  – Quality policy
  – Quality objectives (and how they are measured)
  – A description of how the quality management system works
■ A description of how the system is monitored and improved
■ Who, by job title, has the authority to review and modify the system based on the systems inputs and outputs.

A preventative and corrective actions program that documents (and records) the following:

■ A description of all the inputs (such as customer satisfaction surveys)
■ A description of all outputs
■ A description of the processes that the inputs and outputs are subject to

An internal audit program, which may be referred to as a project review program. It should include the following elements:

■ A database or spreadsheet of projects
  – Who is the project manager
  – Current status
■ A quality assurance review checklist that includes the mandatory and non-mandatory elements of the quality management system
■ A form, or a repeatable way to record the results of the audit or quality assurance review. It is important to understand that it is the quality system (along with its standards, tools, processes, and techniques) that is being reviewed, *not* the people.

Quality management systems may well include ITIL, Six Sigma, and/or Total Quality Management (TQM) components. Finally, please note that some of the work instructions contain mandatory items. These can be the basis of an auditing checklist.

Tip: *The work instructions contain many helpful hints, embedded tools, and PM-related insights.*

Table 5.1 indicates which team members can most benefit from the standard.

Work Instruction #1: Project Documentation
Objective

To define the standard for all of "Your Organization Name Here" for maintaining program or project management and account documentation.

Table 5.1 Work Instruction Table Indicating Applicable Roles

Work Instruction	Account Team	Project Management	Program Management	Corporate Management	PMO
Work Instruction #1: Project Documentation	✓	✓	✓		
Work Instruction #2: Risk Management		✓	✓		
Work Instruction #3: Project Schedules	✓	✓	✓		✓
Work Instruction #4: Quality Assurance					✓
Work Instruction #5: Escalation	✓	✓	✓	✓	✓
Work Instruction #6: Project Tracking	✓	✓	✓	✓	✓
Work Instruction #7: Communications		✓	✓		
Work Instruction #8: Launch Support	✓	✓	✓		
Work Instruction #9: Acceptance Testing		✓	✓		
Work Instruction #10: Transferring Projects	✓	✓	✓		
Work Instruction #11: Customer Satisfaction Surveys	✓	✓	✓		

	1	2	3	4	5
Work Instruction #12: Document Control Process	✓				
Work Instruction #13: ISO Document Review Process	✓	✓			
Work Instruction #14: Post-Project Reviews			✓	✓	
Work Instruction #15: Scope Change Management			✓	✓	
Work Instruction #16: Presales Process			✓	✓	
Work Instruction #17: Corrective and Preventative Actions	✓				
Work Instruction #18: Tools Development and Review Procedure	✓				
Work Instruction #19: Training Procedure	✓				
Work Instruction #20: Program Resource Management			✓	✓	✓
Work Instruction #21: Master Records Procedure	✓	✓	✓		
Work Instruction #22: Management Review Meeting Procedure	✓	✓			
Work Instruction #23: Project and Program Progress Reporting—(Customer)			✓	✓	

Scope

This procedure applies to all projects and accounts being managed by "Your Organization Name Here."

Reference Documents

> WI#2—Risk Management (Note: Add document control numbers here.)
> WI#3—Program and Project Schedules
> WI#10—Transferring Accounts or Projects
> WI#14—Post-Project Reviews
> Project Completion Notification Letter

Definitions

PM: "manager" or project manager, WI: work instruction (Add other titles or acronyms such as IC: implementation coordinator, IE: implementation engineer, AM: account manager, BDM: business development manager, ISE: Internet systems [sales] engineer, TAM: technical account manager)

Procedure or Process

Every project that has a "manager (PM)" assigned to it, regardless of complexity or contract value, must have a project folder under the "Current Projects" directory (insert location such as "Common Drive E") to ensure that all the required documentation and information is captured. A hard-copy project binder may be kept by the manager as well, at his or her option.

The accuracy and timeliness of updates to the electronic files will be the responsibility of the manager (PM) designated by senior management to manage the implementation or account. This manager may designate the uploading, scanning, or downloading of documents to a member of the account or project team.

The electronic project folder will contain the following mandatory subfolder directory structure:

1. Account Overview
   Can Contain:
       A. A brief description of how the customer uses the Internet and Internet systems today.
       B. Insert any customer-provided business plans or marketing materials, if applicable.
       C. Overview of third-party responsibilities and relationship, if applicable.

D. A brief (generally one paragraph to one page) description of the customer's primary business activity.

E. A description of the ISP or third-party products and services installed or to be installed.

2. Architecture/Drawings

Can Contain:

A. The architecture may be a pictorial representation or word description.

B. The BOM (Bill of Materials), if applicable, should be included or attached. The BOM may be attached to the architectural drawing or listed in the contract document with the customer. (Note: The accuracy and completeness of the BOM is critical.)

3. Communications

(If only hard copy is available, where possible, reference location for faxes, letters, memos, or e-mails containing commitments.)

Must Contain:

A. Meeting minutes from internal and external kick-off meetings.

B. Meeting minutes from progress, launch meetings, including documentation verifying that acceptance tests have been completed.

Can Contain:

C. Copies of customer requests and ISP responses to customer requests.

D. Notifications to (insert group names here, for example, Engineering, Data Center, etc.).

E. Notifications to (insert group names here) for each case in which the project schedule has slipped by 5 or more days.

F. Telephone Log—tracks communications that contain commitments.

4. Contacts

Must Contain:

A. Customer contacts—Name, company, title, telephone #, e-mail address, role/responsibilities (e.g., is this the primary contact?).

B. If applicable, third party vendor contact—Name, company, title, telephone #, e-mail address, role/responsibilities (e.g., is this the primary contact?).

C. Internal project team numbers and contacts.

5. Customer Support Plan

Can Contain:

Any documentation describing support plans specific to this customer.

Must Contain:

A. Account or Project Transition Plan, including Transition Schedule.

B. Project Completion Notification Letter.

6. Legal Documents

Must Contain:

A. (Insert lines for copies of documents such as Contract, Statement of Work, etc.)

7. Other Deliverables
   Can Contain:
   A. Intellectual property deliverables such as customer reports and analyses.
   B. Line item descriptions of any hardware deliverables.
8. Other Documentation
   Can Contain:
   This location is designed for *any* additional documentation that, in the judgment of the PM, should be included.
9. Pricing Information
   Must Contain:
   A basis of estimates.
   Can Contain:
   A. (Insert other pricing documents here, one line for each, such as the one below.)
   B. Vendor quotes.
10. Project Plan and Supporting Documents
    Must Contain:
    A. Project Schedule using (insert software application name here).
    B. Risk Assessment such as a Risk Management Checklist.
    Can Contain:
    C. E-mail confirmation of Risk Management Checklist transmission.
    D. If there are multiple subprojects, provide the Master Schedule.
    E. Staffing Plan, if applicable.
    F. Action Items Log.
    G. Documentation of outstanding issues, concerns, unusual circumstances, or mismatched expectations.
11. Project Reviews
    Must Contain:
    A completed Post-Project Review form.
12. Sales Documentation
    Can Contain: (Add or subtract items that your company employs.)
    A. Final proposals submitted to the customer.
    B. Data-gathering forms.
    C. Final orders.

Special Instructions

For programs, the initial directory structure as described above is established; the program manager has the discretion to create subfolders as he or she deems appropriate.

Reporting

None.

Records (List of Documents that Your Company Will Retain)

Contact information
Basis of estimates
Applicable architecture or drawing with Bill of Materials
Meeting minutes
Transition Schedule
Project Completion Notification Letter
Acceptance Test results
Legal documents
Other contractual documents
Project schedule
Risk assessment
Project reviews

Training

Updates will be communicated via e-mail as needed.

Attachments

(Add samples as appropriate.)

Work Instruction #2: Risk Management

Objective

This procedure provides the standard for "Your Organization" program and project managers for developing a Risk Assessment Plan and identifying risk issues.

Scope

This procedure is mandatory for all projects. It is recommended for use when planning a customer Program Management Office (PMO) or program.

Reference Documents

Risk Management Checklist.

Definitions

The term *manager* or acronym PM refers to the project manager. WI represents a work instruction.

Procedure or Process

Anticipated and unanticipated risks can cause schedule delays, increase cost, and even force scope changes. Managers should analyze risk as early, and as often in the project life cycle, as possible. Completion of a Risk Management Checklist is to be done *before* developing the project schedule/plan (see WI#3—Program and Project Schedules).

Managers should, in addition to the initial Risk Assessment, examine and manage the risk issues throughout the project life cycle.

Assessments and checklists are not a substitute for good judgment. As professionals, managers should be prepared to identify issues that may not be listed on the forms. Other items might include answers to the question, "Are there any internal or external customer concerns that may force me to extend the schedule or add tasks to my project plan?" such as:

A. Hardware delivery lead-time
B. Unrealistic customer expectations (e.g., delivery dates)
C. Functionality of customer-provided software
D. Misinterpretation of scope by ISP or customer
E. Telco access and facility issues
F. Circuit capacity issues
G. Carrier or vendor dependencies
H. Undefined scope issues
I. Segment testing
J. Regulatory issues with international accounts
K. XLOB coordination issues
L. Subcontractor constraints
M. Strategic account constraints

For all risks identified, the following should be done:

1. Identify impact in terms of schedule time, added cost, or increased effort.
2. Develop risk mitigation to reduce or eliminate impact should the risk occur.
3. Establish Risk Management Action Plan to prevent, transfer, avoid, or control and mitigate the risk should it occur.
4. The results of the Risk Management Action Plan should be communicated to management.

The decision may be to assume the risk for now and take no action. If this is the case:

Quantify impact in terms of:
■ Time
■ Cost
■ Level of effort

- Scope
- Customer satisfaction and/or loyalty
- Quality

Determine what actions may be taken to mitigate or transfer the risk.

Adjust the schedule up front. For example, if procurement lead time is an issue, then schedule the tasks associated with purchasing earlier in the schedule.

Address the concern with your customer at the external kick-off meeting. For example, if the customer's anticipated go-live date is not realistic, you can begin by describing all the activities needed, and the time it takes them to happen. This will clearly show a timeline that is realistic.

Special Instructions

None.

Reporting

None.

Records (Examples Listed Below. List Those Specific to Your Company.)

Risk Management Checklist
Risk Event Summary Log
Risk Event Identification Log

Training

Risk Management training by a PMI-Registered Education Provider.

Attachments

Risk Management Checklist is in Tools and Templates section in Chapter 6 of book. (Attach your company's checklist.)

Work Instruction #3: Project Schedules

Objective

To define the procedure for all of "Your Organization" project and program managers for creating project schedules.

Scope

This procedure applies to all projects under the management control of "Your Organization."

Reference Documents

(Insert either "None" or list any schedule templates that project and program managers can access.)

Definitions

None.

Procedure or Process

All projects, regardless of contract value or complexity, must have an associated schedule with copies in the Project Plan and Supporting documentation subfolder of the Project folder. (As per WI#1—Program and Project Documentation.) Software Application X available on the PMO Intranet (if not, delete line), in the Tools section. The templates are not mandatory. It is, however, required that the following scheduling elements be included in a project schedule:

Note: For every project schedule, specify minimum requirements such as milestones, task owners, start–end dates, subtasks, and relationships between tasks (FS, SS, SF, etc.). The minimum requirements are the elements cited below in the checklist.

In addition to the requirement that all projects have an associated schedule, programs or Customer Program Offices, and Program Management Offices, regardless of contract value or complexity, they *must* have an associated Master Schedule as well, with copies in the Project Plan and Supporting documentation subfolder of the Project folder. (As per WI#1—Program and Project Documentation.) Table 5.2 displays the minimum elements a schedule should contain.

Special Instructions

1. If multiple schedule templates are available, describe them here.
2. Upon completion of the project and handoff to the customer, it is required that the PM or program manager confirm that the account manager has reviewed the first invoice for accuracy. (Item 2 is an example of a special instruction.)
3. If you have a program with multiple related projects, each project should have its own schedule. Program managers may compile the individual project schedules into a single program schedule. MS Project 98, MS Project 2000,

Table 5.2 Scheduling Elements Checklist

Internal kick-off meeting
External (customer-facing) kick-off meeting
Progress meetings
Provisioning tasks
Site launch support meeting, if applicable
Risk mitigation tasks
Third party deliverables
Customer dependencies
Acceptance testing tasks
Launch support tasks
Confirmation that all contractual deliverables have been provided to the customer
Quality assurance tasks, if applicable
Project closure or disengagement

MS Project 2003, and MS Project 2007 have functionality that allows you to insert project schedules, in their entirety, into a program-level schedule.

4. The project manager can add a column to the scheduling software that will contain hyperlinks to documentation referenced in the task description.
5. Use a Tracking Gantt format to view Actual versus Baseline.

Reporting

Corporate management will access the project folders to view the project schedules.

Records

Project Schedule
Project Plan

Training

New project managers will receive a minimum of 24 classroom hours of instruction in MS Project. Updates to this standard will be communicated, as needed, via e-mail.

Attachments

None. (If templates are available, they can be listed here and attached. Templates are available in the Tools section of the book.)

Work Instruction #4: Quality Assurance

Objective

To define the process to be used for conducting independent assessments of our quality program to ensure conformance to our documented procedures, effective process implementation, and the effective use of resources.

Note: Quality Assurance reviews are performed to check on the quality and tools employed by program and project management staff; they are not designed to evaluate individual performance.

Scope

This procedure is *mandatory* for program and project managers to provide evidence of adherence to our quality procedures, quality policy, quality manual and quality plans, and goals.

Reference Documents

Add the review schedule document here.
Add the Auditor's Checklist here.
Add Sample QA Audit Form.
WI#17 Corrective and Preventative Actions.

Definitions

1. Corrective action: Action taken to solve or fix a problem
2. Preventative action: Action taken to eliminate the cause of a potential nonconformity or other potentially undesirable situation
3. Nonconformity: Nonfulfillment of a requirement

Procedure or Process

We will create an internal audit schedule to ensure that all areas of the quality system, including internal procedures and corporate-level procedures, are being followed. The areas defined on the schedule will be audited at least once a year based on the importance of the activities being conducted and the results of prior audits. Also defined on the audit schedule will be the scope of the audit, its frequency, and the methodology to be used. All audits will be conducted by personnel other than those who perform the activity being audited. All auditors will use the appropriate sections of approved checklists to conduct internal audits. Internal audits will ensure that all procedures are reviewed periodically for accuracy, and are effectively implemented and maintained.

The audit protocol consists of the following:

A. Audit notification: The auditee will be notified by the auditors prior to the upcoming audit, and a date will be agreed upon.
B. Auditors will prepare a checklist outlining what questions they will ask and what they will be looking for during the audit.
C. A brief opening meeting with the auditee and/or auditee management to review the audit plan.
D. Conducting the audit, including interviewing all the people who have to complete the questions on the checklist. The department manager may be present during the entire audit process.
E. A closing report meeting identifying all the findings of the audit. Management will take timely corrective action on deficiencies found during the audit.

Post Audit

Follow-up actions will include the verification of the implementation of corrective action, and verification activities will be recorded on the audit report.

Special Instructions

Types of Findings:

A. Observation: An observed condition that could affect the quality of our product/service which does not necessarily contradict what is outlined in our procedures or the ISO standard.
B. Minor nonconformance occurs when an observation indicates a departure from controlled procedures, documented specified requirements, or other applicable documents. A minor nonconformance is also where planned arrangements have been followed, but not strictly to the letter.
C. Major nonconformance occurs when an observation indicates a departure from controlled procedures, documented specified requirements, or other applicable documents; when there is an absence of a procedure or the total breakdown of its implementation; a number of findings against the same clause of the standard or paragraph of the procedure; or a number of findings reported in the same area or section of the organization.

Failure to comply with mandatory policies as stated in the work instructions are considered "nonconformities" and are categorized as major (failure to comply with the basic tenets of the WI) or minor (failure to comply with selected elements of the WI). A report summarizing the results of the review, including any nonconformities and recommended corrective actions, is sent to the reporting manager and department director.

Reporting

Upon completion of the audit and the verification of the corrective action, the results of the audit (consisting of the audit report and all findings) will be recorded and maintained. A summary of internal audit results will be reported to senior leadership at management review meetings. (The meeting stated is designed to review the integrity of the quality system.)

Records (Recommended Record Items Below)

Internal Audit Schedule
Audit Report Form

Retention

Records of internal audits will be maintained for a minimum of 1 year or for one full audit cycle of the specific area being audited. After that time, records shall be destroyed. Previous audit results may be useful to current auditors for specific areas to audit, areas in need of a reaudit, and to verify effective implementation of previous corrective actions. Records will be stored in such a way that they are protected from loss and readily retrievable. Records may be in electronic or paper format and shall be stored with the person responsible for the internal audit program.

Training

Internal Auditor Qualification/Certification Requirements

All internal auditors will be trained on how to conduct an audit. This training requirement can be met by attending a course given by an accredited ISO training body, or given by a trained auditor within the company. Evidence of training will be recorded on the employee's training record.

Attachments

None.

Work Instruction #5: Escalation

Objective

This work instruction defines the escalation standard for program and project management.

Scope

This procedure applies to everyone in "Insert Your Department Name Here" (add this note if your company has a helpdesk).

Note: This procedure serves as a guideline and does not substitute for the Event Management process.

Reference Documents

(Add this note if your company has a helpdesk) Escalation Matrix: Insert the Helpdesk Escalation Matrix; usually combined with specific time frames for each escalation.

Definitions

Party: Refers to the person who is responsible for the deliverables, action, or response. *Manager:* Refers to the program or project manager.

Procedure or Process

An issue should be escalated when attempts to obtain a satisfactory response through the primary contact have failed. Each escalation step assumes the following:

- Previous escalations resulted in an unacceptable or unsatisfactory response.
- The issue is still unresolved.
- The manager has received no response to previous escalations.

Guidelines for escalation:
Calls or e-mails should be supported by existing documentation such as (note that you should revise the job titles in *italic* so they match your company titles):

- Project plans signed by internal stakeholders
- Internal kick-off meeting minutes
- External kick-off meeting minutes
- Prior e-mail commitments
- Written confirmation of telephone commitments

(In some companies, certain departments state their response times. If your organization has this, it should be mentioned here.)

The initial escalation step should be in e-mail *and* voicemail to the party's direct supervisor (*first line manager*) with e-mail copies to the manager's *supervisor*.

The second escalation step should be in e-mail *and* voicemail to the party's *second line manager* (e.g., *director*) with e-mail copies to the manager's *supervisor*.

The third escalation step should be directly to the manager's supervisor for direct involvement in escalating the issue to the party's third line manager (e.g., *vice president*) with an e-mail copy to the manager's *director*, and the PMO *manager*.

The fourth escalation step should be initiated by the manager's supervisor in e-mail *and* voicemail to the manager's *director* for further escalation and resolution with copies to all parties engaged up to this point. The *director* may elect to initiate a project recovery effort if necessary.

Notes: The amount of time you should wait for a response before escalating a step further should depend on the urgency/severity of the issue. This is a judgment call managers must make, but as a *guideline*. For issues that place the project scope, schedule, or cost in jeopardy, wait no more than a maximum of 4 to 8 h between escalations. Each escalation communication should indicate the time frame in which you need a response and any previous escalation attempts.

Prior to escalating an issue, it is advisable that the project manager inquire as to the cause of the delay or lack of response. Apply common sense to that information. If, for example, the data center is not responding because they are experiencing a power outage, it might be better to give them more time.

Special Instructions

None. (If your company has a published escalation policy, it can be referenced here.)

Reporting

None.

Records

Documented history of the problem in need of escalation. Please add this to the project's documentation folder.

Training

None.

Attachments

None. (If your company has a published escalation policy, it can be attached here.)

Work Instruction #6: Project Tracking

Objective

These procedures define the requirements for all of "Your Department" program and project managers, for updating the status of programs and projects. (This work instruction assumes that senior management proactively monitors the health of active projects. If your company is currently managing projects by exception [only when there is a problem], the implementation of this quality management system is an opportunity to move toward a more proactive management approach.)

Scope

These procedures are *mandatory* for all programs and projects.

Reference Documents

(If your company has developed a project progress report template or software-enabled roll-up reporting, it should be referenced here. Please note that the latter is often referred to as *portfolio reporting* or *portfolio management*.)

Tip: *Project roll-up reports should be designed to gauge the project's health at a high level. The temptation to micromanage the work of the project managers should be avoided to maintain a PM-empowered culture. Try to keep the report to a major milestones level to control the level of effort needed by staff to generate this report.*

Definitions

PM designates project and program managers.

Procedure or Process

(Insert the reporting process here.)

Tip: *It is highly recommended that the labor hours of project team members along with Actual versus Baseline Gantt charts be included in the process for two reasons: It will allow the PM to manage using earned value management, and it will positively influence the corporate culture by raising awareness of project costs.*

Special Instructions

None.

Reporting

None. (If the company has a customer reporting policy, it can be inserted here.)

Records

None.

Training

It is recommended that the company's PMO (or designated senior-level project manager) provide training on internal and external progress reporting.

Attachments

None.

Work Instruction #7: Communications

Objective

This procedure provides standard *guidelines*, for program and project management, on communications protocols.

Scope

This procedure applies to all programs and projects being managed by "Your Department."

Reference Documents

WI#1—Program and Project Documentation
WI#3—Program and Project Schedules
WI#8—Launch Support
WI#22—Management Review Meeting Procedure

Tip: *List similar tools here; bear in mind that the next part of this book includes a number of communication tool templates.*

Launch Support Meeting Template
Project Kick-Off Meeting Template
Enterprise VoIP Kick-Off Meeting Template
Progress Report Template

Definitions

PM: Project or program manager, "manager"; project or program manager PPOC: primary point of contact.

Procedure or Process

Tip: *The PPOC concept described here is a helpful way to avoid scope creep.*

Project communications management is one of the basic elements of the Project Management Body of Knowledge. Communications comprise all interactions with internal and external stakeholders, including meetings, telephone conversations, and correspondence.

Once the contract has been signed and the PM assumes responsibility for the implementation, PMs serve as the PPOC with the customer. During the implementation, and launch support, the PPOC is responsible for defining the "rules of engagement" based on the following considerations.

The PPOC is the only individual with the authority to communicate changes to the program, project, or project plan, including:

- The quantity, specification, architecture, or performance criteria of the deliverables
- Milestone, summary task, or task dates in the project schedule (see WI#3—Program and Project Schedules)
- Risk Management Plan (see WI#2—Risk Management)
- Project budget
- Customer price
- Contractual provisions

It is understood that the PPOC shall make every effort to coordinate communications between members of the project team and the customer to ensure that there is no duplication of questions or inquiries. (Duplication of inquiries, particularly those related to Requirements Gathering or Definition, should alert the project manager that this may be a problem area.) This is further defined when refining the "rules of engagement."

Tip: *It should be noted that the PPOC function helps the management of customer expectations. It, additionally, prevents the intentional or unintentional playing off of one project team member against another. Finally, it is understood that other job functions such as sales need to be respected.*

The manager establishes the communication protocols for the project during the internal and external kick-off meetings. During the kick-off meetings, the manager should establish the following rules of engagement.

The manager is the PPOC and the leader of project-related meetings for the duration of the implementation. (The customer may have a different PPOC once the project is completed. That individual may be, for example, an account or service manager.)

At the internal kick-off, or shortly thereafter, the PPOC establishes the frequency (generally weekly) of progress meetings, including participants, date, time, location, and con-call number if necessary.

The manager will manage to the project plan, and will send updates to attendees well in advance of meetings, identifying key upcoming milestones and high-risk issues. The PPOC will develop a concise agenda for all formal meetings. (If templates have been developed, mention them here.)

The PPOC will be responsible for ensuring that the meeting minutes are written and that an Action Item Log for formal meetings is created.

Team members must document *significant* communications with the customer for review and subsequent filing (see WI#1—Program and Project Documentation).

Internal Kick-Off Meeting Objectives

From the manager's perspective, the primary objectives of the internal kick-off meeting are:

- Review the scope of work to ensure consistency with contractual obligations.
- Ensure that the team members and their functional groups have the information required to proceed.
- Identify any new risk issues that may have developed or that individual team members are concerned about.
- Define internal escalation paths.
- Define which milestones or activities must be reported on between progress meetings, how these updates will be communicated, and on what schedule.
- Identify any customer expectation issues that either exist or may develop.
- Define the milestone delivery dates.
- Ensure stakeholder buy-in.
- Establish schedule for progress meeting.

External Kick-Off Meeting Objectives

From the manager's perspective, the primary objectives of the external kick-off meetings are:

- Identify the manager as PPOC.
- Review the scope of work.
- Review or develop the program or project schedule.
- Discuss customer-controlled dependencies and their impact (e.g., deliverables that must be provided by the customer to keep the schedule on track).

- Manage the customer's expectations.
- Secure verbal customer buy-in on the program or project plan (this element should be documented in the minutes).
- Identify or discuss risk issues that may impact the implementation.
- Discuss third-party milestones, if any, that are schedule dependencies.
- Define the communication protocols (including ISP and customer escalation paths).

Launch Support Meeting Objectives

(See WI#8—Launch Support and the Launch Support Meeting Template for additional guidelines.) Although many of these items are hosting specific, some of these may be applicable for other products and services of the business.

From the manager's perspective, the primary objectives of the launch support meeting are:

- Reiterate the manager's role as the PPOC.
- Review risk, and identify any new risk issues.
- Review escalation paths during Launch Support phase.
- Solicit and gain (or reiterate, if already known) understanding of what the customer will be doing during the Launch Support period, such as applications that will be loaded or tested.
- Review customer expectations.
- Identify potential issues with content development and production environments.
- Confirm access rights to servers.
- Discuss acceptance testing and customer validation plan.
- Discuss the role of third-party integrators (if applicable).
- Schedule dates with the data center (provisioning) for hosting projects, engineering assistance, as needed for content loading to meet customer's schedule requirements.
- Identify run book. (The term *run book* refers to a data center document that contains the architecture, Bill of Materials, list of customer applications, maintenance requirements such as daily software patch installations, and emergency customer contact information.) Identify customer launch ("go live") date.

E-mail Distribution Protocol

The manager is responsible for ensuring that all team members receive timely and accurate information related to the tasks they are responsible for. For e-mail-based programs, project, or Program Management Office communications, the manager may set up mailing lists for each project. It is suggested that one be created for internal communications only, and one for all stakeholders, both internal and external.

An all-stakeholders list might include:

■ The internal list.
■ Customer's senior management.
■ Primary customer project interface.
■ Any third-party developers.
■ At no time should we *only* be communicating through third-party developers.
■ Subcontractors.
■ Vendors.

If the manager or other team members send e-mail updates on a regular basis, they may find it helpful to use sequential naming conventions (e.g., date or meeting number) to identify each correspondence.

Tips for Managing Successful Meetings

■ The PPOC will manage to a structured agenda that is as concise as possible. It is suggested that standard (consistent across all meetings of the same type) agendas be used, so as to set the expectations of participants appropriately.
■ If an individual has been identified to handle this project post-implementation, the PPOC should invite him or her to the last two or three meetings to facilitate the transition.
■ The project team members should forward questions or issues to the PPOC in advance of the meeting so they may be added to the agenda.

Possible Agenda for Progress Meetings

■ Roll call of attendees.
■ Review questions on minutes from last meeting, if any.
■ Review action items.
■ Technical staff asks/answers questions of customer.
■ Review schedule at a milestone level.
■ Review your company's delivery dates.
■ Discuss required deliverables from customer.
■ Update on status of identified risk issues.
■ Report on scope changes, if any.
■ Report on customer questions or concerns.
■ Assign new action items, if any.
■ Confirm next meeting date and location.

Special Instructions

None.

Reporting

None.

Records

Customer contracts
Project plan
Program or project schedule
Customer communications

Meeting minutes including:

- External kick-off meeting minutes
- Launch support meeting minutes

Training

When implementing the quality management system, it might be a good idea to determine the need, if any, for soft skill training, such as that required to effectively manage meetings.

Attachments

None.

Work Instruction #8: Launch Support

Objective

This procedure defines the standards and requirements, for all of "Your Organization" program and project managers, for projects that are hosting specific, during the Launch Support phase of an implementation.

Scope

This procedure is *mandatory* for hosting projects.

Reference Documents

WI#3—Program and Project Schedules
WI#9—Acceptance Testing
Launch Support Meeting Template

Definitions

The Launch Support phase begins after the architecture (servers) has been tested and handed over to the customer and ends when the customer's applications and/or content have been loaded and tested.

Procedure or Process

Activities associated with this phase of the project include the following:

Note: The launch support meeting is scheduled in lieu of one of the progress meetings, and subsequent progress meetings would address the action items from the launch support meeting.

Preparing for the Launch Support phase:

- Review risk assessment; identify issues pertaining to the Launch Support phase.
- Schedule and manage a launch support meeting after the external kick-off meeting. This meeting should occur in advance of any acceptance test and, as a general guide, should be conducted after 30% of the provisioning tasks are complete, or earlier where possible.
- If your company has help documents or written procedures for customers working on their services, make sure the customer has them.
- If the customer requires a password for access, make sure he or she has it.
- If there are any customer acceptance issues, resolve them at the upcoming meeting.
- If the implementation is phased (in other words, the customer's server hand-offs are in groups), this is the time to work out any scheduling issues.

The attendees should include:

- The customer (make sure the customer brings his or her technical personnel who will be working on the servers)
- Data center or provisioning representative implementation coordinator, if applicable
- Order manager, if applicable
- Your company's technical personnel
- Account support representative, if assigned
- Technical account manager, if assigned
- Your company's customer support staff representative, if assigned

During the Launch Support phase:

- Continue to act as the customer's primary point of contact (PPOC).
- Report on the status of risks identified at the external kick-off, as well as any new risks identified during the launch support meeting.

- Make sure the run book is up to date.
- Identify and proactively resolve potential issues with content development and/or production environments.
- Confirm access rights to servers.
- Discuss acceptance testing and customer validation plans, if changed.
- Discuss the role of customer service if appropriate.
- Discuss role of third-party integrators (if applicable) during Launch Support phase.
- Confirm internally scheduled delivery or milestone dates.
- Review open tasks, schedule, and dependencies.

After launch support has been provided and either the customer has loaded content or your company's contractual obligations have been completed, the manager:

- Issues a Project Completion and/or Transition Letter to the customer, confirming that
- the project has been successfully completed
- Transfers the customer to your company's customer support staff

Special Instructions

None.

Reporting

None.

Records

Launch support meeting minutes.

Training

(Your company may wish to consider opportunities for cross or awareness training.)

Attachments

None.

Work Instruction #9: Acceptance Testing

Objective

This procedure will define the standards and requirements, for all of "Your Organization" program and project managers, for projects that are hosting specific, during the Acceptance Testing phase of an implementation.

Scope

This procedure is *mandatory* for all hosting projects.

Reference Documents

WI#1—Project Documentation
WI#3—Project Schedules

Definitions

UAT is an acronym for unit acceptance test, which confirms that the unit has been installed and that it is possible to communicate with the unit. (The respective data center performs a ping test, using a software script that confirms that the unit is accessible via the Internet.)

System test is a test of the entire architecture including routers, data backup devices, firewalls, etc. This will require the development of a testing protocol that may include testing scripts. The testing should be planned bearing in mind risk issues and contractual obligations.

Customer acceptance testing is the protocol, mutually agreed to, as to how the customer will confirm that the contractual deliverables have been provided. (To the extent that the customer requests this type of test, the associated tasks are defined at the launch support meeting and subsequently included in the project schedule.) Both your company and the customer perform this.

Note: In many cases, this represents activities coordinated between the customer and your company's technical staff.

Results of the UAT and or system acceptance testing should be obtained and stored in the project folder as per WI#1—Project Documentation.

Procedure or Process

Managers are responsible for the scope management (a keystone in the Project Management Body of Knowledge) of their projects, which includes ensuring that all the contractual deliverables are provided to the customer in good working order. Managers are responsible for ensuring that acceptance testing, or its equivalent, has been conducted for all service elements, including hardware and software, and that the tests confirm that the deliverables have passed these tests. The project manager must perform confirmation of testing and results.

Project deliverables may include hardware, software, and services or a combination of these. Hardware deliverables include devices and all their components. Software deliverables include applications provided by your company or others, such as CHP. Customer-provided software installed by your company personnel is considered a service. It is the manager's responsibility to ensure that each item is delivered as specified in the contractual documents, and in the manner specified in your company's service descriptions. The task associated with Acceptance Testing must be included in the project schedule. (See WI#3—Project Schedules)

After the internal unit acceptance testing (UAT) or system testing is completed and the Launch Support phase is complete, the customer will validate the entire solution. Although technical expertise will vary from customer to customer, every customer should be able to confirm that he or she has access to or can use the basic products and services implemented by your company. An example of this, in a hosting environment, the customer has tested access to the installed servers as specified in the contract. If the solution includes a firewall, the customer should verify that the access rights have been set properly.

Special Instructions

None.

Reporting

None.

Records

None.

Training

None.

Attachments

None.

Work Instruction #10: Transferring Projects

Objective

This procedure defines the standards and requirements for "Your Organization" when transferring accounts or projects from the project management group to your company's service organization. It is also applicable to project transfers within the project management group.

Scope

This procedure applies to "Your Organization" program and project management staff.

Reference Documents

WI#1—Program and Project Documentation
Account or Project Transition Checklist
Project Completion Notification Letter

Definitions

PM: Project or program manager.

Procedure or Process

The objective of this process is to ensure that projects, when transferred, are done so in a seamless way. Two types of transfers are possible: Between project managers or between a project manager and your company's service organization. The transfer is accomplished by using a Transition Checklist.

This transition plan contains four stages:

1. *Stage One* encompasses data collection relevant to reviewing and assessing the account and customer's needs.
2. In *Stage Two*, this data will be reviewed by the "transfer team" for accuracy and posted to the appropriate electronic customer folder per WI#1—Project Documentation. The new (individual to whom the project or account is transferred) "manager" will be responsible for keeping the documentation up to date upon transfer.
3. *Stage Three* will gradually migrate the account or project responsibilities from the originating "manager" to the "manager," who will then take on the leadership role on the account.
4. *Stage Four* covers the official handoff.

Special Instructions

1. The Transition Checklist and Project Completion Notification Letter are required if all four stages of the plan apply to your account or project transfer (see guide for details).
2. The new manager taking over the project or account needs to ensure that all the electronic documentation (see WI#1—Project Documentation) has been edited to include the new manager's name for all the folios contained in the project folders.

Reporting

A transition schedule baseline is sent to the *director*.

Records

The completed transition schedule, checkpoint table, and Project Completion Notification letter must be stored per WI#1—Project Documentation.

Training

None.

Attachments

None.

Work Instruction #11: Customer Satisfaction Surveys

Objective

This procedure will define the standards and requirements for "Your Organization" for performing customer satisfaction surveys (upon completion of an implementation and, in some cases, for ongoing support), in order to provide the necessary feedback to improve "Your Organization."

Scope

This procedure is *mandatory*.

Reference Documents

WI#1—Project Documentation
WI#3—Program and Project Schedules

Definitions

None.

Procedure

An essential component of continuous improvement, customer satisfaction surveys provide feedback necessary to improve the company.

Tasks have been included in the Project Schedules templates developed by the PMO (see WI#3—Program and Project Schedules) to remind managers to have their customers complete these reviews at the conclusion of every new project.

Online Customer Satisfaction Surveys—Mandatory

Surveys for both implementation and ongoing customers can be found at: http://your-organization's survey URL. (Web-based surveys are suggested as they can be automatically tracked and stored.)

Special Instructions

1. The project management survey is completed once at the conclusion of the project.
2. The ongoing support survey, when appropriate, is on a quarterly basis, beginning one quarter after the completion of the project management survey.
3. If explicitly requested by the customer, the ongoing support survey frequency may be adjusted accordingly, and the project manager should maintain a record of that request.

Reporting

None. (If your company publishes the results, it is suggested that the project and program managers with the highest scores be acknowledged and, when possible, be given a monetary bonus.)

Records

None. (The PMO or the company's QA group should retain the results for future trend analysis.)

Training

None.

Attachments

None.

Work Instruction #12: Document Control Process

Objective

To define the document control system for all Program Management Office documents (PMO) and to establish a standard numbering convention for all PMO-generated documents. (If your company does not have a PMO, name the project manager designated to manage this process. Note: This process may be, at times, labor intensive. It is, however, a process that all ISO quality management systems [as well as most other quality systems] require for certification. Note as well that the individual, ideally in the PMO, responsible for the integrity of the quality system is referred to as the QA manager.)

Scope

This procedure applies to all controlled documentation developed and managed by the Program Management Office. This procedure does not include Customer Project Documentation (Records) that are generated by "Your Organization" program and project manager's staff or any of the following:

(If your company uses an Intranet that records inputs via an accessible database, indicate that here. Similarly, if your company has enterprise project management software that automatically records and stores data input, indicate that here as well.)

Reference Documents

WI#13—Management Document Review Process

(Create the templates listed below for your quality management system. This will ensure professional quality consistency regardless of the project or program manager's office location.)

  WI Template
  Tools Template
  Excel Template
  PPT Template
  Visio Template
  Word Template
  Help Template
  PMO Documentation Library Log

Definitions

There are three types of documents that are considered controlled documents:

1. Procedures/process: These documents outline a procedure or process that must be followed. These documents must contain a document control page with a revision history. Procedures/process documents can be in any format, i.e., MS Word, MS Excel, MS PowerPoint, etc.
2. Supporting documentation: These documents support a procedure or process document, contain guideline information, or just contain general information to be used as a reference. These documents do not need a document control page, nor do prior revisions need to be maintained. These documents must contain a document #, date, and revision level identified somewhere on the document, i.e., footer, bottom of page, or header, and must be approved prior to use as outlined in this procedure. Training presentations and self-study guides are considered supporting documents.
3. Form/Template: These documents are empty shells that outline specific requirements that need to be filled in by the user. A separate document control page with revision history is needed as defined in this procedure. The document control page should be in MS Word format. The form/template can be in any format, i.e., MS Word, MS Excel, MS PowerPoint, etc. There should not be any document control information contained on the form/template itself. Forms/templates do not need to have prior revisions maintained. The type of each document will be identified on the PMO Documentation Library Log.
   A. PMO ID#—Distinct 9-digit ID number assigned by the QA Manager for a document.
   B. Version—The # of the document issue.
   C. Issue Date—The date the document was revised.
   D. Effective Date—When applicable and where appropriate, an effective date may be established. The effective date is the date to start using/implementing the procedure. There may be a delay from the issue date to the effective date due to training, software upgrades (or new systems) not being available, or other circumstances to allow for a time to transition from the old process to the new one.
   E. Change Details—A record of what has been released and edited.
   F. Document Owner/Author—The author and individual responsible for maintaining and updating the document. The originating author may transfer a document to a new owner; hence, this new individual becomes the new author.
   G. Document Location—Where the document is located: Web site, etc.
   H. Approver—Individuals who are responsible for approving documents prior to release.

I. Reviewer—Any individuals deemed appropriate by the owner/author to review the document for accuracy and comments.
J. Attachments—Any supporting documentation attached to the procedure, including but not limited to, process maps that may be unique to this process.
K. Objective—Goal or purpose of the process.
L. Scope—A clear description of whom the procedure affects and what the procedure applies to.
M. Reference documents—Additional documents, forms, or subprocesses that apply or should be used in conjunction with the procedure. Add the PMO ID# if applicable.
N. Definitions—Any acronyms or technical terms may be defined here.
O. Reporting—Are any special reporting requirements?
P. Special instructions—Do any special requirements or instructions apply?
Q. Procedure or process—The details of the process.
R. Records—Are any customer/quality records produced as a result of this procedure?
S. Training—Define who needs to be trained prior to making the content of the document enforceable.

Procedures

New Documents

When a new controlled document is developed, the owner/author must complete the required document control template. In addition to completing the appropriate template, the owner/author needs to add the development of this new document to the PMO Master Activity Log as a distinct activity. The document is then sent to the QA manager for review and approval. Table 5.3 indicates which document control template should be used for new documents.

Amending an Existing Document

When updating an existing document, the document owner/author must download the most current version from the Web (if you do not have Web capability, indicate location of the templates) and update the existing document control template to reflect the changes that have been made by adding comments in the Change Details section, and editing the version #, issue date, and any applicable reviewer name requests. The desired updates or changes are then to be made to the document. The review and approvals process is the same for amendments to documents.

Anyone in "Your Organization" may make suggestions to the owner/author via e-mail or phone for suggested updates or may enter comments into the latest version and submit for review.

Table 5.3   Document Control Table by Type

New Document Type	Document Control Template to Use
Work Instructions	WI Template—PMO ID#
Tools	Tools Template—PMO ID#
Process/Procedure Documents	Word Template—PMO ID#
Help documentation	Help Template—PMO ID#
Process Map/Graphics	Visio Template—PMO ID# or Word Template—PMO ID#
Form/Template	Use document control sheet as outlined in WI template ID# (no set template for new forms; just create the new Form/Template) Form/Template; use document control sheet as outlined in WI template ID#

Obsolete or Retired Documents

When a document is determined to be obsolete, it must be sent through the review and approvals process to be removed from circulation. A justification must be made for the document to be deemed obsolete, in the Change Details section on the document control page. Anyone in "Your Organization" may make suggestions to the owner/author via e-mail or phone to recommend making a document obsolete or may enter comments into the latest version and submit for review.

External Documents

"Your Organization" staff will exercise care with external documentation while it is under the control of the project manager. Documents that are external to "Your Organization" program and project managers will be identified by customer's name and documentation location. They will be considered records and will be listed on the Records Master Log.

Numbering Convention

The QA manager will review the document to ensure that the document control template elements are included, and assign a document control #. The QA manager will maintain the PMO Documentation Library Log and will be responsible for issuing PMO ID numbers for all controlled documents. Document ID numbers start with PMO ID# and a 5-digit sequential # (example of a PMO ID#: 1082-00012).

Document Reviews and Approvals Process

(Note: Change job titles "PMO director" and/or "QA manager" to fit your company or department.) The QA manager will approve all PMO documentation. The PMO director will approve any documents developed by the QA manager.

Approvals will be provided electronically. The QA manager (and PMO director, if applicable) will initial the document control template ("Approvals" section) and add the approval date; with the approvals enclosed, the QA manager will forward the document back to the owner/author.

The QA manager will ensure that the appropriate subject matter experts are engaged for document reviews and feedback. The owner/author may identify specific reviewers in the document control template "Reviewer" section.

The QA manager will determine if the document requires a management team review. (The "management team" refers to the senior-level managers sponsoring the quality management system.) If this is required, the QA manager will send the document to (insert e-mail address) with a request to review, following the procedures outlined in Work Instruction #13.

The QA manager will update the PMO Library Log (which can be substituted for your company's document management system) to reflect the new revised date and version # for all reviewed and approved documents.

Training Determination and Method

For all PMO documentation, the QA manager will determine if training is required and the training method to be employed. A document containing a procedure/process cannot be considered fully implemented until all training has been completed. Once a determination has been made regarding training, the QA manager forwards the document to the document owner/author.

Exceptions: There may be some exceptions whereby training is delivered in phases and the process is effective in those areas that have received the required training. If no training for the document or procedure is required, the QA manager will forward the approved document to the owner/author with the assigned PMO ID#.

Examples of the method of delivery include:

- Informal—user reads document.
- Formal—on-site classroom training.
- Web-based.
- E-mail notification with instructions.

Posting Documents to the PMO Intranet

(References to the Web or Web team may be substituted for your company's document management system.) The document owner/author will forward the reviewed and approved document to the Web team, using the required Quick Web form (PMO-ID#).

The Web team will have the document posted within 48 h of receipt of the required information and document. Once the document is posted to the PMO intranet, the intranet project manager or assigned person from the Web team will send an e-mail notification indicating that the document has been posted.

Control of Originals and Archiving

The PMO QA manager will maintain an electronic copy of the most current version of all PMO documentation, including the approvals, in native format, in a password-protected area, and will back up all files on a monthly basis, using online backup.

The PMO QA manager will also maintain a copy of one prior revision and a record of its approval in a secure site for all procedure/process documents. No prior versions or approvals need to be maintained for supporting documents or forms/templates.

Special Instructions

Paper copies of procedures are not under control, nor are they considered controlled documents. Only the version that is available on the (may be substituted for your company's document management system) PMO intranet or another approved Web-based, electronic media is controlled.

Reporting

None.

Records

None.

Training

None.

Attachments

Embedded process map.

Document Control Process Flow Map as displayed in Figure 5.1. (The Web Team swim lane may be substituted for the document management system team.)

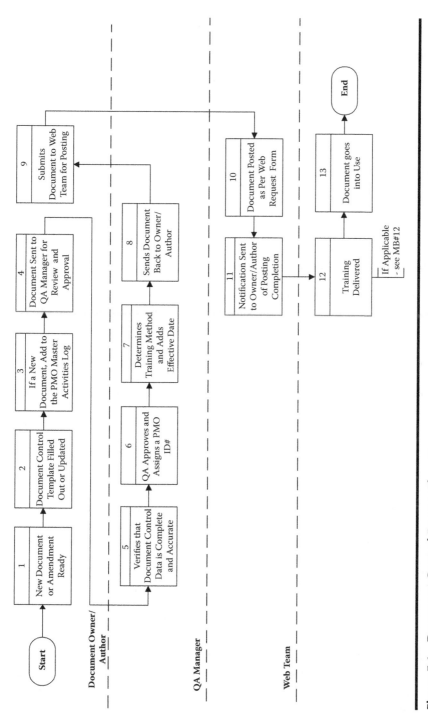

Figure 5.1 Document Control Process Flow Map.

Work Instruction #13: ISO Document Review Process

Objective

This procedure defines the process by which the management team (the "management team" refers to your company's senior management that sponsored the quality system and is responsible for its integrity) can review controlled documents before they are approved and released.

Scope

This procedure is *mandatory* for all quality system documentation that applies to "Your Organization" program and project managers, with the exception of PMO-specific procedures or documentation.

Reference Documents

WI#12—Document Control Process—PMO ID-#.

ISO Charter—This refers to the Charter for the ISO Implementation Project. The charter is an ideal mechanism for initiating an ISO certification effort.

Definitions

(Substitute the titles in *italic* with the corresponding job titles of your organization.)

Management team—Composed of the *regional directors* and the *director* of "Your Organization" will follow the steps outlined below when reviewing a new document.

Procedure

1. Draft copy #1 of every new document will be circulated to the management team for a 5-business-day review period. A reviewer may request another 5-business-day review period. The QA manager will ensure that all reviewers are listed on the document control template and that they have completed the table and initialed a completed review date.
2. Management team members may elect to include his or her management team in the review process: If a management team member elects to include his or her management team, the timelines associated with this process will still apply. If the comments do not conflict with other reviewer comments or ISO standards, they will be incorporated and posted on business day 6.
3. If comments received conflict, a conference call will be scheduled by the PMO director with the management team to resolve these conflicts and reach agreement on the final edits. If comments conflict with basic ISO standards, an explanation will be provided by the PMO director with supporting information or examples.

4. Nonpolicy or nonmaterial updates, such as a new URL or group name, will be completed and posted by the PMO on a quarterly basis, within the first 3 weeks of each new quarter.

5. A PMO-proposed policy change to any of the documents defined in the scope of this procedure will be handled as if it were a brand new document per steps 1–3.

6. Changes or updates to these defined documents will be communicated via e-mail to the management team.

7. If the conference call does not conclude with resolution, the director of "Your Organization" will make the final decision.

8. The PMO director will address nonpolicy updates, such as new URLs or technical corrections to existing work instructions or similar previously approved documents.

Special Instructions

None.

Reporting

None.

Records

None.

Training

This work instruction will be explained at the next management team meeting.

Attachments

None.

Work Instruction #14: Post-Project Reviews

Objective

This procedure defines the standards and requirements, for all of "Your Company or Department" program and project managers, for performing post-project reviews.

Scope

This procedure applies to all projects and accounts being managed by "Insert department name here" program and project managers.

Reference Documents

MB#1—Project Documentation
Post-Project Review Form

Definitions

PPR Form: Post-Project Review Form.

Procedure or Process

After a project has been completed, it is *mandatory* that the project/program manager conduct a post-project review and submit a completed PPR document.

The PPR submission is the posting of this document (in your document management system) in the Project Reviews folder in the appropriate Customer Folder as per MB#1.

The PPR form provided by the PMO is not required, but is strongly recommended. If the PM chooses not to use the PPR form, then the instructions outlined below in Section 6, item 3, will apply.

See Section 6 below for special instructions and notes.

Special Instructions

1. The QA and process and tools program managers will review the post-project reviews on a monthly basis (monthly meeting) to identify potential preventative or corrective actions, and when applicable, manage them in accordance with MB#17 Corrective Action.
2. After the monthly review meeting, select PPRs will be chosen for posting on the PMO intranet (or your document management system).
3. The PPR form is not required; however, if the PPR form is not used, then the details and questions that appear in the PPR form provided by the PMO *must* be provided as part of the PM's submission in their preferred format (this can be done by cut and paste into any format). It is highly recommended that the PPR form be used so that additional work is avoided with cutting and pasting into other formats.

Special Notes:

If possible, the PPR form should be developed in a meeting with the project team. If a team meeting is not possible, it is suggested that input be obtained through e-mail. If a project team meeting is not feasible or team member inputs via e-mail have not been successful, the project/program manager should fill out the form using his or her best judgment. Although the project team meeting is not required, it is recommended because:

1. It gives the PM opportunity to exercise leadership, which may positively influence future projects.
2. The team meeting synergy often yields insights for opportunities for continuous improvement.

Tip: *One way of getting a better response from the project team is by sending them the PPR form developed by the PMO and asking them to answer any of the questions they would like to answer, as they see fit.*

Reporting

None.

Records

Post-Project Review Form.

Training

None.

Attachments

None.

Work Instruction #15: Scope Change Management

Objective

To define the standard for all of "Your Company or Department" program and project managers, for managing program and project scope changes.

Scope

This work instruction applies to all programs and projects being managed by "Your Company or Department" program and project managers and is *mandatory* for the following:

1. Any change in contractual scope obligations.
2. Any scope changes that significantly impact the cost or schedule of a project or program. It is within the discretion of the project manager to determine which noncontractual scope changes represent "significant impacts."

Tip: *Remember the Triangle of Truth; a change in scope will almost always require changes to the schedule and budget. This is also known as the "triple constraints."*

Reference Documents

Scope Change Management Checklist
Scope Change Form

Definitions

None.

Procedure or Process

The Scope Change Management Checklist should be completed by the program or project manager: Copy of checklist is in Tools section of the book.

Special Instructions

This work instruction is applicable to all LOBs.

Reporting

None.

Records

Scope Change Management Checklist

Training

Updates will be communicated via e-mail for version 3.0.

Attachments

Embedded in this work instruction:

Scope Change Management Checklist
Scope Change Form

Work Instruction #16: Presales Process

TIP: *In many companies the sales organization and the delivery or project management organization are two different departments each with its own management team.*

The selling organization works to provide the best customer solution at the best price. The delivery organization wants to make sure that the commitments to the customer take into account potential risk issues, potential schedule issues, and potential resource issues. To avoid conflicts, a work instruction that includes a Roles and Responsibilities Matrix along with a clear presales process can be of immeasurable help.

Objective

This document defines the Presales process via a graphical representation and provides a Roles and Responsibilities Matrix for the sales and project management communities during the Presales phase of the project life cycle.

Scope

This process is applicable to all of "Insert department name here" sales personnel and project management staff.

Reference Documents

Presales Process Map—Mapping out the process can help define roles and responsibilities.
Roles and Responsibilities Matrix—Embedded.
Scope Review Guide (a tool that facilitates a scope analysis).

Definitions

(Change the acronym and job titles to match your company's organizational structure.) BDM—business development/sales manager, PM—program or project manager, SE—sales engineer

Procedure or Process

Process Map identified workflow.
Refer to Roles and Responsibilities Matrix for distinct BDM and PM activities associated with the Presales Phase.

Special Instructions

Insert items such as password access to sales and pricing applications.

Reporting

Statement of Work sign-offs from sales and project management supervisors.

Records

Scope Review Guide
Statement of Work

Training

Joint (BDM and PM) training sessions.

Attachments

1. Roles and Responsibilities Matrix as depicted in Table 5.4—Embedded
2. Presales Process Map—Embedded

(Insert sales process map here.)

Table 5.4   Roles and Responsibilities

Activity	BDM	SE	PM
Complete requirement questionnaires		✓	
Design architecture		✓	
Engineering risk analysis		✓	
Define Bill of Materials		✓	
Obtain resource labor hours (if needed)			✓
Determine delivery dates			✓
Draft Statement of Work	✓		
Pricing	✓		
Finalize Statement of Work			✓
Obtain customer signature on Statement of Work	✓		
Sets up internal and external kick-off meetings			✓
Chairs and documents internal kick-off			✓
Chairs and documents external kick-off			✓

Work Instruction #17: Corrective and Preventative Actions

Objective

To define the process to identify and manage improvements. Use appropriate sources of data to detect, validate, analyze, and eliminate causes and potential causes of nonconformities. Assign and track actions necessary to assure timely and effective preventative and corrective actions have been taken. Enable management review of relevant information for actions taken, including changes to procedures. To document actions taken as a part of "Your Company's or Department's" continuous improvement process.

Scope

This procedure shall be used to correct any problems or nonconformities identified at any time. This procedure shall also be used to implement actions that will prevent problems from occurring or reoccurring.

Reference Documents

Corrective and Preventative Actions Log
Notice of Corrective Action, Preventative Action, or Continuous Improvement Opportunity Form

Definitions

Conformity indicates that the work process or product meet the quality standard. Nonconformity indicates that the work process or product does not meet the quality standard.

Procedure or Process

We will use appropriate sources of information that affect project quality, including quality assurance review results, customer satisfaction surveys, results of after-action reviews, and information gathered from customer phone calls to detect, analyze, and eliminate causes and potential causes of nonconformities.

A corrective action can be generated from any of the following sources:

■ A breakdown of an internal process
■ Internal audit results

- Key measurement reports
- Benchmarking information
- Feedback (i.e., customer complaints, customer satisfaction surveys)

When a nonconformance is identified through an internal audit, it will be identified in the Audit Report.

(Titles in *italic* should be changed to reflect your organization.)

When a nonconformance is identified, whether in-house or from a customer complaint, a Notice of Corrective Action, Preventative Action, or Continuous Improvement Opportunity Form (PMO ID #) will be filled out, stating the problem/nonconformance in full detail, by the person who identified the problem or received the complaint. The form will be forwarded to the *manager for quality assurance.*

The *manager for quality assurance* will review the nonconformance, and a tracking number will be assigned. A determination will be made as to who the most appropriate person is to address the nonconformance, and the CAR (with all details) will be forwarded to that person's *regional manager* for further investigation and action.

Tip: *Determine the root cause on nonconformities by simply asking "why" and challenging unspoken assumptions.*

The person assigned will own the nonconformance and is responsible for correcting it. He or she will:

a. Launch an investigation to determine the causes of the nonconformity.
b. Evaluate the need for action to ensure that nonconformities do not recur.
c. Determine and implement action needed.
d. Record the results of action taken.
e. Review corrective action taken.

(If your company has a corporatewide quality program and you want your quality system to link with theirs, the interface can be placed here. It may simply be that the link is activated in two ways.

1. Send audit results and corrective action database at a given frequency.
2. Secure their assistance when the cause of the nonconformity resides in a department outside of program and project management.)

Once the corrective action has been identified, an evaluation to determine the action needed to ensure the nonconformities do not recur (preventative action) will be identified and documented on the Corrective Action Request Log and implemented.

Preventative action will include:

a. Determining potential nonconformities and their causes
b. Evaluating the need for action to prevent occurrence of nonconformities
c. Determining and implementing action needed
d. Recording the results of action taken
e. Reviewing preventative action taken

All required corrective and preventative action that is identified will be implemented. Upon implementation, a reevaluation/reaudit will be completed to determine if the corrective and preventative action taken was appropriate and effective. If the corrective and preventative action was successfully implemented, the Correct Action Request will be closed. If the corrective and preventative action taken was not successful, further investigation into the root cause of the problem will be required, and this process will begin again until resolution.

The program manager for quality assurance is responsible for performing a follow-up review to ensure that the corrective action has been effective in preventing or eliminating the cause of the nonconformance. The program manager for quality assurance will determine the appropriate timing or schedule for performing the follow-up review according to the nature of the cause and/or corrective action taken.

Special Instructions

Continuous Improvement:

The Notice of Corrective Action, Preventative Action, or Continuous Improvement Opportunity Form (PMO ID #1082-00057) can be used by anyone in the department to provide opportunities for continuous improvement. When a best practice is developed, the project team should be acknowledged and the work product posted for use by other project teams.

Reporting

All corrective and preventative action requests and actions taken will be recorded and maintained in the Corrective and Preventative Actions Log. A summary of corrective and preventative actions will be reviewed by senior leadership at management review meetings.

Records

Records of corrective and preventative action will be maintained for a minimum of one (1) year. After that time, records shall be destroyed. Previous corrective and preventative action information may be useful in current situations and may be maintained longer than one (1) year. Corrective action requests will be assigned a unique number; records will be stored in such a way that they are protected from loss and readily retrievable. Records may be in electronic or paper format and shall be stored with the person responsible for the corrective action program.

Training

The process defined in this work instruction will be part of the New Hire Training Program.

Attachments

None.

Work Instruction #18: Tools Development and Review Procedure

Objective

Provide the procedure followed by the PMO to review proposals for new tools, update existing tools, and respond to comments and suggestions for improvement of tools by staff.

Scope

This procedure is applicable to all of "Your Company or Department" program and project managers and includes the roles and responsibilities for the Tools Review Committee.

Reference Documents

TRC Meetings Log
New Tool Request Form (form in Attachments section)

Definitions

TRC: Tools Review Committee (this is a representative group of line staff that test-drive and evaluate new or improved tools).
PMO: Program Management Office (or designated senior-level project manager).

Procedure or Process

New Tools

When a new tool idea or suggestion has been made, the requestor needs to complete a New Tool Request form for review and consideration by the PMO.

The PMO will review the proposed idea and provide a response status of any of the following: Approved (estimated target date), Declined (with why), or Tabled (added to list for future development).

The development of new tools is subject to constraints such as the availability of resources, budget, time, and existing projects being managed by the program manager for process and tools.

Updates to Existing Tools

Tools are reviewed, and if updates are needed, revised and posted on a quarterly basis. Often, the TRC is engaged to review existing tools and related processes for continuous improvement. The PMO facilitates TRC review meetings, tracks comments and new ideas, and logs all TRC review meetings in the TRC Meetings Log.

Updates to tools are also made when there has been a change in a process or work instruction and the tool is a dependency to completing a task or procedure. If this is the case, the PMO makes updates, and a notification of these updates is announced in the PMO Pipeline Quarterly Newsletter. (The electronic newsletter vehicle can keep the project management community informed, is a medium to recognize performance, and can serve as a training mechanism.) If work instructions are impacted by these changes, the *QA manager* is notified via e-mail for recommended updates to the work instructions.

Anyone in "Insert company or department name here" may send suggestions via e-mail for consideration and review. The TRC is the established forum for reviewing suggestions, but the PMO may choose to respond independently.

Tools Review Committee—Objectives and Protocols

The Tools Review Committee is composed of delivery staff of every functional role. The scope of this group is limited to reviews for implementation services; however, some of the tools that are reviewed may, in fact, impact other organizations, i.e., provisioning. In general, the Tools Review Committee is engaged when a new tool or related process change is being developed or reviewed. The TRC does not have a formal charter or process; instead, the objective and TRC requirements for a particular TRC meeting are provided in an e-mail, and any available samples, history, or documentation are forwarded prior to the scheduled date. If advance reviewing of the product or process and specific preparation for the meeting is required, the TRC members are notified in advance.

On average, TRC members are asked to contribute 4 h per month for reviews. The requirements for the TRC are that each member, when asked to participate in a TRC meeting (customer meetings being priority one), review the materials or tools and provide feedback on the functionality of the tool or process as it relates to their specific job function or provide a set of new criteria in the form of specific needs.

Based on the feedback received from the TRC, the PMO will review the recommendations and determine if the suggestions or comments for changes are incorporated.

The PMO is responsible for managing the TRC-related functions, meetings, members, establishing priorities for TRC reviews, and communicating the objectives and requirements for all TRC reviews.

Special Instructions

None.

Reporting

None.

Records

E-mail suggestions from staff
E-mail responses to suggestions or proposed new tools
Log of TRC review meetings

Training

Updates will be communicated via the PMO Pipeline Newsletter.

Attachments

Embedded attachment—New Tool Request Form as displayed in Figure 5.2.

Work Instruction #19: Training Procedure

Objective

To identify and document how training requirements will be determined and delivered.

Requester:	Enter your name
Audience for tool:	Enter user community
Purpose	What is the purpose and how will this tool be used? What process is being impacted?
Scope	What is covered by this tool?
Functional requirements	What are the specific functional requirements?
Format requirements	Are there any format requirements?
Access requirements	How will this tool be accessed?
Special comments	Any additional info that is helpful or special guidelines.
Samples provided	Include attachments, if available, with request form.
Special contacts	Provide contact names and information. For additional subject matter experts that may be engaged by the Program Manager for assistance.
Request submitted on:	Enter date
Status of proposal: Approved/Tabled/Declined	Program Manager for Process and Tools to return form with status
Target date	Enter the date this tool is needed
Initials: (Tool developer)	Individual developing tool

Figure 5.2 Tool Request Form.

Scope

All "Insert company or department name here" staff shall have the appropriate skills required to perform their job responsibilities. In the pursuit of professional growth, when additional duties are added to people's responsibilities, additional training requirements will be identified. A plan will be created to ensure everyone receives the required training: Based on entry-level, basic, and advanced training paths for assistant, associate, project manager, and senior project manager job titles.

Tip: *Job descriptions that include requirements such as CAPM® or PMP® certification facilitate a uniform knowledge base. The Tools section of this book includes a Project Management Interview Guide that can be used as part of the new hire screening process.*

Reference Documents

Staff Roles and Responsibilities Matrix
Professional Growth and Development Plan
Company and departmental organization charts
Training paths
Training schedule
Self-study guides
Training database

Definitions

None.

Procedure or Process

Job descriptions including required competencies for positions within "Insert company or department name here" are available at the following URL: (if not Web-based, indicate location) http://Your company URL.

Through the use of the job descriptions, "Insert company or department name here" will ensure that personnel are aware of the relevance and importance of their activities and how they contribute to the achievement of the quality objectives.

The senior managers identify gaps in the educational background of their direct reports that require additional training. This training will be added to a professional growth and development training plan for employees, as needed. The senior manager notifies the PMO Training Group of the employee's training requirements. This professional growth and development training plan is tracked and maintained by employees' senior manager to ensure that employees are getting the required training. Employees are responsible for signing up for any courses they need. The training group is available to coordinate with employees to provide information on schedules and assist in registering for the required training.

Additionally, training on PMO tools and work instructions will be provided by the PMO Training Group.

Adequate and appropriate training of personnel will be provided to satisfy identified skill or training requirements or training needs as a component of the company's quality assurance system. Training is to be provided to all new employees, and on a periodic or "as-needed" basis to experienced employees. Training records are considered quality records and are controlled in accordance with the Quality Record Procedure.

Effective use of the PMO training is tracked during Quality Assurance Review audits. If training is found to be ineffective, the PMO Training Group is notified and corrective action is required. Additionally, level 1 evaluation will be conducted via participant evaluation forms to determine the effectiveness of the training. Where training is not effective, the training materials are revised and the training is readministered.

Special Instructions

The Human Resource Department procedures to be specifically followed for implementation of this policy are:

- Tuition Reimbursement Policy.
- Job Description and Requirements Policy.

Where appropriate, the Human Resources Department will retain records of these transactions and activities.

Reporting

None.

Records

Training records and records of training needs are quality records and are controlled in accordance with the Quality Record Procedure except those controlled by Human Resources.

Records of education, training, skills, and experience will be maintained by the PMO for the term of employment.

Training

Semiannual management training session led by the PMO Training Group. Version 2.0.

Attachments

None.

Work Instruction #20: Program Resource Management

Objective

To define the standard for all "Insert company or department name here" program and project managers, for managing program resources.

Tip: *This work instruction is designed to address situations where the project or program manager needs resources above and beyond those available to him in his cost center.*

Note: This work instruction is based on the following assumptions:

■ Program managers are a higher level that project managers.
■ Program managers report to a regional director.
■ Program managers may have project managers reporting to them as matrix resources.
■ Some program managers work at customer sites.

Scope

This work instruction applies to all programs being managed by "Insert company or department name here" program and project managers.

Reference Documents

None.

Definitions

LOE: Level of effort—Translated into labor hours per activity to be input in the Task Authorization Form
PPOC: Primary point of communication

Procedure or Process

1. If a member of a program team requires additional resources:
   ■ The request should include LOE data extracted from a project plan, to the extent possible.
   ■ A request is then made to the program manager.
2. If the program manager approves the request and the required resource is within this department:
   ■ The department's regional manager's Task Authorization Form will be processed by the program manager and sent to the regional manager to whom the program manager reports.
   ■ The regional manager will work with the program manager to determine the appropriate resource.

3. If the required resource is external to this department:
   - The program manager will act as the PPOC.
   - The program manager will contact the supervisor or manager of the department that is being asked to provide the additional resource.
   - The regional manager will be kept copied and informed.
   - If an escalation is required, the program manager will follow the procedure outlined in MB#5—Escalation. If the program manager elects to involve departmental management:
     - The regional manager will be engaged and the program manager will participate in the joint discussion, continuing the PPOC role (but with the regional manager's support).
   - If the director of all the regional directors is engaged, the regional manager will be kept informed, and any joint discussions will have the program manager as the PPOC (but with the director's support). If the director elects to have a private one-on-one discussion with a manager external to the department:
     - The director will communicate this to both the program manager and the regional manager.
     - The director will become the acting PPOC.
     - The program manager and the regional manager will be kept informed.
     - Per the PPOC function, while the director is the acting PPOC, neither the program manager nor the regional manager will have communications prior to fully coordinating this with the director.
4. The program manager should schedule and chair weekly resource meetings.
5. Whenever another department or group has an identified PPOC, the program manager should communicate with that individual. The program manager is accountable to the regional manager for any financial impact associated to program-related matters. The program manager is accountable for ensuring that any existing or new resources are employed correctly and efficiently by having the resource track hours logged against deliverables or activities.
   - The program manager must ensure that the labor hours are tracked against the Task Authorization Form.
6. If a performance or behavioral issue develops, the program manager will address this directly with the resource's manager.
   - The regional manager will be kept informed if the resource is external to his or her cost center.
   - If the resource is internal to his or her cost center, the regional manager to whom the resource reports will be contacted directly by the program manager.
   - The program manager will be responsible for accurate documentation of the issue up to the point the issue is completely turned over to the resource's supervisor or manager.

7. Vacation approvals and the corresponding coverage will be managed as follows:
   - Vacation requests made by department staff members working on a program will require final authorization by the regional manager.
   - The regional manager will work with the program manager to ensure appropriate coverage is in place before final vacation authorization is granted to the requesting staff member by the regional manager.
   - If a member of the program team that is external to this cost center makes a vacation request, the program manager will work with the requesting team member and his or her supervisor or manager to ensure appropriate coverage is in place.
8. The addition, deletion, or reallocation of resources that will translate into a contract change or amendment will be managed by the program manager (and when appropriate, salesperson) in consultation with the regional manager.

Special Instructions

None.

Reporting

None.

Records

Regional manager's Task Authorization Form (this form specifies the activities, deliverables, time frame, and required labor hours)

Training

None.

Attachments

None.

Work Instruction #21: Master Records Procedure

Objective

To define the procedure for maintaining records within "Insert company or department name here" as well as define how quality records are identified, filed, stored, accessed, and maintained.

All records should be destroyed when the retention time is exceeded, unless it is specifically stated that they will be archived.

Scope

This procedure applies to the quality management program, and all records generated by "Insert company name or department here" program and project management.

Reference Documents

None.

Definitions

Record: A document stating results achieved or providing evidence of activities performed. Records can be electronic or in paper format. Records can be created by this department or provided to this department for use and maintenance.

Procedures, tools, and training materials: These are released documents and are not records until the tools are in use, at which time they become a record—in the form of checklists, completed forms, and training database records.

Quality Records: Any documented output to the customer (customer records, project schedule, meeting minutes, contracts) as well as internally used records (training records, survey results).

Life of Project: Customer records are maintained while the project is active. After delivery of the product/service, records are archived on (insert location here).

Procedure or Process

Master List

Records will be identified on the master list, which will identify the record's name, its media format, its minimum retention time, the person/department responsible for its maintenance, the location where the record is stored, and how the record will be handled after the retention time expires.

All records will be legible and readily available, whether in paper form or electronic media of any type.

Access

In general, everyone can access any quality record at any time. Customers may also request to see quality records that affect them or products they have received. In some cases, records will be considered confidential and access will be restricted. The quality manager will determine what records are confidential. Confidential records will include employee's personnel and training records, and these records can only be accessed by the individual and his or her manager. Salary information is also confidential, and access to these records is restricted. This information is outside the control of the quality management system.

Filing Storage and Maintenance

Customer records are filed, stored, and maintained by, and reside with, the person who is responsible for the creation, use, and/or maintenance of that record. Internally used records are filed and stored by the quality assurance manager but are updated by the holder (person responsible for ensuring the document is up to date and contains document control elements) of the record. Records must be stored in a manner that prevents damage or loss, and allows for ease of access. Filing cabinets, desk drawers, computer hard drives, diskettes, and network servers are all acceptable methods of filing and storage. Computer storage must be backed up regularly. Internal records are backed up by the quality assurance manager. Customer records, stored on (Indicate location) are automatically backed up.

Miscellaneous

Any records or documents that are received from either our customers or suppliers will be handled:

  a. As specified in a signed contract with that customer or supplier
  b. In accordance with specified guidelines received with the documentation
  c. In accordance with our own procedures as we deem appropriate

Special Instructions

None.

Reporting

None.

Records

  Records Master List—Embedded (add list to this work instruction).

Training

Updates will be communicated via e-mail.

Attachments

Records Master List

Work Instruction #22: Management Review Meeting Procedure

Objective

This procedure outlines the process for the management review meetings.

Scope

This procedure is *mandatory* and applies to the QA manager and the ("Insert company or department name here") management team. (This work instruction is meant for the managers who sponsored the quality certification and are charged with ensuring its integrity. This is typically at the departmental level.)

Reference Documents

Management Review Meeting Template

Definitions

Management Team—Composed, at minimum, of the regional directors, the PMO director, and the director of the regional directors (change if job titles are different in your company).

Procedure or Process

The QA manager will hold a management review meeting, at minimum, on a semi-annual basis to review the quality management system to ensure its continuing suitability, adequacy, and effectiveness. The agenda for the meeting will be based on the Management Review Meeting Template. The input to management review shall include information on:

A. Results of internal audits, and, when applicable, external surveillance or recertification audits
B. Customer feedback
C. Process performance and product conformity
D. Status of preventive and corrective actions
E. Follow-up actions from previous management reviews

F. Planned changes that could affect the quality management system

G. Recommendations for improvement

The output from the management review shall include any decisions and actions related to:

A. Improvement of the effectiveness of the quality management system and its processes

B. Improvement of product related to customer requirements

C. Resource needs

Notes of this meeting will be taken by the QA manager and distributed to the management team and filed in accordance with the Master Records Procedure MB#21.

Special Instructions

None.

Reporting

None.

Records

Management review meeting minutes.

Training

Updates will be communicated via e-mail for version 8.0.

Attachments

None.

Work Instruction #23: Project and Program Progress Reporting—(Customer)

Objective

Provide a standard process and format for reporting on the status of projects and or programs to the customer.

Scope

This procedure applies to projects and programs managed by project managers and program managers. The frequency for progress reporting is weekly, unless otherwise requested by the customer. The weekly progress report may be e-mailed prior to, in conjunction with, or after scheduled calls with the customer. This procedure is *mandatory*.

Reference Documents

> Progress Report Template
> MB#1—Project Documentation

Definitions

None.

Procedure or Process

The referenced Progress Report template will be used as the standard reporting tool for all projects and programs. See Section 6 below for exceptions.

The template contains specific elements that must appear in each weekly report:

A. Agenda.
   Introductions and Attendance.
   Brief recap of previous meeting and minutes.
   Report on Project Percent Complete and Status of Scheduled Milestones.
   Review status and record updates for action items, issues, and risks.
   Discuss scope changes (if applicable).
   New Business.
   Next Steps.
   Schedule next meeting.
B. Scheduled Attendees list.
C. Accomplishments since the last report.
D. Project Schedule Status (requires MS Project 2003/7 or other application)—If you do not wish to paste it into the template, it may be attached. If attached, indicate in this section of the template. Please remember to format the schedule to indicate percent complete as well as Actual versus Baseline dates.
E. Issues and Action Items Matrix.
F. Risk Register (alternate formats, to preclude duplication, for risk reporting may be used).
G. Scope Change Record.

Special Instructions

1. The use of the Progress Report Template may be waived if we have signed a contract that includes reporting requirements that overlap or duplicate the contents of this template. Although the use of the template may be waived, the requirement for reporting to the customer on a weekly basis remains *mandatory*.
2. If the template requirement has not been waived due to contract provisions, use the referenced progress report template.

Reporting

Copies of submitted progress reports need to be posted or filed per MB#1—Project Documentation—PMO ID# 1082-00044 (sample number).

Records

Progress reports produced as a result of completing the reporting template.

Training

None.

Attachments

None.

Chapter 6

Tools and Templates

Chapter 5 included a collection of work instructions that formalized the project management methodology described earlier in the book. The beginning of the book simply described the methodology from a purely project management perspective. The previous chapter placed the methodology in the context of a quality management system, formalizing it with specific directives.

Each directive, when appropriate, includes specific references to tools and templates that will support the project manager deploying the methodology. This chapter contains all those tools and templates.

This section of the book includes reproducible tools and templates. (Please feel free to scan or copy.) Additionally it includes activity lists that can be used to create network diagrams and schedules. Some tools may require minor adjustments to match the job titles of your organization. Every tool and template has been used in the field and reflects both best practices and lessons learned. The tools can be copied and will prove invaluable. For example, the SOW template has been designed to provide the basic information for developing a project plan. The Project Change Control Plan and the Risk Management Plan may be copied as tool suites and can be embedded into a more comprehensive Project Management Plan.

Project Change Control Plan

Any project stakeholder can either cause or request a project change. As a general rule, we can assume that a change in scope, cost, or schedule will almost always impact the other two. These three in combination are often referred to as the "Triple Constraints" as shown in Figure 6.1.

To manage planned changes the following process will be put in place. To facilitate the Project Change Control Plan, the forms in Table 6.1 will be deployed.

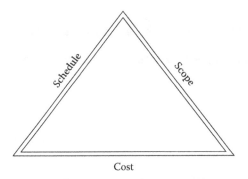

Figure 6.1   The Triple Constraints.

Table 6.1   Change Control Forms

Form Name	Filled Out by	Comment
Change Request Form	Stakeholder requesting change	This is used to request the change.
Change Review Checklist	Project Manager	This is used to evaluate the impacts of the requested change.
Risk Management Checklist	Project Manager	This is used to assess the potential risks of the change.
Change Log	Project Manager	Tracks requested changes and their disposition.

Project Change Management Process Steps

1. Any member of the team fills out the Change Request Form.
2. Upon receipt, the project manager enters the request in the Change Log.

3. The project manager, working with the appropriate stakeholders, fills out the Change Review Checklist.
4. The project manager, working with the appropriate stakeholders, fills out the Risk Management Checklist (shown later).
5. If required, all three forms are submitted to the Change Control Board (CCB) for disposition.
6. If the CCB approves or partially approves the change, the plans are re-baselined as needed.
7. If the CCB rejects the change, the submitter is informed.
8. If the change is below the CCB threshold for disposition and is approved by the project manager, the plans are re-baselined as needed.
9. If the change is below the CCB threshold and is rejected, the submitter is informed.
10. The disposition of the change is noted in the Change Log.

For typical programs the CCB threshold will be scope changes impacting the schedule 10 business days and/or increasing the budget $10,000. The process is displayed later.

The Change Control Board (CCB) will have the authority to determine the disposition of Change Orders. As a general rule, Change Orders may be initiated by any stakeholder and may imply a change of any of the following:

■ Scope
■ Budget/cost
■ Schedule

The CCB will have representation from:

■ Program sponsor
■ Program director
■ Project manager
■ Program SME, as appropriate
■ Workstream lead, as appropriate

The Project Change Control Process is displayed in Figure 6.2.

The following tools round out the Project Change Control Plan tool suite.

Project Change Request Form

Table 6.2 is a template Project Change Request Form. This is filled out by any member of the team seeking a change.

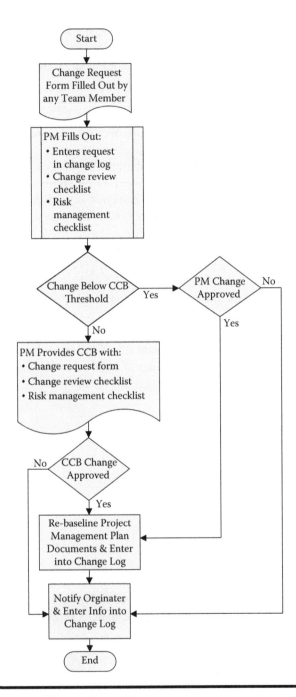

Figure 6.2 Project Change Control Process map.

Table 6.2   Change Request Form

Please describe the scope change you are requesting. If you require additional deliverable(s), please be as specific as possible.
_____
_____
_____
_____
Kindly indicate (if applicable) the date by which you need the change completed: _____ / _____ / _____
From your perspective are there any risks the Program Team should be aware of? If so, please describe below.
_____
_____
_____
_____
If you know the estimated or allocated cost or funding or hours for this change please indicate: $ _____ hours _____
Please submit this form to the Project Manager at your earliest convenience. Thank you.
Print Name: _____
Print Title: _____
Signature: _____ Date: ____ / ____ / ____

Project Manager's Project Scope Review Checklist

The project manager's Scope Review Checklist in Table 6.3 makes sure all the key potential impacts and dependencies are addressed as part of the assessment process.

Scope Change Log

The Scope Change Log in Table 6.4 is where all proposed changes are registered and tracked.

Table 6.3 PM Project Scope Review Checklist

Project Manager Ensures the Following:	
Checkpoint	*Action*
1. Identify all the Stakeholders	List Stakeholders
Notes:	Internal: List Names
	External: List Names
	Vendors: List Names
	Developers: List Names
	Consultants: List Names
	Third Party: List Names
	Others: List Names
2. Address Risks	Use Risk Checklist
Notes:	Risk Management Checklist
3. Is this a Viable Schedule?	
Notes:	
4. Identify Customer Dependencies	List Dependencies
Notes:	
5. Third-Party Deliverables	List with due dates
Notes:	

Table 6.3 (continued)   PM Project Scope Review Checklist

Checkpoint	Action
6. Commitments are consistent with PM or PMO Process	Insert Notes below as needed
Notes:	
7. Soft Requirements are being addressed—Example: (hosting) Launch Support or post-hand-off	Insert Notes below as needed
Notes:	

Risk Management Plan

The project's Risk Management Plan will be based on the following processes:

1. Risk Identification
2. Risk Qualification
3. Risk Quantification
4. Risk Response Planning
5. Risk Monitoring and Control

Risk Identification, as a best practice, will include the participation of all the project stakeholders. Risk Identification will be embedded in key document reviews as well as all changes to the Project Plan.

Risk Qualification will be as follows: This is "Priority" in the Risk Register with a scale of 1 to 5. The prioritization is as follows: 1 being the lowest, 5 being the highest. When appropriate the categorization will be associated with its potential impact to the Project Schedule's critical path. Risks qualified as negligible, or below 2 and with no impact to the critical path will not require moving on to the next step in the process. All other identified risks will move on to the Quantification step.

To facilitate Risk Quantification and, in some cases the risk event's impact on program or project quality, the following categories will be employed. As we progress, new categories may be created.

■ Technical
■ Quality
■ Project Management
■ Organizational
■ External

Table 6.4 Scope Change Log

SC.No#	Description of Change Request	Requested by	Request Date	Deadline to Resolve	Impact on Schedule	Impact on Cost	Required Action/ Comments	Approval Status		Approved By
					Days	Cost		Date	Yes/No	Name

Risk Quantification will include, as appropriate, the following components:

- The risk event's dollar value
- The effect the risk issue may have on the project schedule
- The effect the risk event may have on scope and quality
- The risk issue's potential impact on project resources

Once the risk has been quantified, we are finally in a position to begin Risk Response Planning. The project manager, in consultation with the project sponsor, can determine any of the following courses of action:

- Risk Avoidance: Take immediate actions such as adding activities to the program schedule or provide direction to a vendor to preclude the risk event from occurring.
- Risk Mitigation: Adjust the Program Plan to reduce the potential impact of the risk event. Typical examples include time buffers and risk funding.
- Risk Transfer: In some cases the optimal course of action is deflecting the risk issue to a third party. In large complex programs this would, for example, take the form of requiring Contractors to secure performance bonds.
- Risk Acceptance: There are times when the reality of a risk event must be accepted and simply planned for. In those cases, the program manager creates a set of backup plans that will go into immediate effect when and if the risk event materializes. This might include, for example, a backup schedule that is ready if and when a Sole Source Supplier's materials (though ordered early) are nevertheless delivered late.

Risk Monitoring and Control: Represents the final part of the process wherein the project manager continually assures the following:

- The Risk Register (spreadsheet shown later) is continually monitored and kept current.
- That risk response planning activities in the Program Plan are adhered to.
- Risks are reported on at regularly scheduled meetings as stipulated in the Program Communications Plan.

Finally, to round out the Risk Management Plan, the team has developed a Risk Checklist to facilitate deliverable and document reviews, as well as the development of contracts, purchase orders, and scope changes. The Risk Checklist is shown later.

Risks that exceed a quantification threshold of 10 schedule days or $10,000 may be monitored in the schedule.

Risks are generally discussed and continually identified and monitored at progress meetings.

A summary of the Risk Management Process is depicted in Figure 6.3.

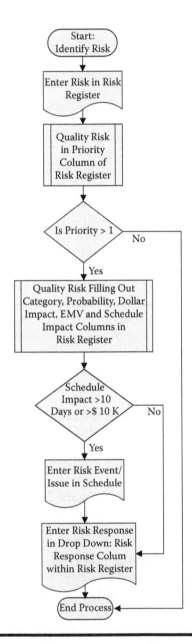

Figure 6.3   Risk Management Process.

Risk Register

An optional tool to supplement the Risk Management Process, the Risk Register, is shown in Table 6.5. This Risk Register is consistent with the process outlined earlier.

Risk Summary Log

Finally, the Risk Management Checklist displayed here rounds out the Risk Management tool suite.

Risk Management Checklist

To help identify risks we have developed a Risk Management Checklist, which is displayed in Table 6.6. The checklist is part of the Risk Management Plan and is also used as part of the Project Change Management Plan as well.

Meetings Checklist

The Meetings Checklist can help the project manager determine what meetings are needed during the project life cycle and what their content should be. The checklist is shown in Table 6.7.

Kick-Off Meeting Template

The template that follows may serve to guide and document the kick-off meeting. See Table 6.8.

Launch Support Meeting Template

The Launch Support Template will aid the project manager as the project moves into the go-live phase. See Table 6.9.

Progress Report Template

Progress reporting is an element of communications and expectations management. The Progress Report Template, shown here, is a tool that can aid in that process. See Table 6.10.

Table 6.5 Risk Register

RISK MANAGEMENT MATRIX

UID	No.	Risk Event Description	Qualification H = High M = Medium L = Low	Impact (1–10) or Qualification $ (Dollar Value)	Schedule Quantification	Quality Impact	Other Impacts (Vendors, Resources, etc.)	Planned Response (Avoid, Mitigate, Deflect, Retain)	Status	Due Date	Owner	Notes
	1											
	2											
	3											
	4											
	5											
	6											
	7											
	8											
	9											

Table 6.6   Risk Management Checklist

1. This Checklist MUST be filled out during each document review.
2. This Checklist MUST be filled out prior to submitting a proposed Project Change Request.

Program/Change Request:	*Project Manager:*
Enter Name or Number	Enter Project Manager Name

Note: Impact could affect schedule, scope, quality, or budget.

Subject/Category of Risk	*Potential Impact of Risk*	*Recommendations*
Enter Category of Risk	Enter Impact of Risk	Enter any recommended actions.
Add lines as needed.		

ACTION ITEMS (as needed)	*Yes*	*No*	*COMMENTS*
Reviewed with (insert stakeholder name)			
Reviewed with (insert stakeholder name)			
Issue identified in Specification/SOW			
Requires input of other Functional Manager(s)			
Requires input of other Key Stakeholder			
Program Plan will require a change			
Program Manager Initials:			

Sample Risks	*Sample Risks*
Hardware Lead Time	Capacity Issues
Unreliable Vendor	Telco Facility Issues
Unknown Technology	Telco Access
Beta Software	Vendor Dependencies
Future Software/Hardware Support	Carrier Dependencies
Ability to Secure Training	Agency Dependencies
Unique Requirements	Testing Issue
Vendor/Contractor's Financial Situation	Unknown Environmental Issues
Unrealistic Completion Date	Regulatory/Legal Issues

Table 6.7   Meetings Checklist

Progress Meeting Agenda

☐ Discuss Status of Existing or New Related Risk Issues

☐ Discuss any Pending or Planned Scope Changes

☐ Compare Actual versus Baseline Milestones

☐ Review Status and Content of Customer Communications Post-Kick-Off

☐ Discuss, if Required, Any Customer Expectations Management Issues or Customer Generated Action Items Raised at PM Progress Meetings

☐ Discuss Plan for Test and Customer Acceptance

☐ Discuss Test Results, and Plan associated with, PM Launch Support Meeting

☐ Lessons Learned to Date

Launch Support Meeting Agenda

☐ Discuss Status of Existing or New Related Risk Issues

☐ Discuss any Pending or Planned Scope Changes

☐ Review needs, if any, for customer access to Servers.

☐ Review needs, if any, for customer loading of applications.

☐ Discuss Plan for Test and Customer Acceptance

☐ Discuss Results (of above items 3,4, and 5), and Plan Dates with Tier II/Tier III

☐ Review Escalation Paths during Launch

Kick-Off Meeting Agenda

☐ Introductions

☐ Review Project Overview (scope description)

☐ Review Hardware solution

☐ Review Software solution

☐ Q&A of solution

☐ Review scheduled milestones

☐ Identify (what & when) deliverables required from customer, if any

☐ Customer run-book requirements

☐ Customer user names and ids

☐ Review risk issues

☐ Define PPOC and Mutual Escalation paths

☐ Action items (Customer) — use status meeting template (to be posted to IS Intranet and or CW)

☐ Final Q&A

☐ Determine date of next call or Progress meeting

Table 6.8   Kick-Off Meeting Template

Customer Name
Your Company Project Team

	Kick-Off Meeting
	IN SUPPORT OF:
	Web Hosting for Customer in the XXXX Data Center
	DATE:
	TIME:
	CONFERENCE DIAL IN # - (800-xxx-xxxx)

Meeting Agenda

Date:

Time:

Conference Dial in # -

- Project Team Introductions
- Review Project Overview (Scope)
- Review Customer or third-party provided software requirements (if applicable)
- Q&A of Scope
- Review Scheduled milestones (status and impact)
- Discuss other open implementation issues/concerns.
- Review Action Items (Your Company & Customer)
- Review Risk Management Process
- Discuss Scope Change Management procedure with team
- Discuss escalation and communication protocols
- Final Q&A
- Schedule next meeting

Attendees: (Include the Name and Title for the following departments; add as needed.)

- Project Manager
- Engineering
- Customer
- Add as needed

(continued on next page)

Table 6.8 (continued)   Kick-Off Meeting Template

Customer Name	
Project Team Contacts	
Customer Contacts:	
Primary Technical Contact:	**Secondary Technical Contact:**
Phone	Phone
Fax	Fax
E-mail	E-mail
Address	Address
Other method of contact (pager/cell)	Other method of contact (pager/cell)
ABC Contacts:	
Project Manager:	**Primary Customer Contact:**
PM Name	IC Name
Project Manager	Implementation Coordinator
ABC	
1 Liberation Road	
New York, NY 10007	
Phone:	Phone:
Fax: 781-xxx-xxxx	Fax:
Pager: 888-xxx-xxxx	
E-mail: XXXX@ABCconsulting.com	

Table 6.8 (continued)   Kick-Off Meeting Template

Customer Name
Project and Solution Overview
INSERT OVERVIEW HERE—USE THE PROJECT OVERVIEW FROM THE PROPOSAL OR CONTRACT. **If an overview is not available in the Proposal or contract, the Project Manager must develop a scope statement.**
Customer Action Items (add or delete items as-needed) 1. Upon receipt of the kick-off meeting notes, review and contact your Project Manager if there any discrepancies or changes you think need to be made. (Each unit will be provisioned to the specifications outlined in this document.) Otherwise, e-mail your Project Manager with confirmation of receipt by the date noted below. Owner: Customer Contact Due Date: XX/XX/XX

(continued on next page)

Table 6.8 (continued)   Kick-Off Meeting Template

2. If applicable, complete the VPN or perimeter security questionnaires and send to the Project Manager. If assistance is required, contact your Project Manager. (Delete action item if not applicable)

   Owner: Customer Contact

   Due Date: XX/XX/XX

3. Complete the letter of agency (LOA) provided by your implementation coordinator. One form for each URL must be completed in its entirety. It is not possible to put multiple URLs on one form. Please return the form to your implementation coordinator as soon as possible. This may impact provisioning schedule if not received promptly. ABC will be applying to VeriSign for all Customer required certificates.

   Owner: Customer Contact

   Due Date: XX/XX/XX

4. If applicable, advise Project Manager on the method and details of receipt for customer-provided software. Software may be transferred or delivered to ABC in one of the following ways:

   (IC will provide the mail to address if that method is chosen)

   FTP—Software is transferred to the designated implementation engineer—Implementation coordinator will coordinate.

   Mail CD—Please make sure CD and CD Case are clearly labeled with your company name.

   URL Access—Please provide license key.

   Owner: Customer Contact

   Due Date: XX/XX/XX

   Method of Delivery: XXXXX

5. Provide ABC with the name, business address, and business phone number for anyone who you are requesting Secure ID's (for access to servers) for that is not registered as a Valid Technical Contact with ABC already. Additionally, open a ticket with the CSC (Customer Support Center) to have those people added as Valid Technical Contacts. Please note: Check with your PM to see how many Secure ids you are being provided with. Additional Secure Ids must be purchased (contact your account manager to order)

   CSC #: 1-800-xxx-xxxx

   Owner: Customer Contact

   Due Date: XX/XX/XX

Table 6.8 (continued)   Kick-Off Meeting Template

6. In order for you to access your NT servers, you will need to purchase "Control IT" (formerly Remote Possible) client software. May purchase at: http://www.cai.com/products/controlit.htm

   Owner: Customer Contact

   Due Date: XX/XX/XX

7. Confirm that you have access to the data center and notify the Project Manager if there are any technical difficulties.

   CSO Url: XXXXX

   Owner: Customer Contact

   Due Date: XX/XX/XX

8. Send beta release, content loading, and public launch dates to the Project Manager, no later than

   XX/XX/XXX

   Owner: Customer Contact

   Due Date: XX/XX/XX

Project Management Notes

Risk Issues Identified:

(see Risk ID Checklist and Risk Management Log)

ABC and Customer Escalation Paths Identified:

May be covered at a high level during the team introductions. Document for the customer in this section—more detail for who and when to escalate to for outages, content migration issues, etc., may be covered in a separate meeting.

ABC:

Primary Point of Contact—**Project Manager**

Customer:

Primary Point of Contact—**Customer**

Scope Change Management:

(Please see the Scope Change Management Process with associated forms.)

Table 6.9 Launch Support Meeting Template

<table>
<tr><td>

Customer Name

and Project Team

Attendees:
PM Project Manager
Tier II Tier 2 Engineer
Tier III Tier 3 Engineer
Implementation Coordinator
Premier Care/Customer Care
Customer Customer Attendees

Month, Day, 200X
</td></tr>
</table>

Table 6.9 (continued)   Launch Support Meeting Template

Launch Support Meeting Agenda	
	Date: 00/00/00
	Time: 5PM EST
1. Discuss Status of Existing or New Related Risk Issues.	
2. Discuss any Pending or Planned Scope Changes.	
3. Review needs, if any, for Customer Access to Servers.	
4. Review needs, if any, for customer loading of applications: Ongoing support for customer managed applications (T&M policy) Content development and production environment needs and access rights.	
5. Discuss Plan for Test and Customer Acceptance	
6. Plan Dates with /Tier II/Tier III for items 3,4,5.	
7. Review Escalation Paths during Launch.	
8. Discuss Customer Care Role and process for customer requests: Special Attention Status Flag.	

(continued on next page)

Table 6.9 (continued) Launch Support Meeting Template

Customer—Implementation Status Update (1–2 on Agenda)	
Risk Issues Reviewed	**Status:**
1. Insert risk that was identified at Kick-Off Meeting	1. Provide Status
2. Insert risk that was identified at Kick-Off Meeting	2. Provide Status
3. Insert risk that was identified at Kick-Off Meeting	3. Provide Status
Notes: **Establish Dates with Tier 2 and Tier 3 as needed.**	
Scope Changes (If applicable)	**Status:**
1. Insert scope change—a Pending or newly identified scope change	1. Provide Status
2. Insert scope change—a Pending or newly identified scope change	2. Provide Status
3. Insert scope change—a Pending or newly identified scope change	3. Provide Status
Notes: **Establish Dates with Tier 2 and Tier 3 as needed.**	
Other/New Requirements:	
Customer–Server Access, Customer-Managed Apps, and Web Content	
Server Access Level Requirements Defined:	
Notes: **Establish Dates with Tier 2 and Tier 3 as needed.**	

Table 6.9 (continued)   Launch Support Meeting Template

Customer-Managed Applications (if applicable)	
1. Has the customer-provided software been received by the IC?	1. ☐ yes ☐ no
2. Has the customer requested an installation by Genuity?	1. ☐ yes ☐ no
3. Will the customer require assistance and or support with the customer-provided software?	1. ☐ yes ☐ no
4. If yes for #3, has a T&M line item been included in the service quotation?	1. ☐ yes ☐ no
Notes:	
Web Content Loading	Contacts:
Customer Needs: (Discuss with customer)	
Development Environment	Contact
Review customer's development environment	
Identify any risks	
Production Environment	Contact
How does the customer transfer data from development to production?	
Identify any risks	
Support:	Contact
Identify contact for support issues with Web content loading	
Notes:	

(continued on next page)

Table 6.9 (continued)   Launch Support Meeting Template

Customer Acceptance Testing, Customer Validation of Systems		
	Date	*Owner*
Testing:		
UAT (Unit Acceptance Testing) — Review process with customer	00/00/00	Data Center
PAS (Production Acceptance Systems) — Solution Testing, if applicable		
Customer Validation Test — Review process with Customer	00/00/00	PM and Customer
Review Testing Components and Plan:		
Access URL(s)		
Loading Content		
Secure IDs working		
SSL(s) activated and working		
Systems validated by customer		
Backups tested		
Notes: **ESTABLISH DATES WITH TIER 2 and TIER 3 as needed.** (Request via e-mail — provide 48 hours notice)		
Follow-Up Action Items: 1. 2. 3. 4.		
Customer-Escalation Paths, Customer Care and Planned Priority Status Reviewed		
Escalation Path Reviewed: (cut and paste from Kick-Off Meeting)		

Table 6.9 (continued)   Launch Support Meeting Template

Notes: **ESTABLISH DATES WITH TIER 2 and TIER 3 as needed.**	
Customer Care Role Reviewed:	
Escalation:	
Requests:	
CSO:	
Notes:	
Special Attention Status	
Enter Provisioning Ticket # Review Process:	
Accessing status updates Requests PPOC	
Internal Notes	
Special Attention Status—(Internal notes)	
1. Request Special Attention status for customer in Launch Support Phase.	Open Ticket with: Process:
2. Review the process and procedure for Planned Priority Status Tickets with your customer.	
3. Provide your customer with the Customer Care Quick Reference Guide.	URL:
4. Give customer the URL to access the "Making Genuity Work for You" welcome process document	Customer URL:
5. PM may access a copy on the K-bank.	

(continued on next page)

Table 6.9 (continued)   Launch Support Meeting Template

Examples of Launch Support Issues — (Internal Notes)

Provided by Tier 3:

1. SW Installation and Configuration:

   Customer requests are automatically opened as Sev 1 tickets. The requests are not always quickly completed. SW installation and configuration can take some time. *(Customers need to be informed that requests will be handled through the Planned Priority Status process and that they should not open Sev. 1 tickets.)*

2. Installation of customer-managed applications:

   Often, Tier 3 is asked to install customer managed apps and then receive requests for support. The challenge faced by Tier 3 is that when there is a problem with the application, the customer will call Tier 3 to resolve it since the customer did not install it. The other side of this is that customers may not be familiar with the application and simply require support. *(As early on as possible, customer-managed application support requirements need to be identified in order to avoid this problem. If support is required, a T&M or special line item needs to be added to the scope of support in the contract, and the roles and responsibilities with regard to customer-managed applications should be reviewed and amended in the contract as needed. The second part relates to problems that are encountered after the application has been installed — and the ownership issue of who is responsible. A customer validation needs to be obtained after the installation; this needs to be documented and approved by the customer.)*

3. Environmental issues which customers encounter:

   Several of our customers develop their environment on either a non-Solaris, non-CHP, nonsecured environment (Securid, secured platform) or nonprivileged (no root) environment. The customer thinks that they'll be able to load content, administer the site, or have privileges on the machine. This is how they developed their content and they have no insight into the platform or environmental issues. *(Review customer's content development environment and needs and identify potential issues at the launch support meeting.)*

Internal Notes

Table 6.9 (continued)   Launch Support Meeting Template

Examples of Launch Support Issues (Internal Notes)

Provided by Customer Care:

1. Verisign certificates not provisioned in a timely fashion, or not ordered, or if problems, no way to work with Verisign in a timely fashion (who are 5 × 12 in California). (*Need to address Verisign requirements at the kick-off meeting and make sure that the customer role is understood in providing specific information.*)

2. Lack of a thorough UAT; UAT comprises a "ping" and a "login" or something very simple such as this. Many times it seems that boxes are provisioned and handed off to the customer without checking that all of the components that are supposed to be delivered are there (missing U boards, missing virtual memory configurations, bad cabling in the data center). (*Use the Acceptance Testing checklist on the IS Intranet.*)

3. ACL/access issues that should be planned with the customer up-front; instead, requests are submitted in the ticketing process with little to no documentation or description for the support orgs to implement. (*Identify access needs at kick-off and launch support meetings.*)

4. Late delivery from provisioning results in "sev 1" behavior on the part of the customer during the launch support phase. (*Review Planned Priority Status process with the customer.*)

5. Monitoring not always set up for all URLs; sometimes not set appropriately (i.e., thresholds or timings) resulting in customer's finding major events before we do. (*Make sure a customer validates acceptance testing. Review plan at launch support meeting.*)

6. Backups sometimes not set up/provisioned. (*Make sure a customer validates acceptance testing. Review plan at launch support meeting to provide a pass/fail for all internal tests.*)

7. T&M Requirements:

   No process to efficiently handle time and materials (one off) requests. (*Need to review scope changes at launch support meeting and include T&M as needed.*)

   No clear way for us to know if a request is within a customer's contract or should be a T&M request. (*If the request is not covered in the scope of the contract and terms, it will most likely be a T&M request.*)

8. Special configurations that require us to design on the fly and put new design through Quality Control process; customer generally feels their request was approved during sales process and are very displeased at the time it takes to process this sort of request. (*Need to review scope changes at launch support meeting and include T&M as needed.*)

Notes:

Table 6.10   Progress Report Template

Insert Customer Name or Logo

Progress Report
Report Date:

Meeting Agenda 59

Accomplishments Since Last Report 60

Project Schedule Status 60

Issues and Action Items Matrix 61

Risk Register 61

Scope Change Record 62

Enter PM Name,

Project Manager

Your address

Table 6.10 (continued)   Progress Report Template

Meeting Agenda

Prepared by: Enter PM Name

Date:
Time:
Conference No.
Pass Code:

- Introductions and attendance
- Brief recap of previous meeting and minutes
- Report on Project Percent Completed and Status of Scheduled Milestones
- Review status and record updates for action items, issues, and risks.
- Discuss scope changes (if applicable)
- New business
- Next steps
- Final Q&A
- Schedule next meeting

Your Company Attendees

Name	Title	Department
		eServices Delivery
		Sales Team
		Customer Provisioning
		Engineering/Data Center
		Customer Care/Premier Care
		Tier III — UNIX/NT
		Tier II
		VPN
		Site Patrol
		Oracle DBA
		Managed Applications
		Engineering

(continued on next page)

Table 6.10 (continued)   Progress Report Template

Customer Attendees		
Name	*Title*	*Department*

Accomplishments Since Last Report

(Deliverables completed, milestones attained, decisions made, issues resolved, etc.)

■

■

■

■

Project Schedule Status

Copy and paste the major milestones from MS Project, developed earlier per Work Instruction #3 by filtering for customer or selecting those that you would like to report on. (Use the snapshot feature to save as a gif file and paste into this document directly.)

Insert MS Project summary level jpeg here

Comments

Miscellaneous comments, public praise for extra effort, announcements, upcoming activities, or any new issues that need to be addressed.

Table 6.10 (continued)   Progress Report Template

Issues and Action Items Matrix
Double-click on the spreadsheet below to launch MS Excel, and enter your data directly into this template. For items entered where a risk is found, use the Risk Register on the next page to record mitigation strategy status, etc. Please note that this matrix and all of its columns are required.
Insert Action Log here—if possible with URL link
Risk Register
Note: Impact could affect schedule, scope, or budget. Use the action items spreadsheet in the previous page to track action items related to Risk. This table should be used to track all the Risk Events that were identified. Refer to Risk Management Checklist for initial data and updates. Also see Work Instruction #2 Risk Management.
Insert Risk Register here—if possible with URL link
Scope Change Record
This table should be used to record all Scope Change requests. Actions taken should be tracked in the action items spreadsheet. If there are any risks associated with a scope change, record them in the Risk Register. Please refer to Work Instruction #15 for access to the Scope Change Form and additional details on our Scope Change policy. (Scope change procedures should be covered with the client in the Kick-Off Meeting.)
Insert Scope Change Log—if possible with URL link

(continued on next page)

Table 6.10 (continued)   Progress Report Template

Help
This is for reference and should be deleted before sending a progress report to the client.

Scope Change Management Discussion Checklist

THIS IS FOR INTERNAL PURPOSES—NOT TO BE DISTRIBUTED TO THE CLIENT

(This may be used to discuss scope changes during the Progress Meeting. Also refer to Work Instruction #15 for process details and use the Scope change form located on the Tools Page under Scope Tools. PLEASE NOTE: If you would like to share this checklist with your client, make sure that all INTERNAL RISK/SCOPE-RELATED items are deleted first.)

Sample Scope Change Items:

ACTION ITEMS	*Yes*	*No*	*COMMENTS*
Have all the new requirements been gathered?			
Have all the new requirements been documented?			
Will the scope change require an addendum?			
Will the scope change require a new Service Quotation?			
If additional Implementation Services' hours are required, has this been addressed?			
If QRT is not required, are any other preapprovals required (i.e., LOB)?			
Has a revised architecture been developed?			
Is the architecture's BOM complete?			
Have we identified and evaluated potential risk elements?			
Should any third-party deliverables or other dependencies be included in the schedule and/or the addendum or Service Quotation?			

Table 6.10 (continued)   Progress Report Template

ACTION ITEMS	Yes	No	COMMENTS
Have we evaluated the effect this will have on the schedule?			
Has the schedule been re-baselined?			
If this project is part of a larger program, should the program schedule be re-baselined?			
Does this scope change affect any performance requirements in the original Service Quotation?			
Are there any launch support issues that should be coordinated and discussed?			

Action Items Matrix

A project manager has to keep track of all the activities requiring follow-up. Activities that may originate in the course of meetings or issues raised by stakeholders need to be tracked. The Action Items Matrix is a tool that facilitates the tracking of follow-up activities. The matrix is displayed in Table 6.11.

After Action Reviews

After a project or major issue has been completed, the project manager will schedule a meeting with the project team. The recommended duration for this meeting is 1 h.

An After Action Review Form is depicted in Table 6.12.

Deliverables Acceptance Process

This process is designed to ensure that the work products received by the client from a vendor, contractor, system integrator, etc., associated with this project meet all contract requirements, are within the scope of work, and are consistent with, when applicable, engineering, industry, project management, and regulatory standards. When appropriate, this process will identify technical and project risks.

Table 6.11   Action Items Matrix

UID	No.	Item	Associated Risk	Track	(Open/ Closed) Status	Due Date	(H/M/L) Priority	Owning Stakeholder	Owner	Notes
	1									
	2									
	3									
	4									
	5									

ACTION/ISSUES ITEM MATRIX

Table 6.12   After Action Reviews

After a project has been completed the PM will schedule a meeting with the project team. The recommended duration for this meeting is one hour. The PM will then complete the form below and submit it to the Regional/Group Manager and the PMO.

Have any issues been escalated? Please be specific with names, dates, and issues. (Limit to key issues.)

_____

_____

_____

_____

_____

_____

_____

_____

Any recommended process changes due to this project experience?

_____

_____

_____

_____

_____

_____

_____

Were any scope constraints (customer generated limits such as brand, time, or performance constraints) identified? (What were they & who identified them?)

_____

_____

_____

_____

_____

_____

_____

Tip: *There are times when organizations retain firms to perform Independent Validation and Verification (IV&V) of work performed. If done correctly, it is implemented in an impartial manner without direct intervention in the management of the production of the deliverables or the project. This process can be leveraged by either the project manager or an IV&V contractor. IV&V teams may be referred to as "QA" (quality assurance), not to be confused with the internal organization that performs testing.*

The process, which many organizations often refer to as the "DAD" (Deliverable Acceptance/Audit Document) process, is as follows.

1. Vendor submits all their work products to both the client and the project's QA team, concurrently.
2. The project's QA team conducts an initial review using the Deliverable Audit Document (shown later).
3. The project's QA team submits the work product with the Deliverable Audit Document attached to the client. If the project's QA team's engineering assessment is issued, it will be attached as well.
4. The client completes the review and, in writing, informs the contractor as to the status of the work product/deliverable received.
   a. If contractor is advised that the work product/deliverable has been accepted the deliverable is deemed closed-out.
   b. If Vendor is requested to resubmit the work product, upon receipt of the transmittal the Deliverable Acceptance Process will be reinitiated.
   c. The status of the work product is tracked in a spreadsheet.

The process is displayed in Figure 6.4.

The Deliverable Acceptance Process is resolved by employing the Deliverable Review Form in Table 6.13.

Daily Event Log

Complete and timely documentation is essential. Minutes, project records, and document and version control are all components of good documentation. Documentation can be facilitated by having tools that facilitate the process. One of them is depicted in Table 6.14 and is a Daily Event Log that allows team members to log key transactions that occur daily in fast moving projects.

Sample Project Schedule

Figure 6.5 depicts a typical project schedule containing a few minimum deliverables and activities.

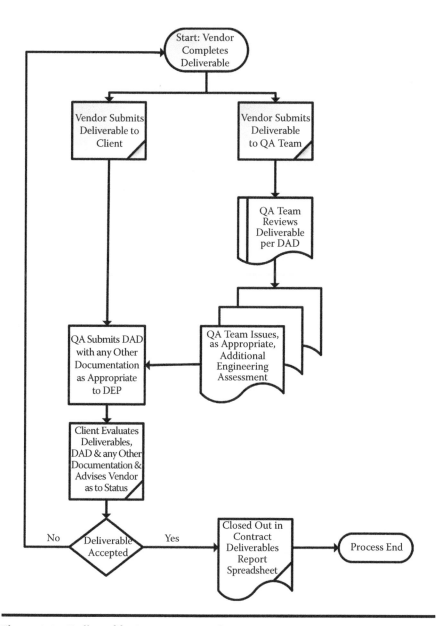

Figure 6.4 Deliverable Acceptance Review Process.

Table 6.13   Deliverable Review Form

Deliverable
Name of Deliverable
Date Received: _____ / _____ / _____ : Version: _____
Major Nonconformities
Minor Nonconformities
Risks
Observations
Findings
Deliverable Conforms to Contract: Yes ☐ No ☐   Deliverable Conforms to Applicable Standards: Yes ☐ No ☐   Deliverable Contains Unresolved Findings: Yes ☐ No ☐
QA Team Signature: _____ Date: _____ / _____ / _____   Print Name & Title: _____   Client Team Signature: _____ Date: _____ / _____ / _____   Print Name & Title: _____

Table 6.14 Daily Event Log

Date	Event/Call	Correspondence	Summary

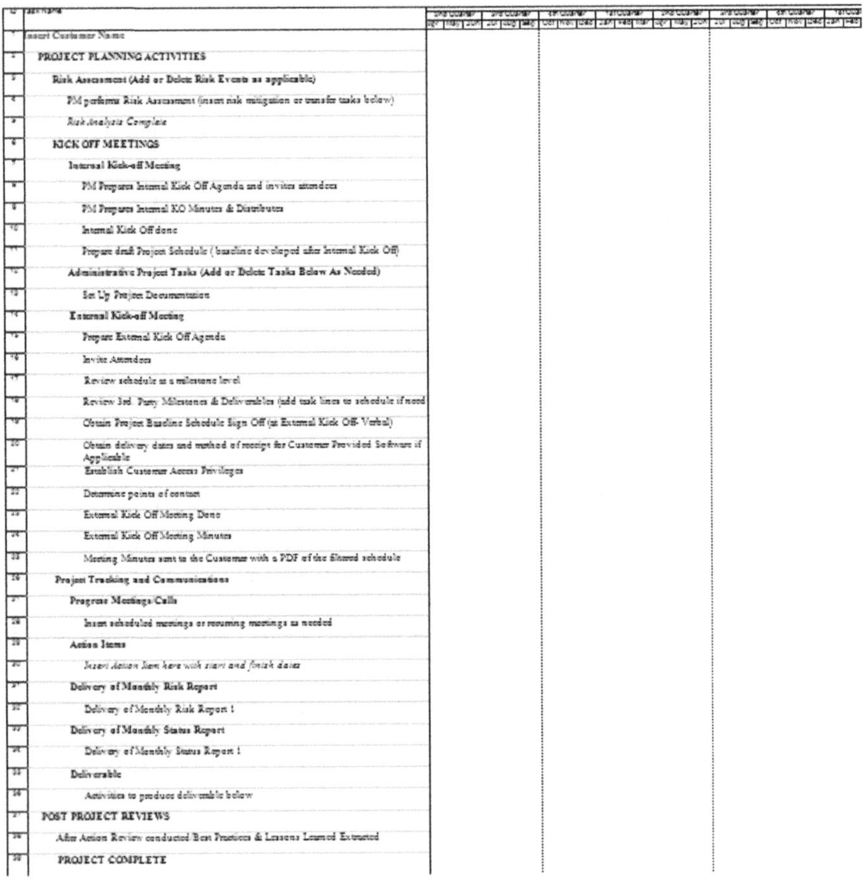

Figure 6.5 Sample project schedule.

Telephone Log Template

The Telephone Log in Table 6.15 is yet another tool to facilitate good documentation.

Resource Authorization Form

The form in Table 6.16 can be used when an organization wants to formalize a process that documents the movement of matrixed resources.

Table 6.15 Telephone Log Template

Date	Time	PM Team Participants	Client Participants	Others	Subject	Summary	PM Team Commitment(s)

Table 6.16 Resource Authorization Form

Program Name	Date

Requesting Organization	Performing Organization
Task Statement	
Task Effort	
Schedule	
Deliverables to Customer Per Contract	
Reporting Requirements	
Requesting Organization's Signature for Task Effort	
Project Manager	
WBS Number (if applicable)	
Performing Organization's Signature for Task Effort	
Task Manager	Regional (functional) Manager

Project Manager's External Resource Authorization Form—Directions for Use

The following describes the information required in each box:

1. Project Name—Enter the project name.
2. Date—Enter the date that the form is initiated.
3. Requesting Organization—Enter the name of the organization making the request for the task.
4. Performing Organization—Enter the name of the organization that will be doing the proposal for the work or actually performing the work.
5. Task Statement—Enter a description of the work to be proposed or performed. Sections for the master contract can be used or referenced.
6. Task Effort—Entered by the requesting project manager. This will include the not to exceed hours and expenses that the performing organization may use in the performance of the work.
7. Schedule—Entered by the requesting project manager. This will identify the period of performance for the work. If there is a unique schedule for different customer deliverables or reports it will be identified here.
8. Deliverables to Customer per Contract—Entered by the requesting project manager. All deliverables will be identified in this section.
9. Reporting Requirements—Entered by the requesting project manager. All reports and metrics will be identified in this section.
10. Requesting Organization's Signature for Task Effort
    a. Project Manager Signature—The project manager signs the form.
    b. WBS number (if applicable)—Entered by the requesting project manager. The work breakdown structure number is entered here. May be done during the proposal effort.
11. Performing Organization's Signature for Task Effort
    a. Task Manager—The task manager signs the TA indicating that the work will be performed in accordance with the Task Statement, Task Effort, Schedule, Deliverables to Customer per Contract, and Reporting requirements.
    b. Regional Manager—The task manager's regional manager signs the form giving authorization to proceed with the work.

Version and Document Control Template

Table 6.17 facilitates document and version control. This is typically a requirement embedded within maturity models and quality management systems. It allows the reader to know who created the document, who reviewed and approved it, and what changes have occurred since the last version was issued.

Table 6.17   Document Control/Revision History

Title of Document	
Description or Purpose	
Location	
PMO ID No.	

Owner/ Author	e-mail	Phone
Dept:	Title:	

Reviewer	Signature/Initials	Date

Approver	Signature/Initials	Date

Change Details

Revision	Change highlights	Author	Date
1	First Release		
	1.		

Business Case Template

The Business Case Template in Table 6.18 helps the project manager work with the team to develop a business case that will advance the project.

Internetworking Requirements Questionnaire

Note: This questionnaire is the first step towards the development of an internetworking solution. The sales executive, architect, business analyst, and project manager begin at a global level and drill down to initiate the technical requirements definition.

Company Background
- What is the overall corporate business model? Does the company have a national or global focus?
- What is the corporate history? What is the structure of the corporation? (Are there any subsidiaries?) How many employees? Where are they located? Is the company public or private?
- What is the size of the company (revenue, financials, public or private)?
- Where is the org chart? Do we have any other relationships within the corporation?
- Have there been any significant news announcements in the last 6 months? If so, what are they?
- What is the overall corporate culture? Is this culture the type that successfully delivers Internet projects? Is there going to need to be a transformation of the culture as part of this project?

Strategy
- What are the key drivers that have caused the customer to propose this initiative?
- What is the value proposition? (market cap, increased revenue, customer acquisition, retention, expansion of wallet, visibility in the organization, protection of client's job, etc.)
- What products/services do they want to sell/provide to their customers via the Web site?
- What is the business case? The goals, objectives, strategies, and tactics.
- Are there going to be channel implications or conflicts? Is there a strategy in place to mitigate them?
- What are the implications for the current organization in doing this initiative?
- What is the main purpose or goal for this site? Identify the priorities as per the design team, the customer, and top-level management.

Table 6.18   Business Case Template

BUSINESS CASE
PROJECT NAME: List project name here
EXECUTIVE SPONSOR: *List executive level or department-head level individual who will sponsor this project; likely to be individual whose functional area will be impacted by the project.*
PROJECT OVERVIEW
Business Context:
Project Description:
PROJECT SCOPE
Included in project scope:
List the functions and systems to be created or impacted by this project. Describe in terms of technical changes, activities, business process, business products, interfaces.
Describes the parameters for the project.
Provides a baseline for controlling changes to the project over the duration.
(Example: Add appropriate CIS product relationship data to CIF and keep these relationships updated on a daily basis in CIF.)
Not included in project scope: *Specify the functions and systems that will not be included in the scope of this project.*
■ *(Example: Roll out of additional CIF installations in Minneapolis.)*
■
PROJECT BENEFITS
Relationship to Strategic Initiatives:
<List any relationships to corporate, divisional or departmental strategic initiatives.>
Dollar Impact:
<Include any anticipated increase in revenue or reduction in cost that the project will realize.>
Other Soft Benefits or relationships w/other projects:
<Many times there are soft benefits to completing a DW project. Having integrated data and conformed dimensions help each organization in many different ways. List as many soft benefits as well as relationships with other projects as possible.>
PROJECT COST
INITIAL ASSUMPTIONS

Internet Presence
- What is the company's current Web address? Are there any related sites? What is the history of the sites? Who currently owns it?
- What is the perception of the current site internally? Externally?
- Is there a specific team in place to work on this project? Is there a specific eCommerce group within the organization? If so, how do they fit within the organization? Who do they report to? How are they funded?
- What are the different roles on the team?
- Who is responsible for the technology supporting the Web site? Are they open to outside involvement in the process or are they afraid of losing control?
- What companies in other industries (may or may not be a competitor) are attempting to do similar things with their Web presence?
- Who are the people who will be responsible for delivering this initiative? What are their current skills? Are they in line with what will be required? What kind of leadership style exists? Are the leaders/managers open to change?
- Who supports the current site? Is the goal to have the site supported in-house or outsourced?

Client Competition
- Who are the client's significant market competitors? How do the company's Internet plans contrast with what their competitors are doing?
- Who are the indirect competitors they should be concerned about?
- Do the competitors currently have a Web presence? If so, to what extent has it been implemented? What has been the level of success?
- Are there specific features/functions on the competitors' Web sites that enhance their competitive position?
- What is the competition doing on the Web that the client either admires or dislikes?
- Are there any alliances or partners that should be considered?
- Should any alliances or partners be included in the process? If none exist, should they? (Is the client open to this consideration?)

Budget
- Has there been a budget allocated for this initiative? If so, how much is it and is it fully allocated or simply budgeted? Who is the decision maker that will release the money? What is the decision-making process?
- If no budget exists, what is the process for getting a budget? Will the project need to include the creation of a compelling business case?
- Find out what the client feels is a reasonable range for the initiative. What is the client willing to spend? (This will assist us in defining the project scope.)

Timing

- Where is the client currently in the process/project?
- Do they have a business plan? Have they done any design? What documentation is available and of that documentation what can be leveraged?
- What would be the ideal start date for the project? If it were possible, what would be the target completion date?
- Have they defined multiple phases for this project? If so, what are they? If not, do they feel that they can get all of the desired functionality into a single phase or are they open to a multiphased approach, aligned to objectives?
- Are there key deadlines (such as an event date) that need to be considered? Are there any times during the project where either the Web systems or affected systems are frozen or unavailable?
- By what date does the customer need information?
- By what date does the customer need a task statement?
- What is the customer's time line for making a decision?
- When does the customer need the system up and active?

Metrics

- What are the company's specific metrics for success (enhanced brand perception, ROI, increased user traffic, other)?
- Have the metrics already been determined? If not, who would need to be involved to create them?
- How will the metrics be used (budget, adjustment and enhancement, prioritization)?
- What action does the client want their users to take as a result of experiencing the site?
- What is the impact if the site is down? Is there any metric or measure for this impact (dollars lost per hours down, number of irate customers, etc.).

Project Overview

- What will be the main function of this Web site? Who will have access to the site?
- What are the overall goals in developing this Web site?
- What are the market/business objectives?
- What are the customer's internal objectives?
- If this application is currently running elsewhere, will the new implementation be phased, pilot, parallel, or cutover?
- What are the key challenges to the success of this initiative?
- What are the time frames required to meet this customer's schedule? Is this a multiphased project?
- What are the consequences of not meeting the customer's preliminary schedule?

Marketing/Branding
- Will the current client identity work within the site or are they looking to create a new online identity?
- With a focus on visual design, what tone/attributes do they want to communicate via their site?
- How does this Web site fit into the larger corporate communications, marketing or sales effort?
- Who is the target audience? What is the primary benefit for this audience?
- Does the client want its potential customers to:
  - Try a new product?
  - Use a product in a new way?
  - Consider the client before choosing a solution?
  - Add the client to its "acceptable" buy list?
  - Switch brands?
  - Trade up?
  - Other
- Will this site be supported by ancillary marketing campaigns? If so, does the client want graphic elements and main messages to be applied consistently across these media?
- Is there an audience/traffic generation process in place? If so, what is it? If not, is one needed?

Site Functionality Requirements
- Has the client identified the type of functionality that the site should have? Have they built a scope document as part of their business plan?
- Are there any deliverables or services that the client already thinks are needed?
- Has the client identified any types of advanced functionality for this site, such as profiling database searches, games, community features, etc.?
- What type of profiling will be necessary on the site? Is there a current data warehouse of customer profiles? If so, is it accessible to the site? Will traffic/activity on the site need to be fed into the warehouse as well as extracted from it?
- Is promotion campaign functionality necessary? Is it currently used?
- Is there a user-registration sequence at the site now? If not, will the customer require users to register to use the site? What type of authentication is used/should be used? Will the user need to be authenticated against multiple back-office systems?

Additional Technical Detail

Content Management
- Does the site contain advertising, and if so, what software is used to manage it (i.e., NetGravity, etc.)?
- Does the client track usage? What software is used to track client usage (e.g., I-Pro)?

- Is the customer open to alternatives with equivalent functionality?
- How does the customer envision updating content (e.g., FTP, Navigator Gold)?
- How often does the customer anticipate updating "content"?
- What protection is needed for the updates (e.g., SecurID, dedicated private-leased line connection)?
- How many users will be using these machines?

Data Architecture
- Where are the data sources for the site? Is there a plan to integrate all the different sources or is that the site goal?

Technical Infrastructure
- Does the company currently host the Web site? If so, what type of equipment is available and how powerful is this equipment?
- What is the target browser platform, delivery system, and transfer speed?
- What web technology is currently used? Are there any corporate standards that need to be followed? What are the current opinions within IT as to the type of technology that should be used for this initiative?
- What type of legacy systems (if any) does the customer require be integrated into this Web site?
- What is the preferred server environment? What is the preferred database?
- Does the customer need access to the operating system to administer its applications?
- What is the current server topology (e.g., database servers behind Web servers, audio servers, standalone)?

Capacity Planning
- What volumes are being driven today in terms of numbers of hits, data/hit, peak hour data transferred?
- What volumes should support be planned for within 12 months in terms of numbers of hits, data/hit, peak hour data transferred?
- Are there any reporting tools required?

Scalability
- Can the customer's Web servers be load balanced based upon if and how the site is managed?

Availability
- Does the customer require RAID 0 or RAID 5 disk?
- Does the customer require a high availability server implementation (e.g., IBM HACMP, Sun Solstice)?

- Does the customer require no single points of failure within the server farm environment (e.g., dual pathing)?
- Does the customer require multiple geographic server farms, and if so, has the customer determined how it would prefer to synchronize its data?
- Is a service level agreement required? What are the requirements?

Security
- What is the customer's security policy for this site and all integration points?
- Where does the customer envision a need for firewalls in the topology?
- What is the customer's interest in our providing protection (e.g., SYN attacks, unauthorized redistribution of customer's material, denial of service, hacking)?
- Does the customer want assistance in responding to attacks?
- Are additional services (e.g., proactive ethical hacking) of interest? Security patch maintenance?

Backup/Recovery
- How often does the customer need full tape backups?
- How often does the customer need incremental tape backups?
- Will backups be just for disaster recovery, or does the customer envision a frequent need to perform other actions (e.g., recovering a single file)?
- How much data would the customer like backed up?

Connectivity
- To what other content providers/back-end systems does the customer need dedicated leased-line connectivity?
- What are the bandwidth requirements of each of those connections?
- How much bandwidth of data transfer capability is needed to the Internet today?
- How much bandwidth of data transfer capability is required on the Internet within 12 months?
- Does the customer have any intranet/extranet requirements?

Support Services
- What other Web hosting services are desired (e.g., DNS)?
- What other affiliated services are of interest (e.g., application development, integration to legacy systems, creative development)?
- What other associated offerings are of interest (e.g., disaster recovery, branded browser dial access kits)?
- Will the customer provide his or her own administrative level support (e.g., DBA, Lotus Notes Administrator)?
- Will the customer provide application-level help desk support?
- Does the customer have a technical focal point identified to work with any third parties for its ongoing Web hosting deployment?

Project Management Service Description Template

If your firm needs a template for contracting purposes, the language below may be useful.

Introduction

This service description (the "Service Description") describes the service offering ("Project and Program Management") of YOUR COMPANY Solutions Inc.'s ("YOUR COMPANY," "we," or "our") eServices Delivery group ("eServices"). The specific Project and Program Management services being provided to you ("you," "your," "Customer") by YOUR COMPANY are set forth in your Service Quotation ("Quotation"). The terms of the YOUR COMPANY Master Agreement for YOUR COMPANY Services ("Master Agreement"), and the Service Quotation, collectively to be known as the "Agreement," shall supersede any statements made in this Service Description. The terms of this Service Description shall supersede any statements made in previous Service Descriptions. This Service Description contains proprietary data that may not be duplicated or disclosed in whole or in part to any third party. YOUR COMPANY reserves the right to amend this Service Description, in whole or in part, without your prior approval.

Service Overview

Summary of Services

These services are provided by YOUR COMPANY project and program managers who adhere to the methodologies of the Project Management Body of Knowledge (PMBOK) to address your needs for the implementation and ongoing support of your YOUR COMPANY services.

The PMBOK contains a set of standards developed by the Project Management Institute and subsequently adopted by the Institute of Electrical and Electronics Engineers, the Engineering Management Society, the IEEE Computer Society, and most recently by the American National Standards Institute (ANSI). YOUR COMPANY's project managers are trained in the PMBOK methodology, which includes project management tools such as Web-based risk analysis and URL-linked scheduling templates.

The Project and Program Management offered by eServices consist of the following:

Project Management

Project management includes the following services:

- Verification of business and technical requirements
- Validation that the proposed solution meets such requirements
- Identification of Customer's key personnel ("Stakeholders") to act as liaisons between Customer and YOUR COMPANY
- Recognition and mitigation of potential risks
- Creation of project plan, including an implementation schedule
- Interaction with YOUR COMPANY constituents to support the on-time delivery of project deliverables
- Monitoring of sales order process to support the Customer from order entry through provisioning

The YOUR COMPANY project manager acts as your primary point of contact throughout the implementation of the solution; interacting with you and with the appropriate YOUR COMPANY personnel to support you through the delivery of the solution. The project manager prepares a project plan and, where appropriate, a list of deliverables, potential risks and mitigation steps, customer dependencies (customer responsibilities on which completion of the project is dependent), and proposed date on which the solutions will be delivered. The project manager schedules a project kick-off meeting (project kick-off meeting) within a reasonable amount of time following the signature of the service quotation. The purpose of the project kick-off meeting is to outline the implementation of the solutions, review the project plan, confirm delivery dates, and provide details regarding YOUR COMPANY and customer deliverables. The customer's stakeholders will be identified as needed to move into implementation.

Upon completion of the tasks outlined in the project plan, the project manager will disengage and transfer the customer's account to Customer Care, or to an ongoing support resource within eServices, as appropriate.

At the conclusion of the project the project manager will conduct a project review meeting and the customer will be asked to take the department's customer satisfaction survey to suggest changes to processes or tools.

Customer Program Office

For large-scale and complex implementations, eServices Project and Program Management offers a Customer Program Office (CPO) to manage each phase of the customer life cycle, which may include: defining business requirements, coordinating project management during implementation, and coordinating ongoing support throughout the remainder of the contract term. A program manager will lead the CPO and coordinate the day-to-day activities and personnel that form the CPO. The CPO will consist of trained YOUR COMPANY personnel, who will perform the tasks necessary to support the Customer throughout the Customer's lifecycle.

The CPO assists the customer in the following:

- Developing a program plan and updating, as necessary
- Defining the requirements of specific projects in support of the overall YOUR COMPANY solution
- Identifying and addressing potential risk issues
- Coordinating and overseeing the installation and integration of all YOUR COMPANY services provided to the Customer
- Providing ongoing status reports throughout the project's life cycle

The CPO may also include the services of a project control analyst, whose responsibilities include:

> Coordinating the implementation of the customer solution through the development of a work breakdown structure (WBS), including a schedule and project plan
>
> Gathering and documenting updates to the schedules and project plans across the CPO
>
> Coordinating and attending all program-related meetings Recording meeting minutes and documenting action items with due dates and responsible individuals on assigned tasks/projects
>
> Communicating and coordinating status updates on action items, tasks, projects, etc. to support a timely closure of all actions
>
> Developing and maintaining reports required by the program; distributing these reports to the Customer and CPO in accordance with an agreed upon schedule
>
> Consolidating billing information for custom reporting to the Customer

Quarterly throughout the life of the program, the program manager will conduct a program review meeting and eServices Customer Satisfaction Survey to suggest changes to processes or tools.

At the conclusion of any projects throughout the program, the Customer will be asked to take the eServices Customer Satisfaction Survey to suggest changes to processes or tools.

Deliverables

The Deliverables (specified below) provided to the Customer are specific to the services provided, and will be presented within the timeframes identified for each.

Project Management

- Project plan to be delivered at the scheduled project kick-off meeting
- Trouble tickets status on demand via the Web

- Network usage on demand
- Status updates and reports to be delivered on a regular schedule at intervals mutually agreed upon between the project manager and the Customer

Program Management

Program plan as mutually agreed upon between the program manager and the Customer

- Project plans as needed
- Project status review weekly (or more often if necessary)
- Program reviews quarterly
- Executive reviews as requested by Customer
- Significant event report weekly via e-mail
- Trouble tickets status on demand via Web
- Network usage on demand
- Project plan/schedule weekly via e-mail

The frequency of any meetings, reports, or other communication can be adjusted upon mutual agreement between the program manager and the Customer.

Customer Responsibilities

Customer's Responsibility to YOUR COMPANY

For Project Management engagements, the Customer agrees to abide by the schedule as referenced in this eService Project and Program Management Service Description and as finalized and agreed to in the project kick-off meeting. In addition, the Customer agrees to:

- Provide YOUR COMPANY with any pertinent available documentation and/or information at or before the project kick-off meeting
- Within a reasonable amount of time following the execution of the Service Quotation, make available all Customer Stakeholders for the project kick-off meeting
- Identify all Customer Stakeholders in advance of project kick-off meeting and ensure their attendance at the meeting
- Commit to ensuring all Customer Stakeholders are available to YOUR COMPANY personnel via phone or e-mail during the program
- Commit to ensuring all Customer Stakeholders attend the regularly scheduled status update meetings throughout the Implementation
- One or more appropriate Customer personnel should respond to the Web-based Customer Satisfaction Survey pertaining to eServices Project and Program Management

For Customer Program Office engagements, the Customer agrees to:

- Provide YOUR COMPANY with any pertinent available documentation and/or information regarding the Customer's ongoing use of YOUR COMPANY's services to support the Customer's overall business needs
- Identify all key Customer Stakeholders for ongoing support interactions and attend regularly scheduled status update meetings
- Commit to ensuring all Customer Stakeholders are available to YOUR COMPANY personnel via phone or e-mail as needed
- One or more appropriate Customer personnel should respond to the quarterly Customer Satisfaction Survey pertaining to eServices Project and Program Management

YOUR COMPANY's Responsibilities

YOUR COMPANY's Responsibility to Customer

For Project Management engagements, YOUR COMPANY agrees to abide by the schedule as referenced in this Service Description and as finalized and agreed to in the Project Kick-off Meeting. In addition, YOUR COMPANY agrees to:

- Schedule a project kick-off meeting in a reasonable amount of time following the execution of the Service Quotation
- Assist in identification of all key personnel at YOUR COMPANY in advance of project kick-off meeting and confirm attendance of those individuals, as necessary, at both the project kick-off meeting and status update meetings
- Prepare detailed agenda and meeting minutes for the project kick-off meeting and status update meetings
- Coordinate delivery of all Deliverables as specified in the project schedule, and agreed to in the project kick-off meeting, to close out the project

For Customer Program Office engagements, YOUR COMPANY agrees to:

- Schedule regular status update meetings with the Customer
- Assist in identification of all key personnel at YOUR COMPANY necessary to support the Customer
- Prepare detailed agenda and meeting minutes for the status update meetings

Pricing and Billing

Pricing and billing terms for the Project and Program Management are set forth in the Service Quotation. Generally, program management involves one program manager. If, prior to or after executing a Service Quotation, it is determined that the Customer needs additional resources dedicated to the program, additional resources may be added. If such additional resources are added after executing a Service Quotation, the additional resource will be subject to additional fees and will be set forth in an additional Service Quotation.

Statement of Work (SOW) Evaluation Tool

This tool displayed in Table 6.19 may be used during the Presales phase to evaluate a Statement of Work.

Statement of Work Template

The template below, if used in its entirety, provides all the information required to provide the basis for developing a foundation for a project management plan.

Statement of Work

(Insert the name of the SOW here.)

This Statement of Work is made this _____ day of _____, 200__ by and between YOUR COMPANY ("YOUR COMPANY") and _____ with a principal place of business at _____ ("Customer") under the Agreement signed by Customer on _____. The Service Period shall commence (the "Effective Date") upon YOUR COMPANY providing the services detailed in this Statement of Work and shall continue until the scope of work is completed. The parties hereby agree as follows.

Executive Summary

The Executive Summary is a short, high-level description of the major objective(s) and value proposition(s).

Scope Description

The Scope Description is a description of the work that will be performed. This is a nontechnical explanation of the tasks that need to be performed to deliver the services and should be broken down in outline format.

YOUR COMPANY, unless otherwise noted below, will perform the tasks and provide the deliverables set forth below:

Table 6.19   Statement of Work Evaluation Template

SOW Evaluation Element	Yes/No/NA	Go/No Go	Comment
Does the opportunity meet the firm's engagement criteria?			
Criteria for Complex Consulting met.			
Criteria for Simple Consulting met.			
Can we deliver on the scope of work?			
The technical resources are available.			
The project resources are available.			
Does solution align with Your Firm/eServices strategic direction?			
Will this pull through business?			
Does this align with an existing LOB product or service?			
What is the estimated pull-through value?			
Has this customer purchased additional products or services in the past?			
Do we feel that the customer will ultimately bid the opportunity elsewhere?			

Have we identified the risks to the point where a business 'go, no-go' determination can be made?			
Technical risks.			
Business risks.			
Project risks.			
Do we have a solid basis for defining a cost estimate?			
Are/is the level of effort commensurate with the deliverables?			
Do the estimated hours include time needed to manage dependencies and third parties?			
Are the costs of Your Firm vendors included?			
Are the costs in line with historical data (when available)?			
Can the SOW be structured for potential up sell opportunities?			
Follow on consulting.			
Structured for Your Firm products and services beyond initial scope.			
Does the opportunity meet the negotiated criteria?			

Table 6.20   Your Company Deliverables

Deliverable	Description

Table 6.21   Partner/Subcontractor Deliverables

Deliverable	Description

YOUR COMPANY Deliverables

The table shown here should list *all* the deliverables the customer is paying for. This may include a Bill of Materials as well as intellectual deliverables such as reports and studies. The description should include the format and content of any written deliverables and any YOUR COMPANY intellectual property must be clearly marked "YOUR COMPANY Confidential" before submission to customer in written format. See Table 6.20.

Partner/Subcontractor Deliverables

The following table should list all the deliverables the Partner or Subcontractor is providing to enable completion of the SOW. The deliverables may be physical (i.e., equipment or software) or intellectual, which require YOUR COMPANY employee expertise or development, such as benchmarking analysis, software code, or hardware. See Table 6.21.

Customer-Provided Deliverables

The following table should list *all* the deliverables the customer will provide such as prior server audits, URLs, documented requirements, or items such as security policies. See Table 6.22.

Table 6.22   Customer-Provided Deliverables

Deliverable	Description

Table 6.23   Team Resources and Responsibilities

Roles	Key Responsibilities	Resource Name

Team Resources and Key Responsibilities

The following table should include the entire project team, the project team may include Partner staff and in some cases customer-named employees.

In addition to the Customer Responsibilities set forth in the Services Agreement, the parties noted below shall:

See Table 6.23.

Summary Tasks and Hours

The following table should describe the amount of hours for either tasks and/or deliverables.

YOUR COMPANY will perform the tasks and provide the deliverables set forth below in accordance with the following Estimated Level of Effort table (Table 6.24).

Please use the applicable Risk Checklist available on the YOUR COMPANY Web site if you think it helpful.

The purpose of the risks and assumptions set forth below is to communicate the basis for the time and cost estimates described in the Statement of Work and to set forth the conditions for completing the services to be provided under this Statement of Work as described in this Statement of Work.

Table 6.24 Tasks and Hours

Task Names	YOUR COMPANY Hours	External Hours

This might include clauses within related contracts, customer developed studies, or Partner documentation. If we reference a YOUR COMPANY contract add the text in red font (change to black prior to submitting to customer)

The (Contact name or number) services described herein shall be provided in connection with the (Contact name or number) services that will be/are provided pursuant to (Contact name or number) and (Contact name or number). The services being provided pursuant to the (Contact name or number) shall be provided pursuant to the terms and conditions of the applicable (Contact name or number).

The references to contracts or other related documents set forth in this section are for reference purposes only.

This might include customer policy statements, industry standards, or codes. Examples may include the customer's security policies and a related SAS 7o report. Describe the impact the references made below may have on the scope of work.

The references to other related documents set forth in this section are for reference purposes only.

This includes the charges for the Level of Effort in the "Tasks and Hours" table (Table 6.24), as well as any other one time YOUR COMPANY or Partner charges associated with the SOW, such as the charge(s) for benchmarking. The "Terms & Conditions" template language should be attached to the SOW. (Sample attached.) For T&M contracts alternate schedules may be developed.

CHOOSE EITHER THE FIXED PRICE OR THE TIME & MATERIALS LANGUAGE.

For Fixed Price Contracts:
The cost of this project shall be a fixed price of **[fill in]**, exclusive of any travel and out-of -pocket expenses, provided there are no changes in the project and the parties fully comply with all of the terms, conditions, and obligations set forth herein. YOUR COMPANY will invoice Customer in accordance with the following schedule:
[fill in] Example: YOUR COMPANY shall invoice Customer 50% of the fixed price upon execution of this Statement of Work and the

Table 6.25 Rates

Role	Rate
Engineer	$fill in/hr
Project Manager	$fill in/hr
Add other personnel as necessary	

remaining 50%, together with all associated travel and out-of pocket expenses, upon completion of the project.

Payment is due within thirty (30) days of receipt of invoice.

Travel and out-of-pocket expenses will be charged for any expenses required to complete the project as set forth herein. Travel expenses include airfare, hotels, meals, rental cars and mileage. Travel and out-of pocket expenses shall not exceed 25% of the contract price without authorization of Customer.

For Time & Material Contracts:

YOUR COMPANY will provide Services as described in this Statement of Work at the time and materials rates specified in the following chart (Table 6.25):

YOUR COMPANY estimates the total fees for the services provided under this Statement of Work will be [fill in], exclusive of travel and out-of-pocket expenses. [Alternative wording: YOUR COMPANY agrees that the total fees will not exceed [fill in] without the prior consent of Customer.] YOUR COMPANY will invoice Customer monthly. [For T&M contracts alternate schedules may be developed.]

[fill in]

Payment is due within thirty (30) days of receipt of invoice.

Travel and out-of-pocket expenses shall be charged for any expenses required to complete the project as set forth herein. Travel expenses include airfare, hotels, meals, rental cars and mileage. Travel and out-of-pocket expenses shall not exceed 25% of the contract price within prior written authorization of Customer.

If a Deliverables Acceptance Form is not required pursuant to Section 3 Acceptance of Deliverables below, then you should reference Section 3 below. If a Deliverables Acceptance Form is required, then you should mention the form below.

Milestone Schedule Dates

The table below should include the YOUR COMPANY and/or Partner deliverables at a Summary Task level.

See Table 6.26.

Table 6.26 Summary Task Table

Task Names	Deliverable if applicable	Completion Date

Agreed to and Accepted by:
This signature section, when completed and signed, transforms the SOW into a binding legal instrument.

By: [Customer Name]

_____

Date: XX/XX/XXXX

By: **YOUR COMPANY**

_____

Date: XX/XX/XXXX

Deliverables Acceptance Form

The table below should include the YOUR COMPANY and/or Partner/ Subcontractor deliverables the SOW requires us to complete.

See Table 6.27.

Table 6.27 Deliverable Acceptance Form

Task Names	Deliverable if applicable	Completion Date

Accepted by:

This signature section, when completed and signed, transforms the SOW into a binding legal instrument. This form documents the customer's acceptance of our work and is a de facto Certificate of Completion.

By: [Customer Name]

_____

Date: XX/XX/XXXX

Terms and Conditions

1. **Termination for Convenience**

   Either party may terminate this Statement of Work in whole or in part at any time by written notice to the other; such notice shall set forth the Termination Date. YOUR COMPANY shall be compensated for the Services rendered and expenses incurred or committed to prior to the Termination Date. For fixed price contracts, YOUR COMPANY will invoice Customer based on the percentage of work performed. In the event of such termination, YOUR COMPANY shall deliver to Customer all deliverables developed pursuant to this Statement of Work prior to the Termination Date, provided Customer pays YOUR COMPANY all amounts owed to YOUR COMPANY.

2. **Additional Terms**

   A. This Statement of Work and all eServices that may be provided hereunder are subject to the terms and conditions of the Services Agreement signed by you (or, if you have not signed such a Services Agreement, the terms and conditions of the current Services Agreement).

   B. This contract is subject to a credit check approval and confirmation of a valid Services Agreement signed by Customer.

   C. Any terms and conditions, including but not limited to those contained in a purchase order issued by Customer, which are different from or in addition to the terms and conditions contained in this Statement of Work and/or the Services Agreement signed by Customer, shall not be binding on YOUR COMPANY unless expressly accepted in writing, herein or otherwise, by YOUR COMPANY's authorized representative, and YOUR COMPANY hereby objects to and rejects all terms and conditions not so accepted.

3. **Acceptance of Deliverables**

   If a Deliverables Acceptance Form is not required pursuant to the Customer Acceptance of Deliverables and Performance Section above or if YOUR COMPANY and Customer agree during the term of Statement of Work that a Deliverables Acceptance Form will not be required, than all Deliverables shall be deemed accepted unless Customer notifies YOUR COMPANY in writing within five (5) business days of receipt that the Deliverable is not acceptable. In the event Customer provides such notification to YOUR COMPANY, Customer must return the Deliverable to YOUR COMPANY and include a detailed description of the reason(s) for not accepting the Deliverable. Upon receipt of a rejection notice, YOUR COMPANY will correct any defects or nonconformities to the extent required so that the Deliverable satisfies the requirements of Section 2 "Deliverables" above. YOUR COMPANY will resubmit the modified Deliverable to Customer for acceptance. All such Deliverables shall be deemed accepted if in compliance with Section 2 "Deliverables" above.

Customer acknowledges that delays in responding to Deliverables could affect the Project Schedule.

If a dispute arises between the parties concerning acceptance of a Deliverable, the parties shall enter into good-faith negotiations and agree upon (1) the work, if any, required for acceptance, and (2) the amount, if any, YOUR COMPANY will be paid for performing such work.

Procurement Matrix Table

Table 6.28 is a Procurement Matrix that will facilitate tracking purchases during the project life cycle.

Customer Program Office Schedule Template

This template shown in Figure 6.9 can help jump-start a schedule when work is being performed at a client site. The kind of work within this template includes application development, testing, setting-up policies and procedures, and more.

Scope Analysis Form

The tool depicted in Table 6.29 can be used to evaluate the scope of work when the project manager is provided with scope documents such as a contract, Statement of Work, Service Quotation, or equivalent. This information will facilitate the project planning effort (see Table 6.29).

Lessons Learned Questionnaire

See Table 6.30.

Table 6.28 Procurement Matrix

Description	Location	Project	Type of Work	Responsibility to Procure	Responsibility to Specify	Procurement Vehicle	Equipment Due Date	Relevance of Date (dependency)	Dependent Activitiy Date	Procurement Start (specify)	Procurement Completion	Work Completion Date	Responsible Entity

PROCUREMENT MATRIX

ID	Task Name	1st Quarter Qtr 1	2nd Quarter Qtr 2	3rd Quarter Qtr 3	4th Quarter Qtr 4	1st Quarter Qtr 1	2nd Quarter Qtr 2	3rd Quarter Qtr 3	4th Quarter Qtr 4	1st Quarter Qtr 1
1	(PMO) Initial Schedule Setup									
2	PROJECT MANAGEMENT ORGANIZATION									
3	(PMO) Office Set Up									
4	Server/Fax/Etc									
5	Prepare/ Move/ Purchase Furniture									
6	PMO Office/ Stationery Supplies									
7	Configure Firewalls at Customer Site for PMO Access to iWeb									
8	Document Management									
9	Initial Directory Structure - Knowledge Repository									
10	Scope Analysis Documentation									
11	Risk Management Documentation									
12	Issues/Action Items Documentation									
13	Asset Management: Arch. Audit (documentation)									
14	ISP Managed Hardware									
15	ISP Managed Software									
16	Bill of Materials									
17	Runbooks									
18	Version Control									
19	Customer Architecture(s) - version control of Asset Management Tas									
20	Validate "As Built"									
21	Validate BOM									
22	Include in BOM, IP addresses, etc..									
23	Update with Revisions									
24	Post to Knowledge Repository									
25	QMS Consistency									
26	Operating Procedure's. etc.									
27	Customer Facing Tools									
28	PMO Internal Tools									
29	MEETINGS									
30	Project/ Program Tracking (Weekly)									
31	Project Tracking (Weekly) 1									
32	Post-Mortem Review - for completed implementations									

(a)

ID	Task Name	1st Quarter Qtr 1	2nd Quarter Qtr 2	3rd Quarter Qtr 3	4th Quarter Qtr 4	1st Quarter Qtr 1	2nd Quarter Qtr 2	3rd Quarter Qtr 3	4th Quarter Qtr 4	1st Quarter Qtr 1
33	Service Level (Monthly)									
34	Service Level (Monthly) 1									
35	Program Activity Progress									
36	Customer Care/ Ticket Status Meetings									
37	ISP- PMO OPERATIONS MANUAL									
38	Manual Sections									
39	1. Organization									
40	a. Organizational Chart									
41	b.Contact list									
42	i. Add ISP Contacts									
43	ii. Add Customer Contacts									
44	iii. Add (sub) Contacts									
45	iiii. Insert into Manual									
46	complete section one									
47	2. Financial Management									
48	a.Financial (flow) Documentation									
49	i. Insert Financial Model									
50	ii. Insert Billing Process									
51	complete section 2a									
52	b. Create SOW Process Map									
53	i. draft the flow (See Operating Procedures 24/25)									
54	ii. Create visio drawing from the draft...									
55	iii. complete and add to manual									
56	d. Create Change Order Process Map									
57	i. draft the flow- see Scope Change Tool on PMO Intranet									
58	ii. Create visio drawing from the draft...									
59	iii. complete and add to manual									
60	e. Create Invoice Process Map									
61	i. draft the flow									
62	ii. complete and add to manual									
63	f. Create Labor log and analysis Process Map									
64	i. draft the flow									
65	ii. Create document and insert screen shots									
66	iii. complete and add to manual									

(b)

Figure 6.9 Customer Program Office Schedule Templates.

ID	Task Name	1st Quarter Qtr 1	2nd Quarter Qtr 2	3rd Quarter Qtr 3	4th Quarter Qtr 4	1st Quarter Qtr 1	2nd Quarter Qtr 2	3rd Quarter Qtr 3	4th Quarter Qtr 4	1st Quarter Qtr 1
67	3. Meetings									
68	a. Insert meeting schedule									
69	b. Insert Attendees Lists									
70	c. Insert Meeting Expectation Documentation Process									
71	4. Documentation									
72	a. Insert Knowledge Repository Manual									
73	5. Subs. Management									
74	a. Schedule of Deliverables									
75	b. Earned Value Reports									
76	6. Reports									
77	a. print and insert into manual									
78	7. Event Management									
79	a. Research owner and insert (Customer Care Information)									
80	8. Change Management									
81	a.Insert Documentation from ISP									
82	9. Security Policies (ISP Policies)									
83	a.Research owner of doc									
84	b. If Customer Information Available- Insert									
85	c. add to manual-									
86	10. Disaster Recovery (ISP T3 Documentation)									
87	a. Research owner of documentation									
88	b. compile report and include all into the tab									
89	c. include in manual									
90	11. Current Architecture									
91	a.Insert Current Architecture/ BOM									
92	b. Insert Runbooks									
93	12. Issues-									
94	Insert Actions Items Matrix Master									
95	Create Hardcopy Notebook									
96	a. Create Table of Contents									
97	b. Create Tabs									
98	c. Design cover									
99	d. Print, Post & Deliver to Customer									

(c)

ID	Task Name	1st Quarter Qtr 1	2nd Quarter Qtr 2	3rd Quarter Qtr 3	4th Quarter Qtr 4	1st Quarter Qtr 1	2nd Quarter Qtr 2	3rd Quarter Qtr 3	4th Quarter Qtr 4	1st Quarter Qtr 1
100	FINANCIALS									
101	Application Development - when needed (See Operating Procedure 20 for									
102	Create Methodology									
103	Identify Resources									
104	Implementation									
105	Create Estimate for Next Month's Work									
106	Deliver the Estimate									
107	Review Previous Month's Actuals									
108	Sign Off									
109	Execute Forward Billing									
110	Nonrecurring Charges									
111	Additional Resource Charges Methodology Development- when needed									
112	Create Methodology									
113	Identify Resources									
114	Implementation									
115	Fee Adjustment Methodology									
116	Customer Request for Adjustment									
117	Management Negotiation									
118	Agreement in Writing									
119	Application of Adjustment									
120	Late Payment Policy Development									
121	One Month Delinquency or Sq/ MSA terms									
122	Invoice Detail									
123	Methodology Development									
124	Monthly Billing									
125	Monthly Billing 1									
126	Pull Data									
127	Sanitize Data									
128	Create Invoice									
129	Deliver Invoice									
130	Resolve Tax Discrepancies, if any									

(d)

Figure 6.9   (continued).

ID	Task Name	1st Quarter Qtr 1	2nd Quarter Qtr 2	3rd Quarter Qtr 3	4th Quarter Qtr 4	1st Quarter Qtr 1	2nd Quarter Qtr 2	3rd Quarter Qtr 3	4th Quarter Qtr 4	1st Quarter Qtr 1
131	**Financial Templates**									
132	Define Scope, Objective, ad Recipients									
133	Assign Resource to Develop Templates									
134	Develop Templates									
135	Approve Templates									
136	Implement Templates									
137	Establish Performance Credit Escrow Account (When required in MSA)									
138	**Billing / Pass-Through**									
139	Define Scope, Objective, and Recipients									
140	Assign Resource to Develop Templates									
141	Develop Templates									
142	Approve Templates									
143	Implement Templates									
144	**QUALITY ASSURANCE**									
145	**Customer Satisfaction**									
146	Coordination of surveys									
147	Baseline Customer Satisfaction via Survey									
148	On-going Customer Satisfaction Surveys performed Annually									
149	Customer Satisfaction Interviews performed Annually									
150	New Installation Satisfaction Surveys performed as needed									
151	Event Management Satisfaction Surveys performed as needed									
152	Survey Response Analysis - in Concert with National PMO									
153	**STATEMENTS OF WORK**									
154	**Statements of Work**									
155	**New Statements**									
156	Record									
157	Check scope with eSd									
158	Perform LOB Buy-In									
159	Staffing Issues									
160	Risk / Dependency									
161	See Rates									
162	Pricing									
163	**Scope Analysis**									
164	1.0									
165	Deliverables									
166	Dependencies/ Constraints									
167	Risk									

(e)

ID	Task Name	1st Quarter Qtr 1	2nd Quarter Qtr 2	3rd Quarter Qtr 3	4th Quarter Qtr 4	1st Quarter Qtr 1	2nd Quarter Qtr 2	3rd Quarter Qtr 3	4th Quarter Qtr 4	1st Quarter Qtr 1
168	**1.0 SOW Sigs. (PMO Template)**									
169	Received Signed Copy									
170	Obtain Work Status									
171	Deliverables List									
172	**Acceptance and Billing**									
173	Signed Acceptance of Work									
174	Billing Status Determined									
175	**Build MPP / Schedule or Revise - for individual SOWs**									
176	1.0									
177	Scheduling									
178	Execute									
179	Sign-Off									
180	**SUBCONTRACTS**									
181	**Subs.**									
182	Determine Potential Outsourcing Opportunities									
183	Communication Protocols									
184	Billing Protocols									
185	Flow-Down Clause									
186	**Validate Scope/ Financials**									
187	ISP									
188	Subs.									
189	**ON-GOING SUPPORT**									
190	Define Activities									
191	**Reports To Customer**									
192	Network Usage									
193	Server Usage									
194	BEA Reports									
195	**Upsell Strategy Development**									
196	Server/System Audit - 'As Builts' for Customer Managed Equipment									
197	Historical Data Analysis									
198	Account Team Selling R&Rs									

(f)

Figure 6.9   (continued).

ID	Task Name
199	Potential P&P Revenue Upsell (Vendor Neutral)
200	P&P Draft Deliverables
201	DSN
202	Draft Submission
203	Define Requirements
204	Present and Review Draft
205	Draft Re-work (as needed)
206	Acceptance of Draft
207	NT Non-Root Permissions
208	Draft Submission
209	Define Requirements
210	Present and Review Draft
211	Draft Re-work (as needed)
212	Acceptance of Draft
213	NT Root Permissions
214	Draft Submission
215	Define Requirements
216	Present and Review Draft
217	Draft Re-work (as needed)
218	Acceptance of Draft
219	Webtrends Log Request
220	Draft Submission
221	Define Requirements
222	Present and Review Draft
223	Draft Re-work (as needed)
224	Acceptance of Draft
225	Server Space Request
226	Draft Submission
227	Define Requirements
228	Present and Review Draft
229	Draft Re-work (as needed)
230	Acceptance of Draft

(g)

ID	Task Name
231	Additional Server Capacity (Non-Priority)
232	Draft Submission
233	Define Requirements
234	Present and Review Draft
235	Draft Re-work (as needed)
236	Acceptance of Draft
237	Additional Server Capacity (Priority)
238	Draft Submission
239	Define Requirements
240	Present and Review Draft
241	Draft Re-work (as needed)
242	Acceptance of Draft
243	Domain Name Registration
244	Draft Submission
245	Define Requirements
246	Present and Review Draft
247	Draft Re-work (as needed)
248	Acceptance of Draft
249	Firewall Port Opening (Standard)
250	ISP Firewall
251	Draft Submission
252	Define Requirements
253	Present and Review Draft
254	Draft Re-work (as needed)
255	Acceptance of Draft
256	Firewall Port Opening (Non-Standard)
257	3rd. Party Firewall
258	Draft Submission
259	Define Requirements
260	Present and Review Draft
261	Draft Re-work (as needed)
262	Acceptance of Draft

(h)

Figure 6.9 (continued).

ID	Task Name	1st Quarter Qtr 1	2nd Quarter Qtr 2	3rd Quarter Qtr 3	4th Quarter Qtr 4	1st Quarter Qtr 1	2nd Quarter Qtr 2	3rd Quarter Qtr 3	4th Quarter Qtr 4	1st Quarter Qtr 1
263	**ISP Firewall**									
264	**Draft Submission**									
265	Define Requirements									
266	Present and Review Draft									
267	Draft Re-work (as needed)									
268	Acceptance of Draft									
269	**Custom DLL Installation**									
270	**Draft Submission**									
271	Define Requirements									
272	Present and Review Draft									
273	Draft Re-work (as needed)									
274	Acceptance of Draft									
275	**View / Obtain Open Ticket Status**									
276	**Draft Submission**									
277	Define Requirements									
278	Present and Review Draft									
279	Draft Re-work (as needed)									
280	Acceptance of Draft									
281	**Replication Applications**									
282	**Draft Submission**									
283	Define Requirements									
284	Present and Review Draft									
285	Draft Re-work (as needed)									
286	Acceptance of Draft									
287	**Replication Basic Content**									
288	**Draft Submission**									
289	Define Requirements									
290	Present and Review Draft									
291	Draft Re-work (as needed)									
292	Acceptance of Draft									

(i)

ID	Task Name	1st Quarter Qtr 1	2nd Quarter Qtr 2	3rd Quarter Qtr 3	4th Quarter Qtr 4	1st Quarter Qtr 1	2nd Quarter Qtr 2	3rd Quarter Qtr 3	4th Quarter Qtr 4	1st Quarter Qtr 1
293	**VPN Configuration**									
294	**Draft Submission**									
295	Define Requirements									
296	Present and Review Draft									
297	Draft Re-work (as needed)									
298	Acceptance of Draft									
299	**SSL Certificate**									
300	**Draft Submission**									
301	Define Requirements									
302	Present and Review Draft									
303	Draft Re-work (as needed)									
304	Acceptance of Draft									
305	**Load Balancing Device Provisioning**									
306	**Draft Submission**									
307	Define Requirements									
308	Present and Review Draft									
309	Draft Re-work (as needed)									
310	Acceptance of Draft									
311	**Load Balancing Service**									
312	**Draft Submission**									
313	Define Requirements									
314	Present and Review Draft									
315	Draft Re-work (as needed)									
316	Acceptance of Draft									
317	**ASP Component Services**									
318	**Draft Submission**									
319	Define Requirements									
320	Present and Review Draft									
321	Draft Re-work (as needed)									
322	Acceptance of Draft									

(j)

Figure 6.9   (continued).

ID	Task Name	1st Quarter Qtr 1	2nd Quarter Qtr 2	3rd Quarter Qtr 3	4th Quarter Qtr 4	1st Quarter Qtr 1	2nd Quarter Qtr 2	3rd Quarter Qtr 3	4th Quarter Qtr 4	1st Quarter Qtr 1
323	Additional Network Capacity									
324	Draft Submission									
325	Define Requirements									
326	Present and Review Draft									
327	Draft Re-work (as needed)									
328	Acceptance of Draft									
329	Install / Uninstall Software									
330	Draft Submission									
331	Define Requirements									
332	Present and Review Draft									
333	Draft Re-work (as needed)									
334	Acceptance of Draft									
335	Install / Uninstall Hardware									
336	Draft Submission									
337	Define Requirements									
338	Present and Review Draft									
339	Draft Re-work (as needed)									
340	Acceptance of Draft									
341	Report a Problem									
342	Draft Submission									
343	Define Requirements									
344	Present and Review Draft									
345	Draft Re-work (as needed)									
346	Acceptance of Draft									
347	Technical Writer Edits									
348	Post Edit Submission									
349	Review Edits									
350	Distribute Policies									
351	Create Manual Forms									
352	Initial Form Creation									
353	Incorporate Tech Writer Information									
354	Post to Intranet									

(k)

ID	Task Name	1st Quarter Qtr 1	2nd Quarter Qtr 2	3rd Quarter Qtr 3	4th Quarter Qtr 4	1st Quarter Qtr 1	2nd Quarter Qtr 2	3rd Quarter Qtr 3	4th Quarter Qtr 4	1st Quarter Qtr 1
355	Written Approvals of All P&P's									
356	3rd. Party Approval if needed									
357	ISP Approval									
358	Customer Approval									
359	Form Creation									
360	Test Manual Forms									
361	Create Web Routing application									
362	Create Web-based Forms									
363	Test Web-based Forms									
364	Potential Upsell Opportunity: (BENCHMARKING)									
365	RISK Mitigation									
366	Define Benchmarking									
367	Negotiate New Benchmarking Definitions and Parameters									
368	Meeting									
369	Sign Off on New Definition									
370	Benchmark									
371	Test Setup, Execution & Review									
372	Meet with customer to determine new scope of Benchmarking									
373	Provide Transaction Details to Compuware									
374	SOW (Benchmarking and Analysis)									
375	Develop SOW (PMO Template)									
376	Sign SOW									
377	Set Up SOW Schedule									
378	Monitor Schedule									
379	Potential Upsell Opportunity (TRAINING)									
380	Enduser Identification & Assessment Phase									
381	Define Scope and Deliverables									
382	Determine In-House Vs. Outsorcing Options									
383	Identify Possible Resources									
384	Negotiate Draft Agreements									
385	Assign Resource									
386	Deliver SOW's (PMO Template)									

(l)

Figure 6.9 (continued).

ID	Task Name	1st Quarter	2nd Quarter	3rd Quarter	4th Quarter	1st Quarter	2nd Quarter	3rd Quarter	4th Quarter	1st Quarter
		Qtr 1	Qtr 2	Qtr 3	Qtr 4	Qtr 1	Qtr 2	Qtr 3	Qtr 4	Qtr 1
387	Identify Training Offers									
388	Define Scope and Deliverables									
389	Determine In-House Vs. Outsorcing Options									
390	Identify Possible Resources									
391	Negotiate Final Agreement									
392	Assign Resource									
393	Deliver									
394	Curriculum Design									
395	Define Scope and Deliverables									
396	Determine In-House Vs. Outsorcing Options									
397	Identify Possible Resources									
398	Negotiate Agreements									
399	Assign Resource									
400	Deliver									
401	Potential Upsell: Security									
402	System Availability and Security									
403	Assign POC									
404	Constant Surveillance									
405	Define Surveillance Operations									
406	Physical datacenter									
407	Documents Operations									
408	Provide Documentation to Customer									
409	Sign-Off									
410	Electronic Data Security									
411	Documents Operations									
412	Provide Documentation to Customer									
413	Sign-Off									
414	Encryption									
415	Documents Operations									
416	Provide Documentation to Customer									
417	Sign-Off									

(m)

ID	Task Name	1st Quarter	2nd Quarter	3rd Quarter	4th Quarter	1st Quarter	2nd Quarter	3rd Quarter	4th Quarter	1st Quarter
		Qtr 1	Qtr 2	Qtr 3	Qtr 4	Qtr 1	Qtr 2	Qtr 3	Qtr 4	Qtr 1
418	Practices									
419	Document Operations									
420	Provide Documentation to Customer									
421	Sign-Off									
422	Provision Security									
423	Firewalls									
424	VPN's									
425	Log-on Procedures									
426	Document Operations									
427	Provide Documentation to Customer									
428	Sign-Off									
429	Recommended Security Procedures									
430	Document Operations									
431	Provide Documentation to Customer									
432	Sign-Off									
433	Management of SSL's									
434	Document Operations									
435	Develop Specific Operational Deviations									
436	Provide Documentation to Customer									
437	Sign-Off									
438	Virus Protection (Staging)									
439	Develop Solution									
440	Obtain Pricing									
441	Obtain ISP Approvals									
442	Document									
443	Sign-Off									
444	Implement									
445	Server Access Site Visit									
446	Coordinate Datacenter Visit									
447	Monitor Intrusion									
448	Document Operations									
449	Provide Documentation to Customer									
450	Sign-Off									

(n)

Figure 6.9   (continued).

ID	Task Name	1st Quarter Qtr 1	2nd Quarter Qtr 2	3rd Quarter Qtr 3	4th Quarter Qtr 4	1st Quarter Qtr 1	2nd Quarter Qtr 2	3rd Quarter Qtr 3	4th Quarter Qtr 4	1st Quarter Qtr 1
451	Patch to Security Bulletins									
452	Document Operations									
453	Provide Documentation to Customer									
454	Sign-Off									
455	Maintain Common Authentication Schemes									
456	Document Operations									
457	Provide Documentation to Customer									
458	Sign-Off									
459	Firewalls									
460	Perform Security Policy Configuration									
461	Assign Resource									
462	Implement Customer's TQ Document									
463	Implement Customer Requested Changes									
464	Document Operations									
465	Provide Documentation to Customer									
466	Sign-Off									
467	Method of Securing Change Requests									
468	Document Operations									
469	Provide Documentation to Customer									
470	Sign-Off									
471	Server Encryption									
472	Document Operations									
473	Provide Documentation to Customer									
474	Sign-Off									
475	24x7x365 Event Monitoring									
476	NOC Response to Urgent Alarms									
477	Document Operations									
478	Provide Documentation to Customer									
479	Sign-Off									
480	Define Response Procedures to Security Breaches									
481	Document Operations									
482	Provide Documentation to Customer									
483	Sign-Off									

(o)

ID	Task Name	1st Quarter Qtr 1	2nd Quarter Qtr 2	3rd Quarter Qtr 3	4th Quarter Qtr 4	1st Quarter Qtr 1	2nd Quarter Qtr 2	3rd Quarter Qtr 3	4th Quarter Qtr 4	1st Quarter Qtr 1
484	Potential Upsell Opportunities (REPORTS)									
485	Develop Reports (Per Service or Fee)									
486	Executive Summary									
487	Project Status									
488	Improvement Action (Bases On Surveys and PMO Quality Program)									
489	Asset Management									
490	Security and Virus Incidents									
491	Helpdesk Trend Analysis									
492	Change Management									
493	Disaster Recovery									
494	RCA									
495	Personnel									
496	Issues and Disputes									
497	Invoices									
498	Registered Domain Names									
499	Implemented Web Applications									
500	Admin and Permissions									
501	Intrusion Detection									
502	Pending Service Quotations and SOW's									
503	Network Usage									
504	Server Utilization									
505	Customer Satisfaction Surveys									
506	Incremental Fees									
507	Webtrends Reports									
508	Trouble Ticket Reports									
509	BMC Reports									
510	(template-future use) Complex Hosting Project w/ Sub.									
511	Formal Sales Opportunity Review Approvals									
512	Contracts									
513	Security									
514	Network Engineering									
515	Finance									
516	Datacenter									
517	Provisioning									
518	Architecture									

(p)

Figure 6.9   (continued).

ID	Task Name	1st Quarter	2nd Quarter	3rd Quarter	4th Quarter	1st Quarter	2nd Quarter	3rd Quarter	4th Quarter	1st Quarter
		Qtr 1	Qtr 2	Qtr 3	Qtr 4	Qtr 1	Qtr 2	Qtr 3	Qtr 4	Qtr 1
819	PM performs Risk Assessment									
820	Customer delivery of customer-provided software									
821	Discrepancy of Customer and Provisioning Timelines									
822	PAS Testing Schedule Impact to Delivery									
823	Risk Assessment Entered in IS Intranet									
824	Verify Receipt of Order									
825	Verify Customer Executes Service Quote									
826	Ensure Order is scanned									
827	Accept Order and Hands off to IC									
828	Internal Project Kick-Off Mtg									
829	Prepare draft Project Schedule (baseline developed after Internal Kick Off)									
830	Prepare Internal Kick Off Agenda (CW tab has minimum agenda items.)									
831	Check Hardware availability and obtain ETA from vendors - if not in inventory									
832	Prepare Confirming Minutes of Internal Kick Off									
833	Send PDF format of schedule to Tier 2 and Tier 3 Management									
834	Internal Kick Off done									
835	External Kick-off Meeting									
836	Prepare External Kick Off Agenda (CW tab contains minimum agenda items									
837	Review Provisioning guidelines and expected Delivery Dates									
838	Review 3rd. Party Milestones & Deliverables (add task lines to schedule if needed)									
839	Obtain Project Baseline Schedule Sign Off (at External Kick Off)									
840	External Kick Off Meeting Minutes									
841	External Kick Off Meeting Done									
842	Progress Updates									
843	Customer update 1									
844	Pre-Close Out Meeting									
845	Provisioning Coordination Activities									
846	Hardware Received by Data Center									
847	Hardware (e.g. servers, RAID devices, Local Directors) installed and configured									
848	Software part I - Server Jump start, O/S Software Installed and tested (CHP)									
849	Perform User Acceptance Testing									

(q)

ID	Task Name	1st Quarter	2nd Quarter	3rd Quarter	4th Quarter	1st Quarter	2nd Quarter	3rd Quarter	4th Quarter	1st Quarter
		Qtr 1	Qtr 2	Qtr 3	Qtr 4	Qtr 1	Qtr 2	Qtr 3	Qtr 4	Qtr 1
850	Software Installation									
851	SQL 2000									
852	Notify Customer of Datacenter Address									
853	Customer Fax License									
854	Confirmation of Receipt									
855	Installation of Software									
856	Commerce 2000									
857	Notify Customer of Datacenter Address									
858	Customer Fax License									
859	Customer FTP Media									
860	Confirmation of Receipt									
861	Installation & Configuration of Software									
862	Customer Support Meeting									
863	Report on the status of risks identified at the External Kick-off meeting and review any new risks that have been identified at the Launch Meeting									
864	Open Special Attention Ticket									
865	Engineering Identifies Run-book details with the Customer									
866	Schedule dates with CP, Tiers II and III as needed for content loading customer requirements									
867	Discuss acceptance testing and customer validation plan									
868	List Tasks for Customer Validation/Acceptance									
869	Handoff to Customer									
870	Customer hand off meeting									
871	Advise Sales - Project Online									
872	Application Work									
873	Load Testing of Applications									
874	Benchmark TQ Completed									
875	TQ Review Conference									
876	Customer revision to TQ									
877	Prepare SOW									
878	Execute SOW									
879	Perform Testing									
880	Review/Feedback from Testing									
881	Testing, HW. and SW Tweaks Complete									
882	Production "Go-Live"									

(r)

ID	Task Name	1st Quarter	2nd Quarter	3rd Quarter	4th Quarter	1st Quarter	2nd Quarter	3rd Quarter	4th Quarter	1st Quarter
		Qtr 1	Qtr 2	Qtr 3	Qtr 4	Qtr 1	Qtr 2	Qtr 3	Qtr 4	Qtr 1
883	Quality Assurance									
884	Request Customer Satisfaction Survey Completion									
885	Customer Responds to Survey									
886	Post Deployment Internal Team Evaluation									

(s)

Figure 6.9   (continued).

Table 6.29   Scope Analysis Form

Scope Analysis

Stakeholder	Deliverable	Dependency	Assumption	Risk	Constraint

Table 6.30 Lessons Learned Questionnaire

[Project Name]
Lessons Learned Questionnaire

Project Questions

1. How clearly defined were the objectives for the project?
   ☐ Very   ☐ Somewhat   ☐ Not Very   ☐ Not at all   ☐ N/A

2. How clearly defined were the objectives for your portion of work on this project?
   ☐ Very   ☐ Somewhat   ☐ Not Very   ☐ Not at all   ☐ N/A

3. How clear were you on your role in the project?
   ☐ Very   ☐ Somewhat   ☐ Not Very   ☐ Not at all   ☐ N/A

4. How adequately involved did you feel in project decisions?
   ☐ Very   ☐ Somewhat   ☐ Not Very   ☐ Not at all   ☐ N/A

   If not at all, what decisions did you feel excluded from?
   _____

5. How efficient and effective were project team/technical meetings?
   ☐ Very   ☐ Somewhat   ☐ Not Very   ☐ Not at all   ☐ N/A

   What would you change or implement?
   _____

6. Do you feel appreciated, recognized, and rewarded for your efforts?
   ☐ Very   ☐ Somewhat   ☐ Not Very   ☐ Not at all   ☐ N/A

   If no, explain what would have made you feel appreciated and rewarded?
   _____

7. What techniques, methodologies, processes, or tools were effective and are worth permanently maintaining?
   _____

8. What specific aspects of the project did you enjoy the most and why?
   _____

9. What technologies, processes, tools, or techniques do you feel would be worth considering for other projects at ABC?
   _____

10. Please provide any additional comments.
    _____

Lessons Learned Report

A template report is displayed below.

[Project Name]

Lessons Learned Report

Overview
[Provide a brief overview of the project.]

Lessons Learned Methodology
[Provide a brief overview of the approach to collect and analyze lessons learned (questionnaires, group sessions, etc.)]

Lessons Learned Report

1. [Describe lesson learned.]
2. [Describe lesson learned.]
3. [Describe lesson learned.]
4. [Describe lesson learned.]
5. [Describe lesson learned.]

[Other lessons learned to be listed]

Summary
[Content here]

Post-Project Review Form

This can be used after a project phase, major deliverable, entire project or program has been completed (see Table 6.31).

Project Review Protocol Review Guide

This tool is an in-depth guide to evaluate projects, gauge their health as well as the methodology employed to deliver them. See Table 6.32.

Configuration Management Process Checklist

See Table 6.33.

Table 6.31   Post-Project Review Form

Post-Project Review Form
Customer Name:
PM Name:
Post-Project Review Date:
Contributors/Attendees:
Project Completion Date:
Project ID: (from Project Form)
Project Name:
1. In retrospect would any changes to the Project Plan be suggested?   Tab to each question and enter your comments here
2. Were there any customer expectation management issues that generated a Lesson Learned?   Tab to each question and enter your comments here
3. In retrospect could any of the Risk, Dependency of Constraint issues have been managed differently?   Tab to each question and enter your comments here
4. Did this project generate a Best Practice that may be shared?   Tab to each question and enter your comments here.
5. Any other Lessons Learned that may be shared.   Tab to each question and enter your comments here.
6. Have any issues been escalated? Please be specific with names, dates, and issues. (Limit to key issues.)   Tab to each question and enter your comments here.
7. Any recommended process changes due to this project experience?   Tab to each question and enter your comments here.
8. Any other comments?   Tab to each question and enter your comments here.

Table 6.32   Project Review Protocol Guide

Project Review Protocol—Guide

Employed by management to proactively review major project status, reinforce best practices and coaching. Questions may fit into any or all of these contexts.

Project Name: _____

Project Manager*: _____Reporting Manager_____

Project Start Date:_____ Percent Complete:___% Completion Date: _____

* May hold any of the following job titles: Account Support Representative, Senior Account Support Representative, Project Manager, Senior Project Manager, Principal Project Manager, Program Manager, Senior Program Manager, Principal Program Manager, Technical Account Manager, or other related title in Implementation Services.

I Project Scope:

1. The Project Manager describes the scope by defining the major deliverables, tasks, and milestones. (Should be documented in one or more of the following: Contract, Service Quotation, Pricing Matrix, Deliverables Document, Unified Configuration Workbook, Task Statement. The scope document(s) should be in either the Project Workbook or Contracts Database)

   _____

2. Describe any changes from the original scope of work. (Since last review. Reference is needed to the PMO Project Scope Change Management Form[s])

   • What were they?

   • How were they processed?

   • How were they communicated to the stakeholders?

   _____

3. Were any scope constraints (customer generated limits such as brand, time, or performance constraints) identified? (What were they and who identified them?)

   _____

4. Have the scope constraints (Your Company generated limitations such as network or architectural constraints) been communicated to the customer? (Should be documented in either e-mail, Doc Repository, or Project Workbook.)

   _____

Table 6.32 (continued)   Project Review Protocol Guide

5. How realistic was the (original) proposal communicated to the customer? (Who developed the proposal? Who communicated it to them? To what extent did the PM ensure scope document integrity?)

6. Were there any expectation management issues?

II Project Risk Management:

1. What risk issues have been identified?

2. How have these risk issues been addressed in the Project Plan (Project Plan includes, but is not limited to, contractual scope definitions, risk management plan, action items and schedules)? (Should be confirmed on PMO Web Risk Management Checklist.)

III Project Schedule:

1. The Project Manager reviews the schedule, employing the template, comparing Actual versus Baseline.

2. Has the Project Manager identified, on the schedule, customer driven schedule dependencies? (Possible coaching opportunity)

3. If an Actual versus Baseline variance, of a key roll up milestone, is identified: Define the actions that were *or* are being taken by the Project Manager to manage this.

4. Were assumptions made for the schedule? Please describe.

5. Have these assumptions worked?

6. Were the (Network Operations) Implementation Coordinator's delivery dates determined (confirmed) at the Internal Kick-Off?

(continued on next page)

Table 6.32 (continued)   Project Review Protocol Guide

7. How have the (Network Operations) Customer Provisioning dates been managed against the project schedule?

_____

8. Was a WBS developed? (Opportunity for coaching)

_____

IV Project Communication:

1. How does the Project Manager assess the customer's expectations and current perceptions?

_____

2. What has been the quality and frequency of communications with the Project Manager's virtual team? (Who composed the core team and in what form: e-mail, in-person, telephone, etc.?)

_____

3. What has been the quality and frequency of communications with the customer? (In what form: e-mail, in-person, telephone, etc.?)

_____

4. Have any issues surfaced that affected scope, risk, or schedule? Please describe how they were addressed.

_____

5. How have newly developed issues changed the Project Plan? (Was a new baseline schedule issued?)

_____

6. Has the initiating sales person (Account Manager, EBC, etc.) been kept informed?

_____

7. How has this project been reported to the Reporting Manager and how frequently?

_____

8. Have escalation paths been identified and communicated at the internal and external kick off meetings? (At Your Company? At customer?)

_____

9. Who has been the primary point of contact? (Possible coaching opportunity)

_____

Table 6.32 (continued)   Project Review Protocol Guide

V Project Quality:

1. Any Lessons Learned thus far? Have they been posted on the intranet site?

   _____

2. What is the customer satisfaction level at this point?

   _____

3. Have Your Company processes been working? If not, please describe issues and potential solutions.

   _____

4. How will we know that the deliverables are installed and working?

   _____

5. How will we obtain customer system acceptance?

   _____

6. Are there any team member roles and responsibilities requiring clarification?

   _____

NOTES:

_____

_____

PM/ASR/TAM Signatuture: _____ Date: ___/___/___

Manager's Signatuture: _____ Date: ___/___/___

Table 6.33   Configuration Management Process Checklist

Checklist Title:	QA Evaluator:	
Review Date:	**Date:**	
Project:		
Project Configuration Management Checklist		
Project:		
Step	*Response (Y or N)*	*Items to Consider*
1		Is there a configuration management (CM) plan for the development effort? Does it include the following: • Roles and responsibilities for CM • Configuration identification activities • Software build activities • Change control activities • Status accounting activities • Audit activities • Reporting and reviews activities
2		Is there someone to perform the configuration management activities?
3		Are sufficient tools and funding allocated for performing the configuration management activities?
4		Are all configuration items identified and documented?
5		Is there a CM library of software baselines?
6		Are software builds being done according to plan and schedule, using the baseline library?
7		Are changes to baselines controlled?
8		Are baseline audits planned and conducted?
9		Is a documented change control process being followed that supports the following: • Documenting a requested change • Reviewing a requested change by a Change Control Board • Examining impact to the project if a change is approved • Modifying project plans to incorporate any approved change • Tracking a change request from submission to completion

Table 6.33 (continued)   Configuration Management Process Checklist

Step	Response (Y or N)	Items to Consider
10		Is there a functioning Change Control Board, with joint representation of supplier, acquirer, and customer (as appropriate)?
11		Are standard reports on CM activities prepared and made available?
12		Are CM activities reviewed with the project manager?
13		Do quality assurance personnel review CM activities and results?
14		Are measures made to determine status of CM activities?
15		Other?

Project Closeout Form

Client Name:

Contract No:

Project Name:

Responsible:

I hereby certify that _____ has fulfilled, to my complete satisfaction, their contractual obligations and transferred to my organization all the project artifacts and deliverables required.

Date:

_____

[Name]

[Title]

[Organization]

[Phone number]

Sample Project Completion Letter

To: PPOC—Client side

        Title

        Company Name

Re: (Name of Project) Project Completion Notification

Project Completion Date: Date

Dear   (PPOC—Client side):

First, allow me to thank you for choosing Your Company as your is this what we want to have in here? provider. As [PM, TAM or ASR] for the (name of Project), it has been a pleasure working with you and the (company name) project team to successfully implement and deliver your new (add name of services—hosting, vpn, etc.)

This letter is to confirm that Your Company has successfully completed the project, handed off all contractual deliverables, and the accepted services and products for Customer's Name as outlined in the (Project Name) Project (contract number) Contract Date.

> To ensure a smooth transition, all relevant project documentation has been transferred to (Name of ASR or Premier Care Rep) for ongoing support services. Name of ASR or Premier Care Rep will be your new primary point of contact as of (enter date).

[THE FOLLOWING PARAGRAPH IS OPTIONAL]

In the next week or two, I will send you a URL for a Your Company eServices Delivery Customer Satisfaction Survey. I would appreciate you taking a moment to complete this survey. If you feel that you cannot submit a response of "Very Satisfied" in any field, please contact me so I may have the opportunity to address any concerns you may have. Please keep in mind that although this survey is only intended to grade my efforts and not that of any other department, I will gladly receive your comments regarding any members of the Your Company team.

Thank you again for your business and support during this project.

Sincerely,

Your Name
Your Title
Your Company

Cc: Project Team
        Sales Team

Requirements Phase Completion Checklist

This can be used to make sure the Requirements phase has been properly completed. See Table 6.34.

Action Item Matrix

This is an alternate template to track action items, some of which may come from JAD/Requirements Sessions. See Table 6.35.

Project Transition Guide

The tool in Table 6.36 will facilitate moving a project from one manager to another.

Audit Plan Matrix

Leveraging the work instructions, tools, and templates: the attached matrix in Table 6.37 is a guide to facilitate PMO conformance with ISO standards.

Table 6.34   Requirements Phase Completion Checklist

#	Requirements Phase Completion Checklist	Yes/No
1	Have the functional application requirements been defined and documented?	
2	Have the functional data requirements been defined and documented?	
3	Have the functional user interface requirements been defined and documented?	
4	Have the functional integration requirements been defined and documented?	
5	Have the nonfunctional usability requirements been defined and documented?	
6	Have the nonfunctional performance requirements been defined and documented?	

(continued on next page)

Table 6.34 (continued)   Requirements Phase Completion Checklist

#	Requirements Phase Completion Checklist	Yes/No
7	Have the nonfunctional operational requirements been defined and documented?	
8	Have all nonfunctional security requirements been defined and documented?	
9	Have the nonfunctional legal requirements been defined and documented?	
10	Have the nonfunctional globalization requirements been defined and documented?	
11	Have the nonfunctional documentation requirements been defined and documented?	
12	Are the stakeholders, their functional relationships, and project dependencies understood and documented?	
13	Are potential interfaces with other systems documented?	
14	Have the identified system requirements issues and risks been documented in the project's risk management system?	
15	Have the issues been documented in project's action/issues tracking system?	
16	Are the Use Cases traceable to System Requirements and documented?	
17	Have the Use Cases been reviewed by the appropriate team members?	
18	Have all actions from review sessions been addressed?	
19	Does the architecture map to the requirements?	
20	Have all actions from review/JAD session been addressed?	
Develop question sets, identify stakeholders, document sessions, validate requirements		

Table 6.35 Action Item Matrix

Action Item Matrix

No.	Unit	Item	[Open/Closed] Status	Open Date	Due Date	Finish Date	Priority	Initiator	Owner	Ticket #	Notes

Table 6.36   Project Training Guide

No.	Transition Milestone Dates	Scheduled Completion Date	Status Check/off
1.	New *(Incoming PM)* Manager drafts preliminary transition schedule and submits to *Outgoing* Manager for review		
2.	Transition Team agrees on the details of the plan and the transition schedule dates. (Baseline created.)		
3.	New *(Incoming PM)* Manager submits transition schedule (baseline) to the Regional Director		
4.	Mandatory documentation has been provided or made available on the *doc repository* for the New *(incoming PM)* Manager		
5.	New *(incoming PM)* Manager reviews all documentation to become familiar with account or project (1 week recommended)		
6.	*Outgoing (incoming PM)* Manager introduces New *(Incoming PM)* "Manager" to Account/Customer (Informal)		
7.	Transition Team works together closely on the Account/Project (2 weeks recommended)		
8.	New *(incoming PM)* Manager assesses level of Maintenance for the account or project		
9.	New *(incoming PM)* Manager reviews project or account issues with *Outgoing* Manager		
10.	*Outgoing (incoming PM)* Manager transfers account to New *(incoming PM)* Manager (formal)		
New (incoming PM) Manager initials confirming that Account or Project has been officially transferred.		Date:_____	

Table 6.36 (continued)   Project Training Guide

Mandatory Documentation or Information	Received
Communications—Meeting Minutes from Kick-Off, Progress and Launch Support Meetings, UAT or PAS Testing results	
Contacts—Customer, Project	
Legal Documents—Master Agreements, Service Schedules, Task Statements, and Service Quotations, Letters of Intent	
Pricing Information	
Project Plan documents—Project Schedule, Risk Assessment	
Billing Verification (Confirm completion)	
Project Completion Notification Letter	

Table 6.37 Audit Plan Matrix

A: Management Team	E: Analyst	I: Quality Assurance
B: Project/Program Mgrs	F: Web Developer	J:
C: Training Department	G: PMO Sponsor	K:
D: Tools and Processes	H: Director PMO	L:

ISO 9001:2000 Requirement Applicability to Each Department/Function/Process

ISO 9001:2000 REQUIREMENT	A	B	C	D	E	F	G	H	I	J	K	L
4 QUALITY MANAGEMENT SYSTEM												
4.1 General Requirements	X	X	X	X	X	X	X	X	X			
4.2.1/2 Documentation requirements Quality Manual				X					X			
4.2.3 Control of documents				X					X			
4.2.4 Control of quality records				X					X			
5 Management responsibility												
5.1 Management Commitment	X				X		X	X	X			
5.2 Customer focus	X				X		X	X	X			
5.3 Quality Policy	X				X		X	X	X			
5.4 Planning	X				X		X	X	X			
5.4.1 Quality objectives/planning	X				X		X	X	X			

5.5 Responsibility and authority, communication	X			X		X	X			
5.6 Management Review	X			X		X	X			
6 HUMAN RESOURCES										
6.1/2 Provision of resources, Human Resources	X		X			X	X			
6.3 Infrastructure	X					X	X			
6.4 Work Environment	X					X	X			
7 PRODUCT REALIZATION										
7.1 Planning of product realization		X				X	X			
7.2.1/2 Requirements/review products requirements		X				X	X			
7.2.2 Review of product requirements		X				X	X			
7.2.3 Customer communication		X				X	X			
7.3 Design and development										
7.4 Purchasing										
7.5.1 Control of production and service provision		X				X	X			
7.5.2 Validation of processes for production/service		X				X	X			
7.5.3 Identification and traceability		X				X	X			
7.5.4 Customer property		X				X	X			

(continued on next page)

Table 6.37 (continued)   Audit Plan Matrix

ISO 9001:2000 Requirement	A	B	C	D	E	F	G	H	I	J	K	L
7.5.5 Preservation of product		X						X	X			
7.6 Control of measuring and monitoring devices		X						X	X			
8 Measurement, analysis, and improvement												
8.1 General	X				X			X	X			
8.2.1 Customer Satisfaction	X	X			X			X	X			
8.2.2 Internal Audit	X	X			X			X	X			
8.2.3 Monitoring and measurement of processes	X							X	X			
8.2.4 Monitoring and measurement of product	X							X	X			
8.3 Control of nonconforming product	X							X	X			
8.4 Analysis of data					X			X	X			
8.5.1 Continual improvement	X				X			X	X			
8.5.2/3 Corrective Action/Preventive action	X							X	X			
Reference to checklist(s) used	Form ACC 101 [x] Form ACC 101-QSA [ ]											
	Form ACC 101-1 (AS 9000) [ ]											

Audit Template

This can be used by the project's internal QA groups or by an IV&V vendor to review conformance with the implementation methodology.

Quality Assurance Review—Final Report

Date of Review: _____   Date of Report: _____

Individual under Review: _____   Title: _____

Regional Manager: _____   Region: _____

Project Name: _____   Status: _____

Reviewer: _____

Review Details

The scope of this review included a review of:

Summary of audit results *(Audit Opinion)***:**

Strengths

Findings with Severity Level *(Major/Minor Nonconformities)***:**

Proposed Corrective Action Plan

The PMO recommends that:

Planned Completion Date:

Verification Date:

Distribution List:

Notice of Preventative and Corrective Action

This form in Table 6.38 aligns with the feedback Work Instruction so that the PMO continually improves. Internal and external stakeholders provide feedback through multiple mechanisms—this tool documents the inputs and facilitates the tracking.

Table 6.38 Notice of Preventative or Corrective Action

NOTICE OF PREVENTATIVE ACTION, CORRECTIVE ACTION or CONTINUOUS IMPROVEMENT OPPORTUNITY	Number: Inserted into C/P Log ☐
PMO	Date:

Source	Check One		Check One
Registrar	☐	cSat Survey	☐
Customer Complaint	☐	QAR	☐
Employee Feedback	☐	Management	☐
Tools Review Committee	☐	Mgmt Review Mtg	☐
ISO Focus Group	☐	PMO	☐

Complaint or Feedback:	
Results of investigation of the root cause:	
Corrective/Preventative Action:	
Document Changes Needed? Yes/ No Which Documents:	
Date of Completion:	Signed
Follow-Up and Close Out:	
Verify Document Changes Yes/No	
Date Closed:	Signed/Initialed:
Closed in C/P Log ☐	

PMO Quality Management System Self-Assessment Tool

This is a tool to help a project organization determine its maturity level in terms of ISO systems. See Table 6.39.

Project Management Quotation Template

Service Quotation for Your Company Services			
to			
<Customer's Name>			
Contact:		Quote Date:	
Company:		Quote Valid to Date:	
Address:		Quote Number:	
Address:			
City			
Country:			
Zip / Postal Code:			

 I. Services Offered: (Please check all applicable boxes.)
  ☐ **Project Management**
  ☐ **Program Management**

II. Service Period: The service period for Project Management services shall commence (the "Effective Date") upon Your Company Solutions Inc. ("Your Company", "we", "our" or "us") providing the service(s) (the "eService(s)") selected in this quotation (the "Quotation") to the Customer indicated above ("Customer", "you" or "your") and shall continue until the scope of work, indicated in this Quotation and the applicable Your Company Service Description(s), is completed. The engagement shall be considered complete when all the Deliverables specified in the applicable Service Description have been delivered to Customer and are accepted pursuant to Section V. below.

 The service period for Program Management shall commence (the "Effective Date") upon execution and shall continue for ___ calendar months from that date. Upon mutual agreement of the Customer and Your Company, the Service Period may be extended on a month-to-month basis during which

Table 6.39 Your Company Quality Program Self-Assessment Checklist

Self-Assessment is the first step in implementing Your Company Quality (GQ) plan for your department. The goal is to identify the "gaps" that will become part of your action plan for meeting Your Company's Quality standards. GQ standards are largely based on ISO 9000:2001, so when you have completed your work you will be well on your way to being "ISO Ready." Gaps are expected, and the more completely you identify them the better your final result will be.

How to Use: The Self-Assessment form is divided into nine sections beginning with "1.0 Quality Planning." Each section begins with a "Standard" that is numbered 1.0, 2.0, 3.0, etc. This is followed by rows stating the "Control Objectives" that must be met, if applicable, to meet the "Standard." These Control Objectives are numbered 1.1, 1.2, 1.3, etc. The Control Objective column is followed by a "Status" column in which you indicate if your department meets the Control Objective (Y), partially meets it (P), or does not meet it (N). If the Control Objective does not apply, simply enter "n/a." In the last column you should note any gaps and reference any supporting documentation for the Control Objective along with its location or URL. You should also use this column for your notes/comments.

Note: The "Standard" is what you need in order to achieve compliance with the Your Company Quality plan; the "Control Objective" is how you demonstrate that you meet the Standard.

1.0	Quality Planning	Status	• **Supporting Documentation with Location/URL**
	Standard: Your Company Organization's plan for quality to assure it meets customer requirements and corporate goals: • Customer Intimacy • Optimize Asset Utilization • Drive Profitable Revenue Generation • Increase Operational Efficiencies **Control Objectives:**	Y N P n/a	• **Gaps** • **Comments or explanation**

		Status Y N P n/a	• **Supporting Documentation with Location/URL** • **Gaps** • **Comments or explanation**
1.1	Quality objectives are established, including those needed to meet requirements for products or services.		
1.2	Plans are in place to meet the requirements of products and services.		
1.3	Business Continuity/ Disaster Recovery plans are implemented.		
2.0	**Documents/Records Control and Management**		
	Standard: Current documented policies, procedures, and forms are controlled and accessible for employee use. Employees can easily access needed documents. **Control Objectives:**		
2.1	• Documents are reviewed and approved prior to issue • Documents are current • Changes shall be identified • Documents are uniquely identified • Revision status is identified • Documents remain legible and identifiable • Prevent unintended use of obsolete documents		
2.2	Documents are stored and available for employees' use.		
2.3	Distribution of documents is controlled.		

(continued on next page)

Table 6.39 (continued)   Your Company Quality Program Self-Assessment Checklist

		Status Y N P n/a	• Supporting Documentation with Location/URL • Gaps • Comments or explanation
2.4	Master list of documents exists and is maintained.		
2.5	Records are: • Maintained for defined period • Legible • Identifiable		
2.6	A documented procedure exists which defines identification, storage, protection, retrieval, retention time, and disposition controls for records specific to products and/or services.		
3.0	**Management Responsibility**		
	Standard: Functional Management provides clear direction to its employees, communicates requirements, roles, responsibilities, results, goals, and regularly reviews performance against company objectives. **Control Objectives:**		
3.1	Mission statements exist and are communicated at functional levels.		
3.2	Functional level roles and responsibilities are defined and communicated (i.e., org chart).		
3.3	Customer requirements are communicated and fulfilled.		
3.4	Business plans supporting corporate strategies exist and are communicated.		

		Status Y N P n/a	• **Supporting Documentation** **with Location/URL** • **Gaps** • **Comments or explanation**
4.0	**Resource Management**		
	Standard: Assure adequate physical and human resources are available to meet customer requirements. **Control Objectives:**		
4.1	Resources exist in order for employees to perform their jobs effectively.		
4.2	Resources exist in order to meet customer requirements.		
4.3	Job descriptions are documented.		
4.4	Employees are provided appropriate training to ensure skills are maintained or improved upon.		
4.5	Training records are maintained.		
5.0	**Customer Related Processes**		
	Standard: Processes exist to assure customer satisfaction with Your Company's products and services. **Control Objectives:**	Status Y N P n/a	• **Supporting Documentation** **with Location/URL** • **Gaps** • **Comments or explanation**

(continued on next page)

Table 6.39 (continued)   Your Company Quality Program Self-Assessment Checklist

5.1	Customer requirements are determined (delivery & post delivery activities) and communicated to required personnel.		
5.2	Requirements are reviewed to ensure they can be met.		
5.3	Records of customer requirements are maintained and reviewed.		
5.4	Records of customer confirmation of requirements are maintained.		
5.5	Design processes exist and cover the following: • Review, verification, and validation of design • Documentation (functional & performance specs, any statutory or regulatory requirements) • Change control • Review of design inputs		
5.6	Built product is tested to ensure it meets customer requirements.		
5.7	Effective customer communication processes exist.		

6.0	Purchasing	Status Y N P n/a	• **Supporting Documentation with Location/URL** • **Gaps** • **Comments or explanation**
	Standard: • Products purchased conform to specified purchase requirements. • Suppliers and vendors are selected based upon their ability to supply products or services in accordance with Your Company's requirements. **Control Objectives:**		
6.1	Products purchased conform to specified requirements.		
6.2	Suppliers and Vendors are selected based on ability to supply products according to requirements.		
6.3	Purchasing process exists and specifies product information needed.		
6.4	Purchasing ensures specified purchase requirements are adequate prior to communicating with the supplier.		
6.5	Product received is inspected to ensure it is free of defects and meets specified purchasing requirements.		

(continued on next page)

Table 6.39 (continued) Your Company Quality Program Self-Assessment Checklist

7.0	Product Realization: Provisioning and Servicing	Status Y N P n/a	• Supporting Documentation with Location/URL • Gaps • Comments or explanation
	Standard: Delivery of products and services is consistently executed and controlled. Processes for product delivery and servicing of solutions are documented, measured, communicated, and available to employees. **Control Objectives:**		
7.1	Product Life-Cycle models exist for products and services.		
7.2	Processes exist for delivery of products according to customer requirements.		
7.3	Processes exist for maintaining products according to SLAs.		
7.4	Products installed are identified by suitable means.		
7.5	Identified product's location is recorded and maintained.		
7.6	Customer Support Program exists to resolve product-related problems.		
7.7	A documented process exists to ensure customers are notified of problems that may affect their services.		
7.8	Problem Severity Levels are assigned for problems.		
7.9	Problem Escalation procedure exists and is documented.		
7.10	Recall process exists and is documented in order to recall products that are unfit to remain in service.		

		Status Y N P n/a	• **Supporting Documentation with Location/URL** • **Gaps** • **Comments or explanation**
7.11	Emergency processes exist, and are documented to ensure services and resources are available to support recovery from emergency failures of services.		
7.12	Established interface exists between problem resolution and configuration management to ensure fixes to problems are incorporated in future installations.		
7.13	Documented patch procedure is established and maintained.		
8.0	**Infrastructure**		
	Standard: Your Company's network infrastructure and systems are secured, available, and maintained to ensure compliance with customer requirements and SLAs. **Control Objectives:**		
8.1	Objectives, standards and policies exist regarding systems security, availability, and maintainability, which are consistent with SLAs.		

(continued on next page)

Table 6.39 (continued)   Your Company Quality Program Self-Assessment Checklist

8.2	Information Security Policies & Program includes, but not limited to: • Audits • Intrusion Detection • Establish Access Levels • Establish Risk Assessment Approach • Clearly defined roles and responsibilities • Access control to systems • Data Classification • Retention Policy • Protection against threats such as sabotage, terrorism, or vandalism			
8.3	Physical Security exists to ensure protection of areas housing system related equipment. Physical Security Program should include: • Access control to system supporting areas • Information Classification • Protection against threats such as loss, sabotage, terrorism, or vandalism			
8.4	Security Awareness Program exists to educate employees on information and physical security issues and procedures.			
8.5	A documented procedure exists for handling changes or modification to systems. As part of the changes there is a "promotion process"; test, stage, production.			

8.6	Adequate off-site storage of maintenance resources: • Program libraries • Data tapes		
8.7	Periodic review of system logs and trends analyzed to identify potential impacts to systems.		
8.8	System users (internal and external) are identified and documented.		
8.9	System availability features are compared and tested to ensure they meet availability objectives.		
8.10	Risk assessments are conducted when internal or external environmental changes occur. Risk assessment should address the protection against: fire, flood, dust, excessive heat, humidity, and labor problems.		
8.11	Business Continuity & Disaster Recovery addresses range of possibilities including minor processing errors, destruction of records, and outages.		
8.12	Monitoring of system performance to ensure SLA compliance.		
8.13	Environmental and technological changes to systems are monitored and impact to system is periodically assessed.		

(continued on next page)

Table 6.39 (continued) Your Company Quality Program Self-Assessment Checklist

9.0	Measurement, Analysis, and Improvement	Status Y N P n/a	• Supporting Documentation with Location/URL • Gaps • Comments or explanation
	Standard: Measure the conformity to processes, SLAs, and customer requirements, as well as foster continuous improvement of processes, products, and services. **Control Objectives:**		
9.1	Monitor information relating to customer perception as to whether customer requirements have been fulfilled.		
9.2	Processes are monitored to ensure they meet planned results.		
9.3	Monitor characteristics of the product to verify that product requirements are fulfilled to ensure customer requirements and SLAs are met.		
9.4	Evidence of product conformity is maintained.		
9.5	Product that does not conform to product requirements is identified and controlled to prevent its unintended use or delivery.		
9.6	Records of product nonconformity and actions taken are maintained.		

9.7	When nonconforming product is corrected it is retested to demonstrate conformity. Retesting records are maintained.				
9.8	Appropriate data is collected and analyzed to assure objectives are met and improvement opportunities are identified.				
9.9	Continuous improvement of product, services, or processes is evident.				
9.10	A corrective action process exists and is documented.				
9.11	Trends are analyzed to identify areas for improvement.				
9.12	Preventive actions are taken to eliminate nonconformities to processes, products, or services.				

time the Customer agrees to pay for the Services provided in accordance with Section III below.

III. Fees:

The Services quoted herein are provided on a fixed price basis, exclusive of travel and out-of-pocket expenses, as follows:

A. Service Fees:

Service Offering		One Time Charge	Monthly Charges
Project Management			
Program Management			

B. Additional Fees: The fee set forth above is for the specific eService(s) described in the applicable Your Company Service Description(s) and such pricing does not cover any services which fall outside the scope work outlined in such Service Description(s). Any additional Your Company e-Services requested by Customer which fall outside the scope of the work outlined under the applicable Service Description(s) may be provided by Your Company pursuant to a separate Service Quotation(s) and/or Statement(s) of Work.

C. Travel and Out-of-Pocket Expenses: In addition to the Service Fees set forth in Section III. A., travel and out-of-pocket expenses will be charged for any expenses required to complete the Services selected herein. Travel expenses include airfare, hotels, meals, rental cars and mileage. Travel and out-of-pocket expenses shall not exceed 25% of the Service Fees without prior written authorization of the Customer.

IV. Billing practices:
Billing for the Services will be on a monthly basis. Payment shall be made by either check or electronic funds transfer and is due within 30 days of receipt of invoice.

V. Acceptance:

All Deliverables shall be deemed accepted unless Customer notifies Your Company in writing within five (5) business days of receipt that the Deliverable is not acceptable. In the event Customer provides such notification to Your Company, Customer must return the Deliverable to Your Company and include a detailed description of the reason(s) for not accepting the Deliverable.

Upon receipt of a rejection notice, Your Company will correct any defects or nonconformities to the extent required so that the Deliverable satisfies the requirements for the Deliverables, as specified in the Service Description. Your Company will resubmit the modified Deliverable to Customer for acceptance. All Deliverables shall be deemed accepted if submitted in compliance with the Deliverables section of the Service Description.

VI. Additional Terms:

This Quotation and all Services that may be provided pursuant to this Quotation are subject to the terms and conditions of the (a) the Your Company Master Agreement (or, if you have not signed such a Your Company Master Agreement, the terms and conditions of the then current Your Company Master Agreement), and (b) the Service Description(s) for the applicable Services you are purchasing as indicated in this Quotation.

By signing in the area designated below, Customer is extending an offer to Your Company and Your Company's subsequent signing below shall constitute our acceptance of this Quotation. Such acceptance is subject to a credit check approval and confirmation of a valid Your Company Master Agreement signed by Customer.

Any terms and conditions, including but not limited to those contained in a purchase order issued by Customer, which are different from or in addition to the terms and conditions contained in the applicable Service Description(s), this Quotation and/or the applicable Your Company Master Agreement signed by Customer, shall not be binding on Your Company unless expressly accepted in writing, herein or otherwise, by Your Company's authorized representative, and Your Company hereby objects to and rejects all terms and conditions not so accepted.

This Quotation is only valid for Services Implementation Services. The Quotation does not entitle you to any future services that we may make available during the Service Period unless separately agreed to in writing by the parties.

Agreed & Accepted by:

CUSTOMER

Signature: _____ DATE: _____

Your Company

Signature: _____ DATE: _____

Launch Support (Go-Live) Discussion Checklist

The tool that follows can be used to help the project manager advance the project into the launch phase. See Table 6.40.

Portfolio Management/Scheduling Requirements Gathering Tool

This tool is an excellent requirements gathering tool to help an organization determine which application it wishes to invest in for scheduling and/or portfolio management. See Table 6.41.

PMO Scheduling Elements Checklist

The code checklist depicted in Table 6.42 can be used to set up a program office that will work on applications and hosting.

Table 6.40 Launch Support Discussion Checklist

1. Discuss status of existing or new provisioning-related Risk Issues.
2. Discuss any pending or planned Scope Changes.
3. Review needs, if any, for customer access to Servers.
4. Review needs, if any, for customer loading of applications:
Ongoing support for customer managed applications (T&M policy)
Content development and production environment needs and access rights.
5. Discuss plan for test and customer acceptance
6. Plan dates with Provisioning/Tier II/Tier III for items 3,4,5.
7. Review Escalation Paths during Launch.
8. Discuss Customer Care Role and process for customer requests:
Special Attention Status Flag.

Table 6.41 Portfolio and Scheduling Software Requirements Gathering Tool

PM Planning Software Requirements		Priority:			Stakeholder Category Rankings:						
		High	Medium	Low	PM	ASR	TAM	Program Manager	Business Analyst	Managers	Executive Level
	Required Product Features and User Requirements: Listed below are the items identified as Requirements for the PM Tracking, Scheduling and Reporting System. Please rank each item High, Medium, or Low in the Stakeholders columns provided. If there are additional requirements you would like added to the matrix, please add at the bottom of this list and rank accordingly.										
	Reporting										
1	Ability to choose/sort project schedule elements to be displayed to the customer on-line	✓	✓		H	L		H	L	H	L
2	Ability to choose/sort project schedule elements to be displayed to the customer in a print format.	✓	✓		H	H		H	L	M	L
3	Ability to provide a status report view on meeting minutes and display to the customer on-line or in printed form. (Able to create a document online or fill out a form that would serve as a status report to send to or view by customer on-line)	✓	✓		H	L		H	L	H	L
4	Ability to create reports on baseline versus actual	✓			H	H		H	H	M	H

(continued on next page)

Table 6.41 (continued) Portfolio and Scheduling Software Requirements Gathering Tool

	PM Planning Software Requirements	Priority:			Stakeholder Category Rankings:						
		High	Medium	Low	PM	ASR	TAM	Program Manager	Business Analyst	Managers	Executive Level
5	Roll-up Milestone Reporting. Ability to create reports for Senior Management that reflect the status of PM Milestones. Specific Milestones: H/W Received, S/W Received, PO numbers generated, Acceptance Testing completed, online, etc.	✓			H	L		H	H	H	H
6	Pert Charts	✓	✓	✓	H	H		H	L	L	L
7	Gantt Charts	✓			H	H		H	L	H	L
8	Generate a report using user defined elements/fields/queries	✓	✓		M	M		H	M	H	M
9	Generate metrics reports based on user defined elements –graphical reports, pie charts/line graphs	✓	✓		M	M		M	M	H	H
10	Resource allocation reporting		✓	✓	M	L		L	M	L	H
11	Ability to save reports on a local drive	✓	✓		M	M		L	H	L	M
12	Variance Analysis reports	✓	✓		H	L		H	H	M	H
13	Ability to import/export with Excel, PowerPoint, Word, HTML	✓	✓		H	H		H	H	H	H

#	Infrastructure/System									
14	100% Web Based:	✓			H	L	M	H	H	H
15	Ability to access projects and update live, via the Web. All users should be able to have the same access.	✓	✓		H	L	M	H	H	M
16	Must be able to provide the same level of access for network and dial-up users (one log-in).	✓			H	M	H	H	H	H
17	Your company would be hosting this Intranet Solution.	✓			H		H	L	H	H
18	Look and feel of Windows environment	✓	✓	✓	H	H	H	M	M	H
19	Compatible with NT/95/98/2000	✓			H	H	H	H	H	H
20	Unlimited number of users		✓		M	M	M	M	M	M
21	Stand-alone user		✓		M	M	M	M	L	M
22	Up to 200 concurrent users	✓		✓	L	L	M	H	L	H
	Security Features:									
23	Configurable access privileges	✓			H	L	H	H	H	H
24	Configurable user privileges	✓			H	L	H	H	H	H
25	Electronic approvals	✓	✓		M	L	M	M	M	L
26	Electronic notification	✓			H	L	H	H	M	H

(continued on next page)

Table 6.41 (continued) Portfolio and Scheduling Software Requirements Gathering Tool

	PM Planning Software Requirements	Priority: High	Medium	Low	PM	ASR	TAM	Program Manager	Business Analyst	Managers	Executive Level
27	Password Protect files	✓			H	H		L	H	H	H
28	Ability to have one login per person with single user ID	✓			H	L		L	H	M	H
	Degradation:										
29	Must be able to handle at least 70 concurrent users without degradation.	✓	✓		H	L			H	M	H
30	Must be able to handle at least 40 concurrent users without degradation	✓	✓		H	L			H	H	H
31	Must be able to handle at least 100 concurrent users without degradation		✓	✓	M	L			M	M	M
	Training										
32	On-site training	✓	✓		M	M		H	H	L	M
33	Web-based training provided as a supplement	✓	✓		M	M		L	M	M	M

No.	Item							
34	Training materials; guide/handouts		✓	H	H	H	H	M	M
35	On-line tutorial/guide		✓	H	M	L	H	M	H
36	Search feature for training help	✓	✓	H	H	H	M	M	M
	Technical Support								
37	800 support number	✓		M	M	H	M	L	M
38	24 X 7 support for severity 1 issues	✓		M	M	L	M	L	M
39	24 X 7 support for all issues		✓	L	M	L	L	L	L
40	On-site support	✓	✓	L	L	L	L	L	L
41	Enhancement requests support		✓	L	M	L	M	L	H
42	Consulting		✓	L	H	L	L	L	M
43	On-line support	✓	✓	M	H	L	M	M	M
	Document Control	✓							
44	Ability to access all project-related documents in one location	✓		H	H	H	H	H	H
45	Access based on user profile to Project Documentation — read/write or admin. rights	✓		H	H	H	M	H	H

(continued on next page)

Table 6.41 (continued) Portfolio and Scheduling Software Requirements Gathering Tool

	PM Planning Software Requirements	Priority: High	Medium	Low	PM	ASR	TAM	Program Manager	Business Analyst	Managers	Executive Level
	Functionality										
46	Ability to have multiple users access different portions of the project at the same time	✓	✓		M	M		M	M	M	M
47	Ability to add specific department codes for costs, users, projects, milestones, companies, resources	✓			H	L		H	M	H	H
48	White boards/chart	✓	✓	✓	L	L		L	L	M	L
49	Notes section	✓	✓		M	H		M	L	M	L
50	Ability to add URL inks for internal guides	✓			H	M		H	L	H	L
	Printing capabilities:	✓	✓	✓							
51	Screen Print	✓	✓	✓	M	H		L	L	M	L
52	Ability to print to network and local printers	✓	✓	✓	M	H		L	L	H	M
53	Ability to print selected data only	✓	✓	✓	H	H		L	L	H	M

Stakeholder Category Rankings:

#											
	Queries:	✓	✓								
54	Dynamic Queries	✓	✓	✓	M	H	M		M	H	M
55	Ability to perform drill down queries	✓	✓	✓	M	M	M		M	H	M
56	Ability to search or query by project characteristics	✓	✓		M	M	M		M	H	H
57	Ease of use	✓			H	H	H		H	H	H
58	Allows functions to be executed using mouse or keyboard	✓	✓	✓	M	H	M		M	M	M
59	Milestone Description/Name	✓	✓	✓	H					H	
60	Planned Date	✓	✓	✓	H	H	H		H	H	H
61	Forecasted Date	✓	✓	✓	H	H	H		H	M	H
62	Actual Date	✓	✓	✓	H	H	H		H	H	H
63	% Completed	✓	✓	✓	H	H	H		H	H	H
64	Variance	✓	✓	✓	H	H	H		H	M	H
65	Notes Field (cause/explanation)	✓	✓	✓	H	H	H		H	H	H
66	Ability to add, delete, or change data	✓	✓	✓	H	H	M		H	H	M
67	Ability to sort by classification and dates, etc.	✓	✓	✓	H	M	M		M	H	M
68	Ability to save a file to a different name	✓	✓	✓	H	H	M		M	H	M

(continued on next page)

Table 6.41 (continued) Portfolio and Scheduling Software Requirements Gathering Tool

PM Planning Software Requirements	Priority:			Stakeholder Category Rankings:						
	High	Medium	Low	PM	ASR	TAM	Program Manager	Business Analyst	Managers	Executive Level
69 Ability to save to another location, file, or drive	✓	✓	✓	H	H		H	M	H	L
70 Ability to baseline project(s) (re-baseline, too)	✓	✓	✓	H	H		H	M	H	H
71 Spell check capabilities	✓	✓	✓	M	M		L	L	M	L
72 Grammar check	✓	✓	✓	M	M		L	L	M	L
73 Define field data type (date, alpha, numeric, etc.)	✓	✓	✓	M	M		M	L	M	L
74 View multiple levels and drill down	✓	✓	✓	M	M		M	H	H	H
75 Calendars — including holiday schedules, 24 hr/shift/minute increments, time-off, resources, multiple daily calendars	✓	✓	✓	H	H		H	M	H	M

No.	Capability									
76	Ability to show critical path	M	H	M	H		M	M	✓	✓
77	Forward and backward pass	M	M	L	M		M	M	✓	✓
78	CPM scheduling for determination of float and critical path	M	M	M	H		M	M	✓	✓
79	Ability to show critical chain scheduling	H	M	H	M		M	M	✓	✓
80	Ability to show project dependencies	H	H	H	M		H	M	✓	✓
81	Time phase	L	M	L	H		H	M	✓	✓
82	Logic Network Diagrams	M	L	L	H		M	M	✓	✓
83	Ability to summarize activities	H	M	H	H		H	M	✓	✓
84	Ability to format/organize and file	H	H	H	H		H	H	✓	✓
85	Sort/select criteria		M		H		H		✓	✓
86	Global change	H	M	H	H		H	M	✓	✓
87	Earned Value Analysis	L	L	M	L		L	L	✓	✓

(continued on next page)

Table 6.41 (continued) Portfolio and Scheduling Software Requirements Gathering Tool

	PM Planning Software Requirements	Priority: High	Priority: Medium	Priority: Low	Stakeholder Category Rankings: PM	ASR	TAM	Program Manager	Business Analyst	Managers	Executive Level
	Integration with Other Products										
	MS Project	✓			H				H	H	H
88	Ability to use MS Project Templates, to import/export using mpp and mpx files	✓			H	H		H	H	H	H
	Vantive, Remedy, or Similar		✓	✓	M	M			L		L
89	Import/export capability		✓	✓	M	H		L		M	H
	Intradoc.com			✓	L	L			L		M
90	Document control software—IT supported			✓	L	L		L		L	M
91	Magma			✓	L	L			L	L	L
	Add additional requirements for consideration (if needed):										

Table 6.42   PMO Scheduling Elements Check

Code	Element
1	(PMO) Initial Schedule Setup
1.1	PROJECT MANAGEMENT ORGANIZATION
1.1.1	(PMO) Office Set Up Structure
1.1.1.1	Server/Fax/etc.
1.1.1.2	Prepare/ Move/ Purchase Furniture
1.1.1.3	PMO Office/ Stationary Supplies
1.1.1.4	Configure Firewalls at Customer Site for PMO Access to iWeb
1.1.2	Document Management System
1.1.2.1	Initial Directory Structure—Knowledge Repository
1.1.2.2	Scope Analysis Documentation
1.1.2.3	Risk Management Documentation
1.1.2.4	Issues/Action Items Documentation
1.1.2.5	Asset Management: Architech Audit (documentation)
1.1.2.5.1	ISP Managed Hardware
1.1.2.5.2	ISP Managed Software
1.1.2.5.3	Bill of Materials
1.1.2.5.4	Runbooks
1.1.2.6	Version Control System
1.1.2.6.1	Customer Architecture(s)—Version control of Asset Management Tasks
1.1.2.6.1.1	Validate "As Built"
1.1.2.6.1.2	Validate BOM
1.1.2.6.1.3	Include in BOM, IP addresses, etc.
1.1.2.6.1.4	Update with Revisions
1.1.2.6.1.5	Post to Knowledge Repository
1.1.3	QMS Consistency Infrastructure

(continued on next page)

Table 6.42 (continued)   PMO Scheduling Elements Check

Code	Element
1.1.3.1	Operating Procedures, etc.
1.1.3.2	Customer Facing Tools
1.1.3.3	PMO Internal Tools
1.2	MEETINGS ORGANIZATION
1.2.1	Project/ Program Tracking (Weekly)
1.2.1.1	Project Tracking (Weekly) 1
1.2.1.2	Post-Mortem Review—for completed implementations
1.2.2	Service Level (Monthly)
1.2.2.1	Service Level (Monthly) 1
1.2.3	Program Activity Progress
1.2.3.1	Customer Care/ Ticket Status Meetings
1.3	ISP-PMO OPERATIONS MANUAL
1.3.1	Manual Sections
1.3.1.1	Organization
1.3.1.1.1	Organizational Chart
1.3.1.1.2	Contact List
1.3.1.1.2.1	Add ISP Contacts
1.3.1.1.2.2	Add Customer Contacts
1.3.1.1.2.3	Add (subtract) Contacts
1.3.1.1.2.4	Insert into Manual
1.3.1.1.2.5	Complete Section One
1.3.1.2	Financial Management
1.3.1.2.1	Financial (Flow) Documentation
1.3.1.2.1.1	Insert Financial Model
1.3.1.2.1.2	Insert Billing Process
1.3.1.2.1.3	Complete Sections Above

Table 6.42 (continued)   PMO Scheduling Elements Check

Code	Element
1.3.1.2.2	Create SOW Process Map
1.3.1.2.2.1	Draft the Flow (See Operating Procedures 24/25)
1.3.1.2.2.2	Create Visio Drawing from the Draft
1.3.1.2.2.3	Complete and Add to Manual
1.3.1.2.3	Create Change Order Process Map
1.3.1.2.3.1	Draft the Flow—See Scope Change Tool on PMO Intranet
1.3.1.2.3.2	Create Visio Drawing from the Draft
1.3.1.2.3.3	Complete and Add to Manual
1.3.1.2.4	Create Invoice Process Map
1.3.1.2.4.1	Draft the Flow
1.3.1.2.4.2	Complete and Add to Manual
1.3.1.2.5	Create Labor Log and Analysis Process Map
1.3.1.2.5.1	Draft the Flow
1.3.1.2.5.2	Create Document and Insert Screen Shots
1.3.1.2.5.3	Complete and Add to Manual
1.3.1.3	Meetings
1.3.1.3.1	Insert Meeting Schedule
1.3.1.3.2	Insert Attendees Lists
1.3.1.3.3	Insert Meeting Expectation Documentation Process
1.3.1.4	Documentation
1.3.1.4.1	Insert Knowledge Repository Manual
1.3.1.5	Subs. Management
1.3.1.5.1	Schedule of Deliverables
1.3.1.5.2	Earned Value Reports
1.3.1.6	Reports

(continued on next page)

Table 6.42 (continued)   PMO Scheduling Elements Check

Code	Element
1.3.1.6.1	Print and Insert into Manual
1.3.1.7	Event Management
1.3.1.7.1	Research owner and insert (Customer Care Information)
1.3.1.8	Change Management
1.3.1.8.1	Insert Documentation from ISP
1.3.1.9	Security Policies (ISP Policies)
1.3.1.9.1	Research Owner of Document
1.3.1.9.2	If Customer Information Available, Insert
1.3.1.9.3	Add to Manual
1.3.1.10	Disaster Recovery (ISP T3 Documentation)
1.3.1.10.1	Research Owner of Documentation
1.3.1.10.2	Compile Report and Include All into the Tab
1.3.1.10.3	Include in Manual
1.3.1.11	Current Architecture
1.3.1.11.1	Insert Current Architecture/ BOM
1.3.1.11.2	Insert Runbooks
1.3.1.12	Issues
1.3.1.12.1	Insert Actions Items Matrix Master
1.3.2	Create Hardcopy Notebook
1.3.2.1	Create Table of Contents
1.3.2.2	Create Tabs
1.3.2.3	Design Cover
1.3.2.4	Print, Post, and Deliver to Customer
1.4	FINANCIAL SYSTEM
1.4.1	Application Development, When Needed (See Operating Procedure 20 for This Section)
1.4.1.1	Create Methodology

Table 6.42 (continued)   PMO Scheduling Elements Check

Code	Element
1.4.1.1.1	Identify Resources
1.4.1.1.2	Implementation
1.4.1.2	Create Estimate for Next Month's Work
1.4.1.3	Deliver the Estimate
1.4.1.4	Review Previous Month's Actuals
1.4.1.5	Sign Off
1.4.2	Execute Forward Billing
1.4.3	Nonrecurring Charges
1.4.4	Additional Resource Charges Methodology Development, When Needed
1.4.4.1	Create Methodology
1.4.4.1.1	Identify Resources
1.4.4.1.2	Implementation
1.4.5	Fee Adjustment Methodology
1.4.5.1	Customer Request for Adjustment
1.4.5.2	Management Negotiation
1.4.5.3	Agreement in Writing
1.4.5.4	Application of Adjustment
1.4.6	Late Payment Policy Development
1.4.6.1	One Month Delinquency or Sq/ MSA terms
1.4.7	Invoice Detail
1.4.7.1	Methodology Development
1.4.7.2	Monthly Billing
1.4.7.2.1	Monthly Billing 1
1.4.7.2.1.1	Pull Data
1.4.7.2.1.2	Sanitize Data

(continued on next page)

Table 6.42 (continued)   PMO Scheduling Elements Check

Code	Element
1.4.7.2.1.3	Create Invoice
1.4.7.2.1.4	Deliver Invoice
1.4.8	Resolve Tax Discrepancies, if any
1.4.9	Financial Templates
1.4.9.1	Define Scope, Objective, and Recipients
1.4.9.2	Assign Resource to Develop Templates
1.4.9.3	Develop Templates
1.4.9.4	Approve Templates
1.4.9.5	Implement Templates
1.4.10	Establish Performance Credit Escrow Account (When Required in MSA)
1.4.11	Billing/Pass-Through
1.4.11.1	Define Scope, Objective, and Recipients
1.4.11.2	Assign Resource to Develop Templates
1.4.11.3	Develop Templates
1.4.11.4	Approve Templates
1.4.11.5	Implement Templates
1.5	QUALITY ASSURANCE SYSTEM
1.5.1	Customer Satisfaction
1.5.1.1	Coordination of surveys
1.5.1.2	Baseline Customer Satisfaction via Survey
1.5.1.3	On-going Customer Satisfaction Surveys Performed Annually
1.5.1.4	Customer Satisfaction Interviews Performed Annually
1.5.1.5	New Installation Satisfaction Surveys Performed as Needed
1.5.1.6	Event Management Satisfaction Surveys Performed as Needed
1.5.1.7	Survey Response Analysis in Concert with National PMO
1.6	STATEMENTS OF WORK

Table 6.42 (continued)   PMO Scheduling Elements Check

Code	Element
1.6.1	Statements of Work
1.6.1.1	New Statements
1.6.1.1.1	Record
1.6.1.1.2	Check Scope with eSd
1.6.1.1.3	Perform LOB Buy-In
1.6.1.1.4	Staffing Issues
1.6.1.1.5	Risk/Dependency
1.6.1.1.6	See Rates
1.6.1.1.7	Pricing
1.6.1.1.8	Scope Analysis
1.6.1.1.8.1	1.0
1.6.1.1.8.1.1	Deliverables
1.6.1.1.8.1.2	Dependencies/Constraints
1.6.1.1.8.1.3	Risk
1.6.1.2	1.0 SOW Sigs. (PMO Template)
1.6.1.2.1	Received Signed Copy
1.6.1.2.2	Obtain Work Status
1.6.1.2.3	Deliverables List
1.6.2	Acceptance and Billing
1.6.2.1	Signed Acceptance of Work
1.6.2.2	Billing Status Determined
1.6.3	Build MPP/Schedule or Revise—for Individual SOWs
1.6.3.1	1.0
1.6.3.1.1	Scheduling
1.6.3.1.2	Execute
1.6.3.1.3	Sign-Off

(continued on next page)

Table 6.42 (continued) PMO Scheduling Elements Check

Code	Element
1.7	SUBCONTRACTS
1.7.1	Subs.
1.7.1.1	Determine Potential Outsourcing Opportunities
1.7.1.2	Communication Protocols
1.7.1.3	Billing Protocols
1.7.1.4	Flow-Down Clause
1.7.1.5	Validate Scope/ Financials
1.7.1.5.1	ISP
1.7.1.5.2	Subs.
1.8	ON-GOING SUPPORT
1.8.1	Define Activities
1.8.2	Reports to Customer
1.8.2.1	Network Usage
1.8.2.2	Server Usage
1.8.2.3	BEA Reports
1.9	Upsell Strategy Development
1.9.1	Server/System Audit—"As Builts" for Customer Managed Equipment
1.9.2	Historical Data Analysis
1.9.3	Account Team Selling R&Rs
1.10	Potential P&P Revenue Upsell (Vendor Neutral)
1.10.1	P&P Draft Deliverables
1.10.1.1	DSN
1.10.1.1.1	Draft Submission
1.10.1.1.1.1	Define Requirements
1.10.1.1.1.2	Present and Review Draft
1.10.1.1.1.3	Draft Rework (as needed)

Table 6.42 (continued)   PMO Scheduling Elements Check

Code	Element
1.10.1.1.1.4	Acceptance of Draft
1.10.1.2	NT Non-Root Permissions
1.10.1.2.1	Draft Submission
1.10.1.2.1.1	Define Requirements
1.10.1.2.1.2	Present and Review Draft
1.10.1.2.1.3	Draft Rework (as Needed)
1.10.1.2.1.4	Acceptance of Draft
1.10.1.3	NT Root Permissions
1.10.1.3.1	Draft Submission
1.10.1.3.1.1	Define Requirements
1.10.1.3.1.2	Present and Review Draft
1.10.1.3.1.3	Draft Rework (as Needed)
1.10.1.3.1.4	Acceptance of Draft
1.10.1.4	Webtrends Log Request
1.10.1.4.1	Draft Submission
1.10.1.4.1.1	Define Requirements
1.10.1.4.1.2	Present and Review Draft
1.10.1.4.1.3	Draft Rework (as Needed)
1.10.1.4.1.4	Acceptance of Draft
1.10.1.5	Server Space Request
1.10.1.5.1	Draft Submission
1.10.1.5.1.1	Define Requirements
1.10.1.5.1.2	Present and Review Draft
1.10.1.5.1.3	Draft Rework (as Needed)
1.10.1.5.1.4	Acceptance of Draft
1.10.1.6	Additional Server Capacity (Nonpriority)

(continued on next page)

Table 6.42 (continued)   PMO Scheduling Elements Check

Code	Element
1.10.1.6.1	Draft Submission
1.10.1.6.1.1	Define Requirements
1.10.1.6.1.2	Present and Review Draft
1.10.1.6.1.3	Draft Rework (as Needed)
1.10.1.6.1.4	Acceptance of Draft
1.10.1.7	Additional Server Capacity (Priority)
1.10.1.7.1	Draft Submission
1.10.1.7.1.1	Define Requirements
1.10.1.7.1.2	Present and Review Draft
1.10.1.7.1.3	Draft Rework (as Needed)
1.10.1.7.1.4	Acceptance of Draft
1.10.1.8	Domain Name Registration
1.10.1.8.1	Draft Submission
1.10.1.8.1.1	Define Requirements
1.10.1.8.1.2	Present and Review Draft
1.10.1.8.1.3	Draft Rework (as Needed)
1.10.1.8.1.4	Acceptance of Draft
1.10.1.9	Firewall Port Opening (Standard)
1.10.1.9.1	ISP Firewall
1.10.1.9.1.1	Draft Submission
1.10.1.9.1.1.1	Define Requirements
1.10.1.9.1.1.2	Present and Review Draft
1.10.1.9.1.1.3	Draft Rework (as Needed)
1.10.1.9.1.1.4	Acceptance of Draft
1.10.1.10	Firewall Port Opening (Nonstandard)
1.10.1.10.1	Third-Party Firewall

Table 6.42 (continued)   PMO Scheduling Elements Check

Code	Element
1.10.1.10.1.1	Draft Submission
1.10.1.10.1.1.1	Define Requirements
1.10.1.10.1.1.2	Present and Review Draft
1.10.1.10.1.1.3	Draft Rework (as Needed)
1.10.1.10.1.1.4	Acceptance of Draft
1.10.1.10.2	ISP Firewall
1.10.1.10.2.1	Draft Submission
1.10.1.10.2.1.1	Define Requirements
1.10.1.10.2.1.2	Present and Review Draft
1.10.1.10.2.1.3	Draft Rework (as Needed)
1.10.1.10.2.1.4	Acceptance of Draft
1.10.1.11	Custom DLL Installation
1.10.1.11.1	Draft Submission
1.10.1.11.1.1	Define Requirements
1.10.1.11.1.2	Present and Review Draft
1.10.1.11.1.3	Draft Rework (as Needed)
1.10.1.11.1.4	Acceptance of Draft
1.10.1.12	View/Obtain Open Ticket Status
1.10.1.12.1	Draft Submission
1.10.1.12.1.1	Define Requirements
1.10.1.12.1.2	Present and Review Draft
1.10.1.12.1.3	Draft Rework (as Needed)
1.10.1.12.1.4	Acceptance of Draft
1.10.1.13	Replication Applications
1.10.1.13.1	Draft Submission

(continued on next page)

Table 6.42 (continued)   PMO Scheduling Elements Check

Code	Element
1.10.1.13.1.1	Define Requirements
1.10.1.13.1.2	Present and Review Draft
1.10.1.13.1.3	Draft Rework (as Needed)
1.10.1.13.1.4	Acceptance of Draft
1.10.1.14	Replication Basic Content
1.10.1.14.1	Draft Submission
1.10.1.14.1.1	Define Requirements
1.10.1.14.1.2	Present and Review Draft
1.10.1.14.1.3	Draft Rework (as Needed)
1.10.1.14.1.4	Acceptance of Draft
1.10.1.15	VPN Configuration
1.10.1.15.1	Draft Submission
1.10.1.15.1.1	Define Requirements
1.10.1.15.1.2	Present and Review Draft
1.10.1.15.1.3	Draft Rework (as Needed)
1.10.1.15.1.4	Acceptance of Draft
1.10.1.16	SSL Certificate
1.10.1.16.1	Draft Submission
1.10.1.16.1.1	Define Requirements
1.10.1.16.1.2	Present and Review Draft
1.10.1.16.1.3	Draft Rework (as Needed)
1.10.1.16.1.4	Acceptance of Draft
1.10.1.17	Load Balancing Device Provisioning
1.10.1.17.1	Draft Submission
1.10.1.17.1.1	Define Requirements
1.10.1.17.1.2	Present and Review Draft

Table 6.42 (continued)   PMO Scheduling Elements Check

Code	Element
1.10.1.17.1.3	Draft Rework (as Needed)
1.10.1.17.1.4	Acceptance of Draft
1.10.1.18	Load Balancing Service
1.10.1.18.1	Draft Submission
1.10.1.18.1.1	Define Requirements
1.10.1.18.1.2	Present and Review Draft
1.10.1.18.1.3	Draft Rework (as Needed)
1.10.1.18.1.4	Acceptance of Draft
1.10.1.19	ASP Component Services
1.10.1.19.1	Draft Submission
1.10.1.19.1.1	Define Requirements
1.10.1.19.1.2	Present and Review Draft
1.10.1.19.1.3	Draft Rework (as Needed)
1.10.1.19.1.4	Acceptance of Draft
1.10.1.20	Additional Network Capacity
1.10.1.20.1	Draft Submission
1.10.1.20.1.1	Define Requirements
1.10.1.20.1.2	Present and Review Draft
1.10.1.20.1.3	Draft Rework (as Needed)
1.10.1.20.1.4	Acceptance of Draft
1.10.1.21	Install/Uninstall Software
1.10.1.21.1	Draft Submission
1.10.1.21.1.1	Define Requirements
1.10.1.21.1.2	Present and Review Draft
1.10.1.21.1.3	Draft Rework (as Needed)
1.10.1.21.1.4	Acceptance of Draft

(continued on next page)

Table 6.42 (continued)   PMO Scheduling Elements Check

Code	Element
1.10.1.22	Install/Uninstall Hardware
1.10.1.22.1	Draft Submission
1.10.1.22.1.1	Define Requirements
1.10.1.22.1.2	Present and Review Draft
1.10.1.22.1.3	Draft Rework (as Needed)
1.10.1.22.1.4	Acceptance of Draft
1.10.1.23	Report a Problem
1.10.1.23.1	Draft Submission
1.10.1.23.1.1	Define Requirements
1.10.1.23.1.2	Present and Review Draft
1.10.1.23.1.3	Draft Rework (as Needed)
1.10.1.23.1.4	Acceptance of Draft
1.10.2	Technical Writer Edits
1.10.2.1	Post-Edit Submission
1.10.2.2	Review Edits
1.10.2.3	Distribute Policies
1.10.3	Create Manual Forms
1.10.3.1	Initial Form Creation
1.10.3.2	Incorporate Tech Writer Information
1.10.3.3	Post to Intranet
1.10.4	Written Approvals of All P&Ps
1.10.4.1	Third-Party Approval if Needed
1.10.4.2	ISP Approval
1.10.4.3	Customer Approval
1.10.5	Form Creation
1.5	Test Manual Forms

Table 6.42 (continued)   PMO Scheduling Elements Check

Code	Element
1.6	Create Web Routing application
1.7	Create Web-Based Forms
1.8	Test Web-Based Forms
1.11	Potential Upsell Opportunity: (BENCHMARKING)
1.11.1	RISK Mitigation
1.11.1.1	Define Benchmarking
1.11.1.1.1	Negotiate New Benchmarking Definitions and Parameters
1.11.1.1.1.1	Meeting
1.11.1.2	Sign Off on New Definition
1.11.2	Benchmark
1.11.2.1	Test Setup, Execution, and Review
1.11.2.1.1	Meet with Customer to Determine New Scope of Benchmarking
1.11.2.1.2	Provide Transaction Details to Compuware
1.11.2.1.3	SOW (Benchmarking and Analysis)
1.11.2.1.3.1	Develop SOW (PMO Template)
1.11.2.1.3.2	Sign SOW
1.11.3	Set Up SOW Schedule
1.11.3.1	Monitor Schedule
1.12	Potential Upsell Opportunity (TRAINING)
1.12.1	Enduser Identification and Assessment Phase
1.12.1.1	Define Scope and Deliverables
1.12.1.2	Determine In-House versus Outsourcing Options
1.12.1.3	Identify Possible Resources
1.12.1.4	Negotiate Draft Agreements
1.12.1.5	Assign Resource

(continued on next page)

Table 6.42 (continued)   PMO Scheduling Elements Check

Code	Element
1.12.1.6	Deliver SOWs (PMO Template)
1.12.2	Identify Training Offers
1.12.2.1	Define Scope and Deliverables
1.12.2.2	Determine In-House versus Outsourcing Options
1.12.2.3	Identify Possible Resources
1.12.2.4	Negotiate Final Agreements
1.12.2.5	Assign Resource
1.12.2.6	Deliver
1.12.3	Curriculum Design
1.12.3.1	Define Scope and Deliverables
1.12.3.2	Determine In-House versus Outsourcing Options
1.12.3.3	Identify Possible Resources
1.12.3.4	Negotiate Agreements
1.12.3.5	Assign Resource
1.12.3.6	Deliver
1.13	Potential Upsell: Security
1.13.1	System Availability and Security
1.13.1.1	Assign POC
1.13.1.2	Constant Surveillance
1.13.1.2.1	Define Surveillance Operations
1.13.2	Physical Data Center
1.13.2.1	Documents Operations
1.13.2.2	Provide Documentation to Customer
1.13.2.3	Sign Off
1.13.3	Electronic Data Security
1.13.3.1	Documents Operations

Table 6.42 (continued)   PMO Scheduling Elements Check

Code	Element
1.13.3.2	Provide Documentation to Customer
1.13.3.3	Sign Off
1.13.4	Encryption
1.13.4.1	Documents Operations
1.13.4.2	Provide Documentation to Customer
1.13.4.3	Sign Off
1.13.5	Practices
1.13.5.1	Document Operations
1.13.5.2	Provide Documentation to Customer
1.13.5.3	Sign Off
1.13.6	Provision Security
1.13.6.1	Firewalls
1.13.6.2	VPNs
1.13.7	Log-on Procedures
1.13.7.1	Document Operations
1.13.7.2	Provide Documentation to Customer
1.13.7.3	Sign Off
1.13.8	Recommended Security Procedures
1.13.8.1	Document Operations
1.13.8.2	Provide Documentation to Customer
1.13.8.3	Sign Off
1.13.9	Management of SSLs
1.13.9.1	Document Operations
1.13.9.2	Develop Specific Operational Deviations
1.13.9.3	Provide Documentation to Customer

(continued on next page)

Table 6.42 (continued)   PMO Scheduling Elements Check

Code	Element
1.13.9.4	Sign Off
1.13.10	Virus Protection (Staging)
1.13.10.1	Develop Solution
1.13.10.2	Obtain Pricing
1.13.10.3	Obtain ISP Approvals
1.13.10.4	Document
1.13.10.5	Sign Off
1.13.10.6	Implement
1.13.11	Server Access Site Visit
1.13.11.1	Coordinate Data Center Visit
1.13.12	Monitor Intrusion
1.13.12.1	Document Operations
1.13.12.2	Provide Documentation to Customer
1.13.12.3	Sign Off
1.13.13	Patch to Security Bulletins
1.13.13.1	Document Operations
1.13.13.2	Provide Documentation to Customer
1.13.13.3	Sign Off
1.13.14	Maintain Common Authentication Schemes
1.13.14.1	Document Operations
1.13.14.2	Provide Documentation to Customer
1.13.14.3	Sign Off
1.13.15	Firewalls
1.13.15.1	Perform Security Policy Configuration
1.13.15.1.1	Assign Resource
1.13.15.1.2	Implement Customer's TQ Document

Table 6.42 (continued) PMO Scheduling Elements Check

Code	Element
1.13.15.2	Implement Customer Requested Changes
1.13.15.2.1	Document Operations
1.13.15.2.2	Provide Documentation to Customer
1.13.15.2.3	Sign Off
1.13.16	Method of Securing Change Requests
1.13.16.1	Document Operations
1.13.16.2	Provide Documentation to Customer
1.13.16.3	Sign Off
1.13.17	Server Encryption
1.13.17.1	Document Operations
1.13.17.2	Provide Documentation to Customer
1.13.17.3	Sign Off
1.13.18	24 x 7 x 365 Event Monitoring
1.13.18.1	NOC Response to Urgent Alarms
1.13.18.1.1	Document Operations
1.13.18.1.2	Provide Documentation to Customer
1.13.18.1.3	Sign Off
1.13.18.2	Define Response Procedures to Security Breaches
1.13.18.2.1	Document Operations
1.13.18.2.2	Provide Documentation to Customer
1.13.18.2.3	Sign Off
1.14	Potential Upsell Opportunities (REPORTS)
1.14.1	Develop Reports (Per Service or Fee)
1.14.1.1	Executive Summary
1.14.1.2	Project Status

(continued on next page)

Table 6.42 (continued)   PMO Scheduling Elements Check

Code	Element
1.14.1.3	Improvement Action (Bases On Surveys and PMO Quality Program)
1.14.1.4	Asset Management
1.14.1.5	Security and Virus Incidents
1.14.1.6	Helpdesk Trend Analysis
1.14.1.7	Change Management
1.14.1.8	Disaster Recovery
1.14.1.9	RCA
1.14.1.10	Personnel
1.14.1.11	Issues and Disputes
1.14.1.12	Invoices
1.14.1.13	Registered Domain Names
1.14.1.14	Implemented Web Applications
1.14.1.15	Admin and Permissions
1.14.1.16	Intrusion Detection
1.14.1.17	Pending Service Quotations and SOWs
1.14.1.18	Network Usage
1.14.1.19	Server Utilization
1.14.1.20	Customer Satisfaction Surveys
1.14.1.21	Incremental Fees
1.14.1.22	Webtrends Reports
1.14.1.23	Trouble Ticket Reports
1.14.1.24	BMC Reports
1.15	(Template: Future Use) Complex Hosting Project w/ Sub.
1.15.1	Formal Sales Opportunity Review Approvals
1.15.1.1	Contracts
1.15.1.2	Security

Table 6.42 (continued)   PMO Scheduling Elements Check

Code	Element
1.15.1.3	Network Engineering
1.15.1.4	Finance
1.15.1.5	Datacenter
1.15.1.6	Provisioning
1.15.1.7	Architecture
1.15.2	PM Performs Risk Assessment
1.15.2.1	Customer Delivery of Customer-Provided Software
1.15.2.2	Discrepancy of Customer and Provisioning Timelines
1.15.2.3	PAS Testing Schedule Impact to Delivery
1.15.2.4	Risk Assessment Entered in IS Intranet
1.15.3	Verify Receipt of Order
1.15.3.1	Verify Customer Executes Service Quote
1.15.3.2	Ensure Order Is Scanned
1.15.3.3	Accept Order and Hands-Off to IC
1.15.4	Internal Project Kick-Off Meeting
1.15.4.1	Prepare Draft Project Schedule. (Baseline developed after internal kick-off)
1.15.4.2	Prepare Internal Kick-Off Agenda. (CW Tab has minimum agenda items.)
1.15.4.3	Check Hardware Availability and Obtain ETA from Vendors if not in Inventory
1.15.4.4	Prepare Confirming Minutes of Internal Kick-Off
1.15.4.5	Send PDF format of schedule to Tier 2 and Tier 3 Management
1.15.4.6	Internal Kick-Off done
1.15.5	External Kick-Off Meeting
1.15.5.1	Prepare External Kick-Off Agenda. (CW Tab contains minimum agenda items.)

(continued on next page)

Table 6.42 (continued)   PMO Scheduling Elements Check

Code	Element
1.15.5.2	Review Provisioning Guidelines and Expected Delivery Dates
1.15.5.3	Review Third-Party Milestones and Deliverables. (Add task lines to schedule if needed.)
1.15.5.4	Obtain Project Baseline Schedule Sign Off (at External Kick-Off)
1.15.5.5	External Kick-Off Meeting Minutes
1.15.5.6	External Kick-Off Meeting Done
1.15.6	Progress Updates
1.15.6.1	Customer Update 1
1.15.6.2	Pre-Close-Out Meeting
1.15.7	Provisioning Coordination Activities
1.15.7.1	Hardware Received by Data Center
1.15.7.2	Hardware (e.g, servers, RAID devices, Local Directors) Installed and Configured
1.15.7.3	Software Part 1—Server Jump-Start/ O/S Software Installed and Tested (CHP)
1.15.7.4	Perform User Acceptance Testing
1.15.8	Software Installation
1.15.8.1	SQL 2000
1.15.8.1.1	Notify Customer of Datacenter Address
1.15.8.1.2	Customer Fax License
1.15.8.1.3	Confirmation of Receipt
1.15.8.1.4	Installation of Software
1.15.8.2	Commerce 2000
1.15.8.2.1	Notify Customer of Datacenter Address
1.15.8.2.2	Customer Fax License
1.15.8.2.3	Customer FTP Media
1.15.8.2.4	Confirmation of Receipt
1.15.8.2.5	Installation and Configuration of Software

Table 6.42 (continued)   PMO Scheduling Elements Check

Code	Element
1.10	Customer Support Meeting
1.10.1	Report on the Status of Risks Identified at the External Kick-Off Meeting and Report Any New Risks That Have Been Identified at the Launch Meeting
1.10.2	Open Special Attention Ticket
1.10.3	Engineering Identifies Run-Book Details with the Customer
1.10.4	Schedule Dates with CP, Tiers II, and III, as Needed for Content-Loading Customer Requirements
1.10.5	Discuss Acceptance Testing and Customer Validation Plan
1.10.6	List Tasks for Customer Validation/Acceptance
1.11	Hand-Off to Customer
1.11.1	Customer Hand-Off Meeting
1.11.2	Advise Sales—Project Online
1.12	Application Work
1.12.1	Load Testing of Applications
1.12.1.1	Benchmark TQ Completed
1.12.1.2	TQ Review Conference
1.12.1.3	Customer Revision to TQ
1.12.1.4	Prepare SOW
1.12.1.5	Execute SOW
1.15.11.1.6	Perform Testing
1.15.11.1.7	Review/Feedback from Testing
1.12.2	Testing, HW, and SW Tweaks Complete
1.12.4	Production "Go-Live"
1.12.5	Quality Assurance
1.12.5.1	Request Customer Satisfaction Survey Completion
1.15.12.2	Customer Responds to Survey
1.12.5.2	Post-Deployment Internal Team Evaluation

Project Management and Account Support Mentoring Model

Executive Summary

Mentors facilitate career development by leveraging internal opportunities and training options. This requires maturity, a real desire to coach, and time. A mentor's contribution should be measured and compensated. Mentors may be immediate supervisors.

Currently, senior project managers and senior account support representatives, by virtue of job descriptions, are mentors. The roles and responsibilities associated with this are undefined. The qualifications needed to be a mentor are undefined. Activities associated with mentoring are not measured. Contributions due to mentoring are not rewarded. The need for mentors is immediate and directly impacts our efficiency and individual job satisfaction. It's important to note that an unqualified mentor can cause more harm than help.

The bullets below summarize the mentor's primary activities and functions:

■ Works with individual staff members in a nonsupervisory capacity.
■ Works with individual staff members as a career development coach.
■ Helps contributors identify skill gaps and special training needs.
■ In concert with the business manager, identifies growth potential candidates for succession planning.
■ Assists new staff integration.
■ Serves as a confidante.
■ Provides input in performance, promotion, bonus and merit evaluations.
■ Should be a senior project manager for project management contributors.
■ Should be a senior account support representative for support staff.

This should be linked to individual commitment programs and consistent with job descriptions.

Skills Definition

Project management mentors should have an in-depth knowledge of the PM discipline covering virtually all key knowledge areas. The mentor should have, or be able to quickly gain, an understanding of the internal YOUR COMPANY processes. Mentors must have excellent people and communication skills. Mentors should have prior corporate experience as a coach or mentor. Most importantly, mentors must *want* to coach and develop staff.

Account support mentors should have an in-depth knowledge of our product line and the associated technology. The mentor should have, or be able to quickly gain, an understanding of the internal YOUR COMPANY processes. Mentors must have excellent people and communication skills. Most importantly, mentors must *want* to coach and develop staff.

Both mentor types must understand, or be able to quickly learn, YOUR COMPANY career tracks, YOUR COMPANY education and training opportunities, our group's future leadership needs, and have access to Human Resource policies when needed (i.e., discrimination, harassment, diversity, etc.).

Mentors should have a clear understanding of the skill sets required for different positions and be able to assess alignment.

Activities

Mentoring begins the moment a new employee walks through the door. The mentor should help new employees with the administrative logistics of the new workplace. After the new employee has settled in the mentor and (if the mentor is not the immediate supervisor) the supervisor should formally meet to determine what immediate training needs are required, and the employee should take the steps determined at the meeting. After the first 4 weeks or the completion of the immediate training needs, the supervisor should help the new employee set goals that link to the Commitment Program; the mentor should be advised of the results. After 3 months the mentor should schedule regular career development discussions— bearing in mind staff capabilities, future needs, and the new employee's commitment and career goals.

Mentors should be available when needed. Mentoring ought not to be confused with managing, supervising, or technical expertise.

Metrics

The mentor's account or project workload should be adjusted in light of the number of people being mentored and the time needed for the associated activities. The metrics should take the form of a quantifiable survey measuring, at minimum, the following:

- Degree of assistance during orientation period
- The extent to which the employee feels that his/her personal career path is a reality
- Responsiveness
- Employee's professional development
- Succession planning

Recommendations

Business managers should identify candidates that have the skills required for this role. Based on how many are identified, determine a ratio and effect the assignments.

Adjust the workload to facilitate this activity. Distinguish between mentor, team leader, and manager, and if dual roles are needed, adjust the number of assigned personnel and the workload. Change or enforce the existing job descriptions from this day forward.

Action Items

1. Develop or use (if an existing version exists) a New Employee Checklist covering all the administrative elements required by new staff.
2. Decide if team leader and program manager positions will be added to the organization.
3. Based on the above item, determine if the mentor function should be a separate function or a responsibility in addition to a management assignment.
4. Identify the mentors and assign staff.
5. Adjust the workloads accordingly.
6. Develop a survey or evaluation form.
7. Determine how this is compensated.

Project Manager Interview Guide

This tool can be used when assessing the hard and soft skills of potential project management personnel. See Table 6.43.

Quality Certification Tool Suite

The first part is a guideline for the checklist that will follow in the second part.

Part I Guide

In compliance with the department's efforts to gain and maintain quality certification, the PMO will conduct scheduled and unscheduled audits throughout the year to ensure that the work instructions are in use.

Failures to comply with the policies stated in the work instructions are considered "nonconformities," and are categorized as major (failure to comply with the basic tenets of the bulletin) or minor (failure to comply with selected elements of the bulletin). A report summarizing the results of the review, including any nonconformities and recommended corrective actions, is sent to the reporting manager and department director.

Table 6.43   Project and Program Management Interview Guide

Interviewer: _____   Candidate: _____

Position: _____   Requisition Number: _____

Date of Interview? _____ , 200__ Time: ____:____
Duration of Interview? ____ Hrs. ____ Min.

Resume was supplied: ☐ Human Resources   ☐ Open House
Interview was conducted: ☐ By phone, or   ☐ In person?

Take a moment to review the candidates resume with them and make any pertinent notes below:

Notes

1. Please select a project that you've worked on in the past and walk me through the project life cycle **OR** define the life cycle of a project.

Look For	Caution	Probes	Notes
Candidate might be discussing theory as opposed to real experiences	Should not be jumping into schedule development	Understanding of scope	
Sequence per methodology		Identification of stakeholders	

Table 6.43 (continued)   Project and Program Management Interview Guide

2. Cite an example of bad news that you had to communicate to your customer. What did you do well? What would you do differently if you had it all to do again?

Look For	Caution	Probes	Notes
An understanding of the customer's needs	Extent to which this could have been anticipated.	Was this communicated to the entire team?	
Documentation		Was this communicated to management?	
Empathy			

3. Please detail a time when you were responsible for the creation of a Project Charter or an SOW.

Look For	Caution	Probes	Notes
Understanding functions of Charter & SOW	Should know that contracts and drawings are integral to scope management	Were performance criteria included?	

Table 6.43 (continued)   Project and Program Management Interview Guide

4. How do you assess the potential risk associated with any project? At what point in the project life cycle do you believe it is appropriate to do so?

Look For	Caution	Probes	Notes
Should be prior to developing a Project Plan	Should not be a one-time activity.	Has this been revisited?	
		How was the identified risk managed?	
		Has this been evaluated to root cause?	

5. How do you as a PM define the scope of work? Assume that you are given architecture with 10 servers and 15 are referenced in the scope documentation, your customer notices and is very upset. How would you handle this situation?

Look For	Caution	Probes	Notes
Understanding what is a "controlling" document.	Should not be trying to see "what went wrong." It may not be an error.	How was this communicated?	
Knowing what is a "representative" document.		Understanding of scope integrity.	

(continued on next page)

Table 6.43 (continued)   Project and Program Management Interview Guide

6. Do you need to do WBS as a group?

Look For	Caution	Probes	Notes
Understanding that this precedes developing a schedule.	Not knowing that it's a key part of project planning.	Was the WBS leveraged to include resource management?	
		Was the WBS leveraged to include estimating durations?	

7. You can complete a project under budget and ahead of time and still be a failure. Please explain your understanding of the meaning of this statement.

Look For	Caution	Probes	Notes
Managing customer expectations		Understanding that third constraint is Scope.	
		What about quality?	

Table 6.43 (continued)   Project and Program Management Interview Guide

8. Can you provide an example of a time when a member of your project team was late on a deliverable? What was the deliverable and how did you manage the situation?

Look For	Caution	Probes	Notes
Anticipating issues.	Heavy handedness.	How frequently was the schedule tracked?	
Management of matrix staff.			

9. What steps do you undertake in the preparation of a project schedule? How do you begin to identify your critical path?

Look For	Caution	Probes	Notes
Understanding the true meaning of Critical Path	Understanding that "critical" in this context does not equate to "important"	Difference between "critical path" and "critical chain"	
		How was this handled in the Project Plan?	

(continued on next page)

Table 6.43 (continued)   Project and Program Management Interview Guide

SHORT QUESTIONS:
• How important is managing customer expectations to the Project Manager?
• Could you provide an example of an instance when your empowered yourself?
• What is the highest number of direct reports that you have managed at any one time?
• Have you ever managed nondirect reports? Please name some of the challenges of managing nondirect reports?
• At what point does the Project Manager plan the close out? OR What is your definition of a completed project?
• To what extent should a PM communicate with external and internal customers? OR What activities should the Project Manager engage in to manage the customers' expectations?
Offer an opportunity for questions on the part of the interview candidate.
Notes

Preparing for the Audit

Before the audit, the reviewer interviews several individuals to determine whether the person being reviewed is in compliance with policies pertaining to his or her job. Preaudit subjects include:

- Preparation, presentation, compliance with processes (if applicable)
- Use of the IS Intranet to track projects and create Risk Assessments
- Use of pm-project-plan@Your Company.com mailing list to distribute initial project plan and any updated or re-baselined Project Schedules
- Responsiveness to requests for data reported to senior management (e.g., Top Ten data, survey information, revenue data)
- Problem areas highlighted in Customer Satisfaction Survey responses or in discussions with reporting manager
- Use of Post-Project Review forms for projects

In addition to interviews, the reviewer also researches the projects or accounts managed by the person being reviewed. The reviewer obtains a list of the projects taken to QRT by the person being reviewed and compares it to the list of projects from the IS intranet. Failure to include any active project on the IS intranet is a *major* nonconformity.

The reviewer then randomly selects an active project for review, and checks the IS intranet for a Risk Assessment for that project. Failure to include a Risk Assessment for any active project on the IS intranet is a *major* nonconformity.

Audit Guidelines

Most project-related documentation should be made available (indicated with an * below; see Work Instruction: Documentation and Work Instruction: Project Tracking). The reviewer will follow the outline below to determine whether the policies stated in work instructions are being followed.

1. Work Instruction: Documentation
   The following items are suggested questions for the reviewer to ask
2. Work Instruction: Risk Management
   a. Does the Risk Checklist include items that may arise during Launch Support phase?
   b. Have any issues arisen that would jeopardize the on-time completion of the project that were not identified in the risk checklist?
   c. Were the risks identified truly risks?
   d. What steps were taken to mitigate risk?
3. Work Instruction 3: Project Schedules
   a. Does the schedule sent to pm-project-plan@Your Company.com match the project schedule in the binder (folder)?
   b. Which template was used?
      i. Are we on schedule? If not,
         (1) Why not?
         (2) By how many days are we off?
         (3) If more than 5, was pm-project-plan@Your Company.com notified? (see Work Instruction: Project Tracking; *major* nonconformity)
      ii. What is the current milestone?
      iii. What is the latest communication on this milestone? [probe]
4. Work Instruction: Escalation
   a. Have any issues been escalated?
      i. What was the issue?
      ii. How did you document it? (Examine documentation—telephone log or e-mail printout)
      iii. How long did you wait for your primary contact to respond?
      iv. Whom did you escalate to?

v. Did they respond?
    (1) If yes, did this resolve the issue?
    (2) If no, how long did you wait for a response?
        (a) Whom did you escalate to?
        (b) How did you document it? [examine documentation]
        (c) Did they respond?

5. Work Instruction: Project Tracking
   a. Is the pipeline form up to date?
   b. Have you set up folios on the K-bank for electronic documentation?
   c. When were project documents on doc repository last updated?

6. Work Instruction: Communication
   a. Who is the PPOC for this implementation?
   b. Have any changes been made to the project plan since PPOC was identified?
      i. Who authorized them?
      ii. How were these changes communicated to the stakeholders? By whom?
      iii. How were changes documented?
   c. Has anyone else on the project team been in contact with the customer?
      i. Were these contacts coordinated by the PPOC?
   d. Was there an external kick-off meeting?
      i. Who conducted it?
      ii. Who took the notes?
      iii. What is the distribution list for the meeting notes?
   e. Were regularly scheduled status meetings established?
      i. Who are the attendees?
      ii. Who develops the agenda?
      iii. Who writes minutes?
   f. E-mail protocols
      i. What are your internal and external distribution lists for this project?
      ii. Have the following been included: AM? ISE? EBC? PM? IC? IE? Tech lead? Data center manager?

6. Work Instruction: Launch Support
   a. What is your definition of the beginning of the Launch Support phase?
   b. Was a launch support meeting held?
   c. Were all applications needed by the customer identified at the meeting?
      i. If not, why not?
      ii. Were all applications to be installed by Tier 2 and Tier 3, and content loads by the customer, identified and included in the project schedule?
      iii. Were any additional items added post-external kick-off?
      iv. How were these additions managed?

      v. Has the PM ensured that the customer has received a CSO account?
         (1) Does the customer have a premier care rep?
         (2) Has the premier care rep taken the customer through the Welcome Kit?

   d. Was a closure letter sent to the customer?
(Note: Occurs after the unit acceptance test [UAT] and customer acceptance)

5. Work Instruction: Acceptance Testing
(Note: Acceptance testing refers to internal testing–UAT–only, using the checklist developed by the Implementation PPOC. The IC is asked to complete this checklist. Customer acceptance testing is discussed in the launch support meeting and included in the schedule on dates agreed upon with CP, Tier 2, and Tier 3.)

   e. Was a checklist created for the components of the solution?
   f. Did it include the following:
      i. Confirmation of warm hand-off for each server
      ii. A list of all software to be installed, including version number
      iii. A list of all hardware to be installed
      iv. A review of all Magma tables associated with the site to ensure that what was ordered is what was delivered according to Magma or an equivalent system records the details associated with the order.
   g. Was customer acceptance of these items documented?

6. Work Instruction: Transferring Accounts
Have all issues relating to this customer been properly identified to ensure smooth handoff when PM disengages?

7. Work Instruction: Post-Project Reviews
   a. Were contacts for this customer added to the quarterly survey pool?
   b. Were post-project review templates filled out?

Part II Quality Certification Checklist

The checklist that follows is a tool that can be used by the team implementing and managing the quality system. It aligns with the Work Instructions and the methodology outlined earlier in this book. The checklist will facilitate conformance with the project management's quality system. Table 6.44 is the ISO Audit Checklist. Note that "M" represents what is mandatory, "C" indicated coaching opportunities and "WI" designates the associated work instruction.

Table 6.44 ISO Audit Checklist

	Training WI	Name of the PROJECT		Name of PM — Prompts	Check off Yes	Check off No	Date — Explanation/Remarks
WI		The following are suggested questions for the QA Assessor to ask during the QAR. (M-Mandatory/C-Coaching)					
1		**Work Instruction 1: Program and Project Documentation Control of Quality Records (ISO 4.2.4)**	M				
	a	Is there a Project Folder on Doc Repository?	M	Verify on Doc Repository			
	b	Are all the required subfolders (folios) present and identified? Every project that has a Manager assigned to it, regardless of complexity or contract value, must have a project folder under the Current Projects directory on the Doc Repository. A hardcopy Project Binder may be kept by the Manager, as well, at his or her option.					

1. Account overview		No mandatory components—see WI#1 for recommendations	
2. Architechure/drawings		No mandatory components—see WI#1 for recommendations	
3. Communications	M	Meeting minutes from internal and external kick-off meetings	
	M	Meeting minutes from Progress, and/or Launch meetings	
	M	Documentation verifying that acceptance testing has been completed. Note: UAT results may be accessed online and PAS results are e-mailed by the PAS engineer to the PM, if applicable. (May use Tab 1 in Configuration Workbook if a hosting project.)	X

(continued on next page)

Table 6.44 (continued)   ISO Audit Checklist

Training WI	Name of the PROJECT		Name of PM			Date	
			Prompts	Check off			Explanation/ Remarks
				Yes	No		
	4. Contacts	M	Customer contacts—name, company, title, telephone #, e-mail address, role/ responsibilities (e.g., is this the primary contact?)				
		M	If applicable, Third Party Vendor contact—name, company, title, telephone #, e-mail address, role/ responsibilities (e.g., Is this the primary contact?)				
		M	Your Company Team contacts—name, title, telephone #, e-mail address for PM, AM, ISE, BDM, IC, IE, Tech Leads, ePartners as appropriate for each project				

5. Customer Support Plan	M	Account or Project Transition Plan (includes Transition Schedule, Checkpoint Table)
	M	Project Completion Notification Letter
6. Legal Documents	M	Copy of Master Agreements
	M	Copy of all Service Schedules
	M	Copy of all Task Statements and Service Quotations. The PDF file of the document submitted to the customer for signature
	M	Other contractual documents—all Amendments, Addenda, Letters of Clarification, and Authorization Letters, and Letters of Intent
7. Other Deliverables		No mandatory components—see WI#1 for recommendations

(continued on next page)

Table 6.44 (continued) ISO Audit Checklist

Training WI	Name of the PROJECT		Name of PM — Prompts	Check off — Yes	No	Date — Explanation/ Remarks
	8. Other Documentation		No mandatory components—see WI#1 for recommendations			
	9. Pricing information		A basis of estimates (Pricing Matrices associated with signed Quotation(s) or Task Statement(s), Configuration Center Quotes or Vendor Quotes (i.e., Configuration Workbook tab 5 for hosting projects)			
	10. Project Plan and Supporting Documents	M	Project Schedule employing one of the PMO templates if a hosting-based project.			
		M	Risk Assessment—scope analysis (see WI#2—Risk Management)			

	11. Project Reviews	M	Post-Project Review form—Must be sent to PM-pmo@Your Company.com
	12. Sales Documentationist		No mandatory components—see WI#1 for recommendations
2	**Work Instruction 2: Risk Management Product/Service Realization (ISO 7.0)**		**This procedure is MANDATORY for all projects. It is recommended for use when planning a customer program office (CPO) or program.**
a	Have you filled out a Risk Checklist? May I see it? Available at: http://is.Your Company.com/app/helpfiles/risk_1.asp or Competed Risk Checklist in Project Plan and Supporting Documents Folder on Doc Repository	M	For all risks identified, the following is required: Identify impact in terms of scope, schedule time, added cost, or increased effort
b	Does the Risk Checklist identify risks that may arise during Launch Support?	C	Verify. Recall items, as they should be included in review of schedule per WI#3.

(continued on next page)

Table 6.44 (continued) ISO Audit Checklist

Training WI	Name of the PROJECT	Name of PM				Date	
		Prompts		Check off			Explanation/ Remarks
				Yes	No		
c	Have any issues arisen that would jeopardize the on-time completion of the project that were not identified in the risk checklist?	M	Develop risk mitigation to reduce or eliminate impact, should the risk occur.				
d	Were the risks identified truly determined by cause?	C	Establish Risk Management Action Plan to prevent, control, and mitigate the risk, should it occur.				
e	What steps were taken to mitigate risk?	C	The results of the Risk Management Action Plan should be commuicated with management.				

3		Work Instruction 3: Program and Project Schedules Product/Service Realization (ISO 7.0)	M			
	a	Do you have a Project Schedule created in MS Project 98? This is mandatory for all projects and programs. May I see it?	M			Template is available at https://is.Your Company.com/IS/tools/tools1.asp#Schedules
	b	If a hosting project requires Tier II or III support during Launch Phase, was e-mail sent to Tier II/III management to facilitate resource allocation?				
	c	Verify Mandatory Elements (for Projects)	M			External Kick-Off meeting
			M			Launch Support meeting— mandatory for Hosting Projects.
			M			Confirmation that all contractual deliverables have been provided to the customer.

(continued on next page)

Table 6.44 (continued) ISO Audit Checklist

Training WI	Name of the PROJECT		Prompts	Check off — Yes	Check off — No	Date	Explanation/Remarks
		M	Risk mitigation tasks, if applicable				
		M	Third-party deliverables, if applicable				
		M	Customer dependencies, if applicable				
		M	Acceptance Testing tasks, UAT, or PAS. Mandatory for Hosting Projects				
		M	Launch Support tasks, Mandatory for Hosting Projects				
		M	Quality Assurance tasks, if applicable				
		M	Billing Quality—First Invoice Review Task				

d	Are we on schedule? If not …	C
	Why not?	C
	By how many days are we off?	C
	If schedule is more than 5 days off, was pm-project-plan@Your Company.com notified?	M
	How are you managing the milestones?	C
	What is the current milestone?	C
	What is the latest communication on this milestone? [probe]	C
4	**Work Instruction 4: Quality Assurance Reviews**	
	The PMO will conduct scheduled and unscheduled project reviews with all PM staff to ensure that Work Instructions are being followed.	
	Is there a QAR schedule?	M
	Have all areas of PM Program and Project Management been audited?	M

(continued on next page)

Table 6.44 (continued)   ISO Audit Checklist

	Training WI	Name of the PROJECT	Name of PM		Date	
			Prompts	Check off		Explanation/ Remarks
				Yes	No	
5		**Work Instruction 5: Escalation**	M	**An issue should be escalated when attempts to obtain a satisfactory response from the primary point of contact have failed.**			
	a	Have any issues been escalated?	C	Escalation sequence:			
				1. The initial escalation step should be in e-mail AND voicemail to the party's direct supervisor (first-line manager) with a copy to the Manager's supervisor.			
				2. The second escalation step should be in e-mail AND voicemail to the party's second-line manager with a copy to the Manager's supervisor.			

	3. The third escalation step should be directly to the Manager's supervisor for direct involvement in escalating the issue to the party's third-line manager (e.g., Vice President) with an e-mail copy to the Manager's Director and the PMO Manager.		
b	What was the issue?	C	(Identify the issue)
c	How did you document it? [Examine documentation: telephone log or e-mail printout]	C	Internal stakeholder(s) signed Project Plans
			• Internal kick-off meeting minutes
			• External kick-off meeting minutes
			• Prior e-mail commitments
			• Written confirmation of telephone commitments

(continued on next page)

Table 6.44 (continued)   ISO Audit Checklist

	Training WI	Name of the PROJECT		Prompts	Name of PM			Date	
						Check off			Explanation/ Remarks
						Yes	No		
				• Existing policy memos that include time commitments, as provided by other functional groups.					
d		How long did you wait for your primary contact to respond?	C						
		Whom did you escalate to?	C	Escalation Matrix: http://domino.Your Company.com/iweb/emweb.nsf/index/home-matrix.html					
e		Did they respond?	C						
		If yes, did this resolve the issue?	C						
		If no, how long did you wait for a respnose?	C	As a guideline, for issues that place the project scope, schedule, or cost in jeopardy, wait no more than a maximum of 4 to 8 hours between escalations					

		Whom did you escalate to?	C				
		How did you document it?	C	[Examine documentation]			
		Did they respond?	C				
6		Work Instruction 6: Program and Project Tracking ISO 7.0 Product/Service Realization Product/Service Realization (ISO 7.0)	M	Every hosting project on which PM Program and Project Managers are engaged must be tracked in the PM: PMO Intranet Project Report (http://is.Your Company.com).			
	a	Is the project form up to date?	M	WI1 Entered and tracked in PM: PMO Project Form: https://is.Your Company.com/IS/project/project_1.asp			
	b	Have you set up folios on the Doc Repository for electronic documentation?	M				
	c	When were project documents on Doc Repository last updated?	M	WI#1 for documentation and WI#6 says that any revisions or updates to the status of a project must be posted as soon as possible.			

(continued on next page)

Table 6.44 (continued)   ISO Audit Checklist

	Training WI	Name of the PROJECT		Name of PM				Date	
				Prompts	Check off				Explanation/ Remarks
					Yes	No			
d		Have Labor Hours been entered into the Labor Log for all PM Staff?	M	https://is.Your Company.com/ IS/labortracking/ LaborTracking_ExtraDays.asp					
e		Future Vantive questions not yet effective							
7		**Work Instruction 7: Communication ISO 5.5.1 ISO 7.0 Product/Service Realization** **Product/Service Realization (ISO 7.0)**							
a		Who is the PPOC for this implementation?	C	While Managers are responsible for an implementation, they are the PPOC and the only individual that may communicate changes to the Project Plan					

			(If changes were made)				
b	Have any changes been made to the project plan since PPOC was identified?	C					
	Who authorized them?	C					
	How were these changes communicated to the stakeholders? By whom?	C					
	How were changes documented?	C	WI#1 & 3				
c	Has anyone else on the project team been in contact with the customer? Were these contacts coordinated by the PPOC?	C					
d	Was there an External Kick-Off meeting?	C	WI#3 PM runs the meeting and takes notes.				
	Who conducted it?	C					
	Who took the notes?	C					
	Could you please show me the distribution list for the meeting notes?	C	Confirm all required persons are on the list.				

(continued on next page)

Table 6.44 (continued) ISO Audit Checklist

| | Training WI | Name of the PROJECT | | Name of PM | | Check off | | Date | |
				Prompts		Yes	No		Explanation/ Remarks
	e	E-mail protocols	C						
		What are your internal and external distributions lists for this project?	C						
		Review copy and cc lines	C	(Optional)					
8		**Work Instruction 8: Hosting Launch Support ISO 7.0 Product/Service Realization**	M	**Scope: This procedure is MANDATORY for Hosting Projects**					
		Product/Service Realization (ISO 7.0)							
	a	What is your definition of the beginning of the Launch Support phase?	C	Generally begins after UAT and/or PAS and ends when customer's applications/ contents are initially loaded and when all mutually agreed Launch Support tasks in the Project Schedule have been successfully delivered.					

b				
Was a Launch Support meeting held?	M	Schedule a Launch Support meeting after the External Kick-Off meeting, approx. 30% into the provisioning cycle. Include all applicable attendees. See Launch Support Meeting Template at: http://is.Your Company.com/ app/downloadlinks/tools1.asp		
	C	To request attendance by Tier 2 or Tier 3, a TWO-day advance notice is required. Send requests to:		
		• Tier 2- ronald.rebeiro@ Your Company.com		
		• Tier 3- who-team-leads@ Your Company.com		

(continued on next page)

Table 6.44 (continued) ISO Audit Checklist

	Training WI	Name of the PROJECT		Name of PM				Date	
				Prompts	Check off			Explanation/ Remarks	
					Yes	No			
	c	Was a request made for a "Special Attention" status flag in Vantive by sending e-mail to Account-Priority@ Your Company.com?	M	The updated Planned Priority Status Ticket has a NEW Special Attention Flag and Special Handling Box. Guidelines are available at: https://kbank.Your Company. com/kb/bin/root/home/ Your CompanyServices/ CustomerCare/ PlannedPriorityStatus					
	d	Were all applications needed by the customer identified at the meeting?	M	Identify potential issues with content development and production environments.					
				• Confirm access rights to servers.					
				• Discuss acceptance testing and customer validation plan, if changed.					

		Item	Question	Type	Notes			
			If not, why not?	C	• Discuss role of third-party integrators, if applicable.			
		e	Were all applications to be installed by Tier 2 and Tier 3, and content loads by the customer identified and included in the project schedule?	M	Schedule dates with CP, Tiers 2 and 3 as needed for content loading to meet customer's schedule requirements. Review open tasks, schedule, and dependencies. Verify with Tier III that the Run-book requirements, if applicable, have been met.			
		f	Were any additional items added at post-External Kick-Off?	M	(If answer is YES) Mandatory per WI#3			
			How were these additions managed?	C				
		g	If there were any changes after acceptance testing and customer validation plan, was required e-mail sent?	M	For PAS Testing requests— send e-mail to pas-systemtest@ YourCompany.com To obtain UAT testing results- e-mail to: http://whocweb.sys.gtei.net			

(continued on next page)

Table 6.44 (continued) ISO Audit Checklist

	Training WI	Name of the PROJECT		Name of PM / Prompts	Check off		Date	Explanation/ Remarks
					Yes	No		
h		Has the PM ensured that the customer has received a CSO account?	M					
i		Verify that the customer has received the "Welcome Package" from CSC (Customer Service Center).	M	Ensure the CSC has educated the Customer on the contents of the Welcome Package.				
j		Does the customer have a Premier Care rep?	M	Discuss the role of Customer Care/Premier Care and Ongoing support, if applicable.				
k		Has the Premier Care rep taken the customer through the Welcome Kit?	M					
l		Was a Transition Letter sent to the customer?	M	After the Launch Support has been provided and either the customer has loaded content or Your Company's contractual obligations have been completed, the Manager:				

• issues a Transition Letter to the customer, confirming that the project has been successfully completed. • transfers the customer to an Account Support Representative, and/or a Premier Care Representative or the Customer Service Center, whichever applies.			
		Work Instruction 9: Acceptance Testing **ISO 7.0 Product/Service Realization** **Product/Service Realization (ISO 7.0)** (Note: Acceptance testing refers to internal testing – UAT – only, using the checklist developed by the Implementation PPOC. The IC is asked to complete this checklist. Customer Acceptance Testing is discussed in the Launch Support meeting and included in the schedule on dates agreed upon with CP, Tier 2, and Tier 3.)	
		9	

(continued on next page)

Table 6.44 (continued) ISO Audit Checklist

Training WI	Name of the PROJECT	Name of PM		Check off		Date	
				Yes	No		Explanation/ Remarks
		Prompts					
		M	Acceptance Testing begins with either Unit Acceptance Testing (UAT) or Performance Acceptance System Testing (PAS).				
		M	It is the Manager's responsibility to ensure that each item be delivered as specified in the contractual documents, and in the manner specified in Your Company's service descriptions. The tasks associated with Acceptance Testing must be included in the project schedule.				

a	Were the results of the UAT or PAS Acceptance Testing obtained from the data center conducting the UAT or PAS if a systems solution test is performed?	M	Documented results of the UAT or PAS Acceptance Testing must be obtained from the data center conducting the UAT or PAS if a systems solution test is performed. PAS Testing results are documented by the PAS Engineer and forwarded to the Project Manager in one of the following three ways: 1. Do a query in Vantive (Brio). 2. By engaging PAS (documented) 3. Look at e-mail for pricing matrix, BOM.		

(continued on next page)

Table 6.44 (continued)   ISO Audit Checklist

Training WI	Name of the PROJECT		Name of PM				Date	
			Prompts		Check off			Explanation/ Remarks
					Yes	No		
b	Was a review of all Magma tables associated with the site conducted to ensure that what was ordered is what was delivered according to Magma?		C	Customer satisfaction requires dedication to the delivery of quality service offerings. To ensure satisfaction, CSD-Operations Production Acceptance Services will implement new processes before a customer site is "put into production," which will enforce a readiness standard. These processes will also be followed for service offering upgrades. The purpose of these activities is to make certain the product offering delivers the desired benefits and reduces the costs associated with customer site unplanned production outages.				

c	Was customer acceptance of these items documented?			
	For nonhosting projects customer acceptance is recommended			
	PAS Home page:	M		
	http://domino.bbn.com/8525672700 6aaf41/a40e0 49c3bbacd8c852563b5005ccd 48/82aceba87e396ec5852567c 30060b7da?OpenDocument	M		
	UAT Testing results— obtained from:	M		
	https://yorktown. Your Company.com/del-sys/ cpplus/accept	M		

(continued on next page)

Table 6.44 (continued) ISO Audit Checklist

Training WI	Name of the PROJECT		Name of PM — Prompts	Check off Yes	No	Date	Explanation/ Remarks
10	**Work Instruction 10: Transferring Accounts or Projects Resource Management ISO 6.0 Product/Service Realization (ISO 7.0)**	M	**If a customer requires ongoing support, a transition plan must be developed by the Ongoing Support PPOC and agreed to with the Project Manager.**				
a	Have all issues relating to this customer been properly identified to ensure smooth hand-off when PM disengages?	M	The Account or Transition Plan Guide located on the PM-PMO Intranet is a requirement if there is a transfer of account or project responsibility from one "Manager" to another "Manager."				
		M	The Ongoing Support PPOC must develop a Customer Profile document (or equivalent) and maintain any billing documentation that pertains to the account.				

M	The Ongoing support PPOC is responsible for developing the plan, and both the PM and Ongoing PPOC are responsible for adhering to scheduled dates and milestones.	
M	All the stakeholders must sign off on the Account Transition plan (including PPOCs, the Reporting Manager, and the Account Manager).	
M	Dates need to be identified and scheduled for all the required Milestones (all stakeholders must agree to the dates).	
M	Revisions to milestones must be documented and reported using the Milestones Variance Report.	

(continued on next page)

Table 6.44 (continued)   ISO Audit Checklist

	Training WI	Name of the PROJECT	Name of PM				Date	
					Prompts		Check off			Explanation/ Remarks
						Yes	No		
b		Hand-Off Transition Plan contains four stages. Transition Plan Template available at: http://is.Your Company. com/app/downloadlinks/tools1. asp#TransitionAccounts		1. Stage One encompasses data collection relevant to reviewing and assessing the account and customer's needs.				
				2. In Stage Two, this data will be reviewed by the "transfer team" for accuracy and posted to the appropriate electronic Customer folder located on the Doc Repository. The new Manager will be responsible for keeping this directory up to date upon transfer.				

		3. Stage Three will gradually migrate the account or project responsibilities from the originating Manager to the new Manager who will then take on the leadership role on the account.	
		4. Stage Four covers the official hand-off.	
	M	Were all electronic documentation on the Doc Repository edited to include the new Manager's name?	The New Manager taking over the Project or Account needs to ensure that all the electronic documentation (See WI#1) on the Doc Repository has been edited to include the New Manager's name for all the folios contained in the Project Folders and that the expiration date has been extended; this will ensure that expiration alerts are sent to the New Manager.
c			

(continued on next page)

Table 6.44 (continued)   ISO Audit Checklist

	Training WI	Name of the PROJECT	Name of PM			Date	
			Prompts		Check off		Explanation/ Remarks
					Yes	No	Date
11		**Work Instruction 11: Customer Satisfaction Survey** **ISO 8.2.1 Customer Satisfaction**	M	**Procedure defines the standards and requirements, for all PM Program and Project Managers, for performing Customer Satisfaction Surveys**			
	a	Were contacts for this customer added to the quarterly survey pool? (Implementation and/or Ongoing)	M	Surveys available at: http:// is.Your Company.com/app/ survey/10/splash_survey.html			
	b	How and when did you request that the customer complete the survey?	C	There is a Survey letter template available at: https://is.Your Company. com/IS/tools/tools1. asp#surveys			Date survey sent …

#			Notes
12		**Work Instruction 12: Document Control Process**	
		ISO 4.2.3 Document Control	
		Verify that the version of all documents listed in the PMO Document Log is the same as the version posted on the intranet.	
		Verify the document control for all process documents	These documents must contain a document control page with a revision history.
		Verify the document control for all supporting documents	These documents must contain a document #, date, and revision level identified somewhere on the document.
		Verify the document control for all templates	A separate document control page with revision history.
13		**Work Instruction 13: Management Document Review Process ISO 4.2.3**	
		ISO 4.2.3 Document Control	
		For documents that have gone through review, verify the following:	The document was sent to the Management team for review.

(continued on next page)

Table 6.44 (continued)   ISO Audit Checklist

	Training WI	Name of the PROJECT		Name of PM — Prompts	Check off Yes	Check off No	Date	Explanation/ Remarks
				Comments from the review team have been incorporated in the new revision.				
				If there is a conflict in the comments, was a meeting held to address these conflicts?				
14		**Work Instruction 14: Post-Project Reviews ISO 8.2.1 Customer Satisfaction Product/Service Realization (ISO 7.0)**	M	**Procedure defines the standards for performing Post-Project Reviews**				
	a	Did you conduct a post-project review?	M	In retrospect would any changes to the Project Plan be suggested?				
			M	Were there any customer expectation management issues that generated a Lesson Learned?				

	M	In retrospect could any of the Risk, Dependency of Constraint issues have been managed differently?			
	M	Did this project generate a Best Practice that may be shared?			
	M	Have any issues been escalated? Please be specific with names, dates, and issues. (Limit to key issues.)			
	M	Any recommended process changes due to this project experience?			
b	M	Check to see that the Reviews were sent.	Were the reviews posted on Doc Repository and sent to: PM-pmo@Your Company.com?		
c	C	Take notes about the plan.	Did you do Identify Lessons Learned from the project? If so, have you developed a plan so that we don't repeat the same mistakes?		

(continued on next page)

Table 6.44 (continued)   ISO Audit Checklist

Training WI	Name of the PROJECT		Name of PM — Prompts	Check off Yes	Check off No	Date	Explanation/Remarks
d	Did you recognize the Best Practices? What are your plans to share it with your manager and peers?	C	Take notes of the Best Practice.				
15	**Work Instruction 15: Scope Change Management** **Product/Service Realization (ISO 7.0)**	M	**To define the standard for all of PM Program and Project Management, for maintaining Project scope changes**				
a	Were there any scope changes on the project that involved any change in contractual scope obligations?						
	How did you document them?	M	Use of the scope change management checklist is mandatory.				
	How did you communicate them?	C	The scope change form can be used to discuss changes with the customer.				

b	Were there any scope changes on the project that significantly impacted the cost or schedule of a project or program? It is within the discretion of the project manager to determine which noncontractual scope changes represent "significant impacts".		
	How did you document them?	M	Use of the scope change management checklist is mandatory.
	How did you communicate them?	C	Use the scope change form to discuss changes with the customer.
16	**Work Instruction 16: Presales Process Product/Service Realization (ISO 7.0)**	**M**	
a	Were you involved in the presales process for this project?		
b	Did you use the scope review guide?	C	While not mandatory, it is expected that PMs have one for each project or engagement.
c	Did this project go through Rapid Review?		

(continued on next page)

Table 6.44 (continued) ISO Audit Checklist

	Training WI	Name of the PROJECT	Name of PM		Check off Yes	Check off No	Date / Explanation/ Remarks
d		Did this project go through QRT?					
e		If the project went through Rapid Review, did you check with the assigned quote preparer to ensure that the PM's hours and comments that were posted to Rapid Review were understood and addressed?	C	PMs should be able to show auditor the comments for the Rapid Review.			
f		If the hours and comments were not posted to Rapid Review, what did you do?		The PM should engage Quote Preparer immediately and escalate as needed.			

g	Did you ensure that you were added to both QRT distribution lists?	qrt-dist@YourCompany.com and qrt-agenda@ YourCompany.com		
	Were any risks identified prior to QRT?			
	How were this risks communicated to the team?	Comments should be sent to qrt-dist@YourCompany.com		
	Did you attend QRT?			
17	**Work Instruction 17: Corrective and Preventative Actions** **Corrective Action (ISO 8.5.2) and Preventative Action (ISO 8.5.3)**			
	Review the CA log for the following:	What is the current number of the last item in the log?		
		How many items are not closed out?		
		Record the numbers, date assigned, and the scheduled response dates for all items that are not closed.		

(continued on next page)

Table 6.44 (continued) ISO Audit Checklist

	Training WI	Name of the PROJECT		Name of PM	Prompts		Check off		Date	
							Yes	No		Explanation/ Remarks
18		**Tools Development and Review Procedure**								
		When were the Tool Review Committee meetings held?								
		What new tools were reviewed during the meetings?								
		What updates to existing tools were reviewed during the meeting?								
19		**Work Instruction 19: Training Procedures**								
		Resource Management (ISO 6.0)								
		What training has taken place since the last QAR?								
		Who attended the training?								

20	Work Instruction 20: Program Resource Management Resource Management (ISO 6.0)	M	For Programs and Customer Program Offices Only			
	Have you required additional resources for this program?		The process in this WI is only used when requesting processes outside of the PM region			
	Did you use the Task Authorization Form?	M	The use of this form is mandatory for resources that are either internal and external			
	Did the Program Manager approve this request?					
	Was the required resource inside or outside of PM?	M	This process is mandatory for resources required outside of PM			
	How did you communicate the resource requirements to the appropriate parties?	C				
	Have any performance or behavioral issues developed?					
	How were they addressed?	C				

(continued on next page)

Table 6.44 (continued) ISO Audit Checklist

	Training WI	Name of the PROJECT	Name of PM / Prompts	Check off Yes	No	Date / Explanation/Remarks
21		**Work Instruction 21: Master Records Procedure** **Control of Quality Records (ISO 4.2.4)**	M			
		What is the minimum retention time of project records?	M			Minimum Retention Time is the Life of the Project or contractual requirements— whichever is greater
22		**Work Instruction 22: Management Review Meeting Process** **Management Responsibility (ISO 5.0)**				
		What are the dates of Management Review Meetings since the last QAR?				
		Can I see the minutes of the meetings?				
		Which of the following items was covered during the meeting?				
		Results of audits				

		Description		
		Customer feedback		
		Process performance and product conformity		
		Status of preventative and corrective action		
		Follow-up actions from previous management reviews		
		Planned changes that could affect the quality management system		
		Recommendations for improvement		
23		**Work Instruction 23: Project and Program Reporting Product/Service Realization (ISO 7.0)**	M	**Provide a standard process and format for reporting on the status of projects and or programs to the Customer.**
	a	Were regularly scheduled status meetings established?	M	
	b	How often were they conducted?	M	Progress report meetings should be held weekly unless requested by the customer. This request should be documented on Doc Repository.

(continued on next page)

Table 6.44 (continued) ISO Audit Checklist

Training WI	Name of the PROJECT		Name of PM				Date	
					Check off			
			Prompts		Yes	No	Explanation/ Remarks	
c	Did you use the Progress Report Template?	M	The use of the Progress Report Template may be waived if Your Company has signed a contract which includes reporting requirements that overlap or duplicate the contents of this template. While the use of the template may be waived, the requirement for reporting to the Customer on a weekly basis remains mandatory. See 14b.					
d	If the Progress Report Template was used, review the following from a recent meeting:	M	A. Agenda					
			B. Scheduled Attendees list					
			C. Accomplishments since the last report.					

		D. Project Schedule Status [requires MS Project]. This may be attached to the agenda. If attached, it must indicate in this section of the template. Format the schedule to indicate percent complete as well as Actual v. Baseline dates.			
		E. Issues and Action Items Matrix			
		F. Risk Register [Alternate formats, to preclude duplication, for Risk reporting may be used]			
		G. Scope Change Record			
	e		M	If use of the Template was waived, review weekly progress meeting to verify that required elements were included.	

(continued on next page)

Table 6.44 (continued) ISO Audit Checklist

	Training WI	Name of the PROJECT		Prompts	Check off		Date	
				Name of PM	Yes	No		*Explanation/ Remarks*
24		**Work Instruction 24: Engagement Criteria Policy** **Product/Service Realization (ISO 7.0)**	M					
	a	Did this meet the following criteria for a Consulting Opportunity?	M	1. All eServices engagements for existing customers which have ongoing project/program management, TAM/ASR services				
				2. eServices engagements in excess of 80 hours of effort—as indicated in SOW				
				3. Engagements that require a project plan as a deliverable				

Did this meet the following criteria for engaging Program or Project Management?			
1. Multiple service offerings, with specific requirements not met by standard product offerings	M		
4. eServices engagements requiring funded resources from other Your Company organizations (non-PM)			
5. Performance or outside assessment services (pass-throughs) involving more than 2 parties (ePartner, multiple customer business units, SIs, etc.)			
6. Opportunities that will pull through business that would be supported by a regional PM (per existing PM engagement criteria)			

b

(continued on next page)

Table 6.44 (continued) ISO Audit Checklist

Training WI	Name of the PROJECT	Name of PM				Date	
		Prompts	Check off			Explanation/ Remarks	
			Yes	No			
		2. Implementations involving three or more service lines (i.e., coWlination of the following: eBH, Dial, DSL, IA, VISS, VoIP)					
		3. Solutions requiring development/delivery of custom support processes					
		4. Projects in which Your Company is prime contractor for a multi-vendor delivery					
		5. Beta product, "one-of," "first-of"					
		6. Large scale deployments (at any one time)					

	7. Your Company application development projects					
M	8. Architectures requiring a phased implementation					
	9. ePartner Project					
	10. Strategic opportunity with senior VP sponsorship					
	11. Project Recovery					
c	M	Was an ORF filled out to engage Program or Project Management?				
25	M	**Work Instruction 25: Consulting Practice Opportunities** **Product/Service Realization (ISO 7.0)**				
		Is a consultant working on this project?				
	M	Was the SOW Template used?				
		If yes, is this a complex consulting opportunity?				

(continued on next page)

Table 6.44 (continued)   ISO Audit Checklist

Training WI	Name of the PROJECT		Prompts		Check off		Date
	Name of PM				Yes	No	Explanation/ Remarks
	Did you schedule the SOW review meeting?		What was the date?				
		M	Did sales, PM, and consultants attend?				
		M	The SOW Review Checklist is available on the PM Intranet at: https://is.Your Company.com/ IS/tools/tools1.asp#Quote				
	Did you review and approve the final SOW?	M					
	Can I see the SOW Checklist?	C					

Sample VoIP Connectivity Checklist

The checklist in Table 6.45 can be employed by the team to troubleshoot connectivity issues on VoIP projects.

Sample Customer Satisfaction Letter

[Date]

[Name of Client]
[Title of Client]
[Full name of Company]
[Address of Company]
[e-mail address of Client]

Dear [Client's name]:

First, allow me to thank you for choosing Your Company as your _____ provider. As the [*your title*] working with you, it has certainly been my pleasure to provide you with ongoing support for the account.

In the next week or two, I will send you a URL for a Your Company Customer Satisfaction Survey. I would appreciate you taking a moment to complete this survey. If you feel that you cannot submit a response of "Very Satisfied" in any field, please contact me so I may have the opportunity to address any concerns you may have. Please keep in mind that although this survey is only intended to grade my efforts and not that of any other department, I will gladly receive your comments regarding any members of the Your Company team.

Your satisfaction with the service Your Company and I provide is of the utmost importance to me. If you have any questions regarding my responsibilities to this account please do not hesitate to contact me. I look forward to our continued relationship as we work together to provide [*Name of Client's Company*] with their Web-hosting solutions. Thank you again for your business and support.

Cordially,

[Your Name]
[Your Title]

Table 6.45 Customer Connectivity Checklist

#	Enterprise Voice Element	Customer or Your Firm Managed	Description/ Category	Item Being Validated	Objective	Owner	Customer Action
				Enterprise Voice [VoIP]			
1	Circuit	F	IA element	Circuit	Validate that circuit is in place	Customer	Customer connects PC to verify data traffic
2	IA	F	IA element	IA Service	Validate IA connectivity	Customer	Customer connects PC to verify data traffic
3	Router	F	IA element	Router	Validate that router is working	Customer	Customer connects PC to verify data traffic
4a	VoIP Gateway	F	VoIP element	VoIP Gateway	If applicable, verify ISDN/PRI circuits are working	Customer	ISDN circuits and PRI circuits are up and functioning
4b	PBX	F	Customer element	PBX	If applicable, verify ISDN/PRI circuits are working	Customer	ISDN circuits and PRI circuits are up and functioning

#	Type		Customer element	Cisco connectivity		Customer	
5	Cisco Call Manager	F		Cisco connectivity	If applicable, register and validate with Genuity	Customer	Customer registers with Genuity and validates
6	VoIP Component	F	Dialing Plan	Route Tables and Route Plans	Validate Route Tables and Route Plans	Customer	Customer configures and verifies in either call manager or PBX
7	VoIP Component	F	Calling	Outbound Calls (PBX to World)	If applicable, test outbound calls	Customer	Customer makes calls to test
8	VoIP Component	F	Calling	Onnet Calls (PBX to PBX or Call Manager to Call Manager)	If applicable, test on-net calls	Customer	Customer makes calls to test
9	VoIP Component	F	Calling	Inbound Calls (World to PBX)	If applicable, test inbound calls	Customer	Customer makes calls to test
10	VoIP Component	F	Failover Plan	Failover Settings	Validate Failover Settings	Customer	Customer tests alternate routes
11	VoIP Component	F	Using Test Pop	Quality of calls	Validate quality of Service	Customer	Make several calls to test quality
12	VoIP Component	F	Using the Production Network	Traffic	Validate traffic	Customer	Customer makes calls to test

Transition Letter—To Service Post Go-Live Template

This is used after all the applications have been tested, are live on the Web, and are moving into maintenance mode.

To: Customer Account Manager
        Sales Region

Re: Internal Project Management Transition Notification for [Customer's Name]

Date:

This letter is to confirm that [Your Firm] has successfully handed off an accepted site to [Name of Customer Contact], and thus fulfilled our obligation to provide "Implementation and Planning Project Management services" for Customer's Name as outlined in the contract number [Contract Number] dated [Contract Date].

Customer's Name has purchased [Ongoing Hours] hours per month of ongoing ASR/TAM support as stated in the above mentioned contract. All documentation, including the completed ASR Account Transition Plan Template, has been transferred to the ongoing support representative in accordance with Project Management Work Instruction.

[If customer has not purchased ongoing support, replace the above paragraph with the one below]

Customer's Name has not purchased ongoing account support.

Outstanding Issues: (Include Go Live Date & Add-Ons)		
Ongoing Support Contact(s):		
ASR/TAM Name	ASR/TAM Phone Number	ASR/TAM Email
Premiere Care Name	Premiere Care Phone Number	Premiere Care E-mail
Customer Primary Technical Contact:		
Primary Contact Name	Primary Contact Number	Primary Contact E-mail
Customer Secondary Technical Contact(s):		
Secondary Contact Name	Secondary Contact Number	Secondary Contact E-mail

I will be available to assist, when needed, on any of the outstanding issues listed above.

Sincerely,

Your Name
Your Title
Your Number
Your E-mail

Cc: Team Leader's Name
  Account Representative's Name
  ASR/TAM Name
  Customer Care Name

Project Status Log

Table 6.46 is a type of dashboard focusing on the triple constraints and resources. Each organization defines the thresholds to reach the red, yellow, and green indicators.

Table 6.46 Status Log

No.	Project	Project Status						Notes
		Schedule	Budget	Scope	Resources	Escalation(s)		
1	Project 1							
2								
3								
4								
5								
6								

Appendix

Project Management and Internetworking Glossaries and Formulas

Technical Support Tools

This section of the book contains a number of useful technical tools for Internet and IT project managers. It will also prove helpful for developers and team leads. Here is what you will find:

- Project management acronym table
- Earned value acronyms and formulas
- Project management terms and glossary
- Technical Internet service provider (ISP) terms

Following the technical support tools, you will find information on project quality management along with template work instructions. Finally, there are project management tool templates that are reproducible.

Project Management Acronyms

Table A.1 is a listing of the most typical project management acronyms in the industry.

Table A.1   Project Management Acronyms and Their Definitions

Acronym	Definition
ACWP	Actual cost of work performed
AD	Activity description
AF	Actual finish date
AOA	Activity-on-arrow
AON	Activity-on-node
AS	Actual start date
BAC	Budget at completion
BCWP	Budgeted cost of work performed
BCWS	Budgeted cost of work scheduled
CAPM	Certified Associate Project Manager
CCB	Change Control Board
CCM	Critical chain method
CPFF	Cost plus fixed fee
CPI	Cost performance index
CPIF	Cost plus incentive fee
CPM	Critical path method
CV	Cost variance
EAC	Estimate at completion
EF	Early finish date
ES	Early start date
ETC	Estimate (or estimated) to complete (or completion)
EV	Earned value
EVM	Earned value management
FF	Free Float or Finish-to-Finish
FFP	Firm fixed price
FPIF	Fixed price incentive fee

Table A.1 (continued)   Project Management Acronyms and Their Definitions

Acronym	Definition
GERT	Graphical evaluation and review technique
IFB	Invitation for bid
LF	Late finish date
LOE	Level of effort
LS	Late start date
OBS	Organization breakdown structure
PC	Percent complete
PDM	Precedence diagramming method
PERT	Program evaluation and review technique
PF	Planned finish date
PM	Project management, program manager, or project manager
PMBOK	Project Management Body of Knowledge
PMO	Program or Project Management Office
PMP	Certified Project Management Professional
PS	Planned start date
QA	Quality assurance
QC	Quality control
RAM	Responsibility Assignment Matrix
RDU	Remaining duration
RFI	Request for information
RFP	Request for proposal
RFQ	Request for quotation
SF	Scheduled finish date or Start-to-Finish
SOW	Statement of work
SPI	Schedule performance index
SS	Scheduled start date or Start-to-Start

(continued on next page)

Table A.1 (continued) Project Management Acronyms and Their Definitions

Acronym	Definition
SV	Schedule variance
TC	Target completion date
TF	Total float or target finish date
TS	Target start date
WBS	Work breakdown structure

Earned Value Acronyms and Formulas

Table A.2 contains acronyms and formulas, from different versions of the practice standard, to facilitate earned value management calculations.

Table A.2 Earned Value Management Acronyms and Formulas

Acronym	Definition or Equivalent	Formulas[a]
AC	Actual cost	CPI = BCWP/ACWP
AC	ACWP	CPI = EV/AC
ACWP	Actual cost of work performed	CV = EV – AC
BAC	Budget at completion	EAC = AC + ETC
BCWP	Budgeted cost of work performed	EAC = BAC/CPI * SPI
BCWS	Budgeted cost of work scheduled	ETC = (BAC – EV)/CPI
CPI	Cost performance index	SPI = BCWP/BCWS
CV	Cost variance	SPI = EV/PV
EAC	Estimate at completion	SV = EV – PV
ETC	Estimate to complete	% Complete = EV/BAC
EV	BCWP	% Complete = BCWP/BAC
EV	Earned value	VAC = BAC – EAC
EVM	Earned value management	
PV	Planned value	
PV	BCWS	

Table A.2 (continued)   Earned Value Management Acronyms and Formulas

Acronym	Definition or Equivalent	Formulas[a]
SPI	Schedule performance index	
VAC	Variance at completion	

[a] The above formulas can be used to create other mathematical statements.

Project Management Glossary

A

Activity: A group of related tasks planned for a project. Within the project plan, each activity is associated with a level of effort, duration, cost, human, and/or material resources.

Activity description (AD): A way to describe a group of related tasks that comprise an activity. Activity descriptions are often used in activity sequencing diagrams.

Activity duration estimating: Estimating the amount of time needed (typically based on workforce calendars) to complete an activity.

Actual cost of work performed (ACWP): Total cost of completed work. In earned value management, this is associated with a period of time.

B

Backward pass: A technique within the critical path method that facilitates the calculation, usually in a network activity diagram, of the project's start date by working backward from a predetermined completion date.

Bar chart: A graphic display of scheduling information. In many software applications, it is referred to as a *Gantt chart*. The x-axis (vertical) indicates activities, tasks, and/or milestones. The y-axis (horizontal) represents the duration and time frame.

Baseline: An original element of a project plan. Examples include budget baseline, schedule baseline, etc. Subsequent to a project change (after it has gone through an integrated change management process), the project plan elements may change; *after* the change, the element is called a *re-baseline*.

Budget at completion (BAC): The forecasted cost of the entire project.

Budgeted cost of work performed (BCWP): The sum of all (direct and indirect) estimated cost for the project work completed.

Budgeted cost of work scheduled (BCWS): The sum of all (direct and indirect) estimated cost for a group of activities or tasks within a specific time frame.

C

CAPM®: Acronym for Certified Associate Project Manager. CAPM is an exam-based certification administered by the Project Management Institute.

Change Control Board (CCB): A group (members may be stipulated in a contract, Project Charter, or project management plan) that typically has the authority to accept, partially accept, or reject project changes above specific thresholds. A threshold example is costs above $50,000. Approved changes imply re-baselines to project plan elements such as the schedule, scope, and budget.

Contingency planning: Normally part of a risk management plan. Contingency planning dictates the response to one or more risk events.

Contingency reserve: Normally a percentage of the project budget set aside for planned and unanticipated events that can affect the outcome of a project.

Contract: As per the Guide to the PMBOK®, a contract is a mutually binding agreement that obligates both the seller and buyer. The seller provides a specified product or service that the buyer must pay for. Project managers typically work with one of three types of contract. These contract types are fixed price or lump sum, cost reimbursable, and unit price.

Contract closeout: Formal resolution or settlement of all contract issues. Typically represents the customer's acceptance that all contractual obligations have been fulfilled. It also represents the time at which all costs and charges are resolved.

Control: Actions taken or response mechanisms activated to address positive or negative changes to project plan elements.

Corrective action: Action taken to address changes to project plan elements in such a way as to realign the project activities to the project plan.

Cost budgeting: Allocating costs to budget elements such as budget line items, cost centers, activity codes, and purchases.

Cost control: Monitoring costs and, when appropriate, taking corrective or preventative actions to align expenditures with the project plan budget or cost baseline.

Cost estimating: Estimating the costs required to complete all or part of the project. This includes all human and material resource costs.

Cost of quality: Costs required to ensure quality. The costs are related to the project's quality plan (specific to the project) or the organization's quality management system (specific to a group of projects within a department or cost center).

Cost performance index (CPI): See the earned value management formulas in Table A.2.

Cost plus fixed fee (CPFF) contract: In this type of contract, the buyer is required to pay the costs approved in the contract. In addition to the approved costs, the buyer pays a prenegotiated contractual margin or fixed amount above the costs.

Cost plus incentive fee (CPIF) contract: In this type of contract, the buyer is required to pay the costs approved in the contract. In addition to the approved costs, the buyer pays an incentive fee. The elements required to constitute the incentive are stipulated in the contract.

Cost-reimbursable contracts: In this type of contract, the buyer is required to pay the costs approved in the contract. In addition to the approved costs, the buyer, typically, pays an incentive fee. The elements required to constitute the incentive are stipulated in the contract. In some cases, this is called a T&M contract. (T&M stands for Time & Materials.)

Cost variance (CV): The difference between estimated costs and actual costs for one or more activities. See Table A.2.

Costs: Costs may be direct; in some cases, such as contracts, they may include indirect costs as well. Examples of direct costs are amounts paid for materials or labor hours. Examples of indirect costs are the utility bills for the warehouse that stores the purchased materials or the rental costs for the staff charging labor hours to the project.

Crashing: Reducing the duration of a project by compressing the time required for as many activities and tasks as possible. Time compression may include early starts of activities without predecessor constraints. Time compression, in most cases, implies that it will be accomplished in the most cost-effective manner possible.

Critical activity: In the context of project management, any activity on a critical path using critical path methodology (CPM).

Critical chain (scheduling and buffer management): A relatively new, sometimes disputed, method used in developing project plans that include buffers.

Critical path: The sequence of activities within a project schedule with little or no float. In other words, if any of the activities on the critical path are delayed, it will adversely impact the end date of the project.

Critical Path Method (CPM): A technique employed to estimate which activity sequence contains the least amount of float or flexibility.

D

Deliverable: What the project manager "delivers" to the customer as required in the scope documents. A deliverable can be hardware, intellectual property such as software or reports. Deliverables may be measurable but, in some cases, may not be hardware or intellectual property. An example of this would be the performance criteria of a Web site. Deliverables may be generically viewed as work products.

E

Earned value: The budgeted cost of work performed.

Earned value management (EVM): See Table A.2. In plain English, it is a group of tools and techniques that allows the project manager to leverage the work breakdown structure, a resource-loaded schedule, and agreed-to ways to measure percent complete yielding meaningful metrics that gauge the health of the project and can help the team see trends that allow for preventative and corrective actions when needed. EVM takes the financial data from the resource loaded schedules and compares them with what has been done and what has been spent in different ways.

Effort: Effort as in "level of effort" (LOE). The amount of labor time units such as hours, days, weeks, or months required to complete an activity. It is important to distinguish between level of effort and duration. For example, the LOE to paint a room might be 16 man-hours, the time needed for the paint to dry might be an additional 12 h; in that case, the duration of the room painting activity is 28 h.

Estimate: Essentially a forecast of total hours or total costs. Forecasts may be qualified, such as order of magnitude, conceptual. Other estimate qualifiers include "preliminary," "within ±X%."

Estimate at completion (EAC): The *forecasted cost for the completion* of an activity, group of activities, or a project. Usually calculated by adding actual costs with estimate to complete. See Table A.2.

Estimate to complete (ETC): The expected *remaining* cost needed to complete an activity, a group of activities, or the project. See Table A.2.

F

Fast tracking: A technique for time compression. Implies adjusting the schedule so that, whenever possible, activities are overlapping.

Firm fixed price (FFP) contract: The buyer pays a contractually stipulated price for completion of the project's scope. The seller assumes the responsibility and risk for the costs required to complete the project's scope. The project's scope is contractually defined.

Fixed price incentive fee (FPIF) contract: Similar to a fixed price contract with the additional ability to receive a type of bonus called an *incentive* if performance criteria in the contract are met. For example, the incentive might be early completion.

Fixed price or lump sum: The buyer pays a contractually stipulated price for the completion of specific deliverables or services.

Float: Represents the amount of time that an activity or task may be delayed from its early start without adversely impacting the project's end date. Float may be referred to as *slack*.

Forward pass: A technique within the critical path method that facilitates the calculation, usually in a network activity diagram, of the project's end date by working forward from a predetermined start date.

G

Gantt chart: See Bar chart.

I

Integrated cost/schedule reporting: Can be gleaned from EVM formulas. See Table A.2.

L

Lag: Represents a time delay between two related tasks. For example, a successor task that can't start until 1 week (the lag period) after the predecessor task has been completed.

Level of effort (LOE): In most cases, the amount of work required for the completion of a task or activity. The Guide to the PMBOK® adds the following to this definition: "Support type activity (e.g., vendor or customer liaison) that does not readily lend itself to measurement of discrete accomplishment. It is generally characterized by a uniform rate of activity over a specific period of time."

Life-cycle costing: A holistic cost amount that covers the entire life cycle. For example, the cost of designing, building, maintaining, and disposing of a server.

M

Management reserve: A predetermined amount of time, cost, or materials that are set aside for unplanned and unknown future events. If management reserves are used, the corresponding project plan baseline elements must change as well to take this use into account. The creation of a management reserve is a way to proactively manage unknown risks.

Master schedule: In a program context, it is a schedule that rolls up all the constituent projects. It can also be a high-level project schedule. For example, a project schedule that is limited to milestones.

Matrix organization: Each member of the matrix has direct and indirect supervisors. For example, an engineer may directly report to a chief engineer and indirectly report to the project managers he or she supports. In this type of organization, the project manager negotiates for resources with functional managers.

Milestone: An activity or event that a project stakeholder views as important. More frequently, it designates the completion of a deliverable or project phase. Milestones can be used as decision (such as go or no go) points.

Milestone schedule: A type of schedule limited to showing just milestones. Project managers frequently use this type of schedule for customer meetings and presentations.

P

Parametric estimating: A way to estimate cost typically based on historical or known data. For example, the last three applications cost $5 for each line of code, as we anticipate having 10 lines of code for this project, we estimate that the cost will be $50. This technique is heavily used in the construction industry where there are commercial parametric databases.

Pareto diagram: A graphical representation that correlates results with corresponding causes. Typically, in a histogram broken down by frequency of occurrence.

PCA: Preventative or corrective action. A term that is quite important in project quality and quality management system plans.

Percent complete (PC): The amount of work completed on an activity or project. Typically, an estimated amount based on available information.

Performance reporting: Another term for reporting on the progress of a project or program.

Portfolio: A group of related projects (by project manager or by organization). This term is also applied to project management software applications.

PPOC: Primary point of contact. The individual, usually the project manager, with the authority to negotiate scope, schedule, or cost changes.

Program: A group of related projects managed in a coordinated way. Programs usually include an element of ongoing activity.

Program Evaluation and Review Technique (PERT): An event-oriented network analysis technique used to estimate project duration when there is a high degree of uncertainty with the individual activity duration estimates. PERT applies the critical path method to a weighted average duration estimate.

Project: As per the Guide to the PMBOK®, "a temporary endeavor undertaken to create a unique product or service."

Project charter: A document sponsored by senior management that defines a project and designates a project manager. The charter gives the project manager the authority to obtain and manage the resources needed to complete the defined project.

Project cost management: Part of what the project manager is responsible for, it is an integral element of the project plan. This includes planning, estimating, budgeting, and controlling. Earned value management formulas can facilitate some, but not all, of the associated processes.

Project life cycle: A series of phases that are defined to facilitate the management of a project. The definition of the phases is a function of the level of control desired by the organizational stakeholders.

Project management (PM): An integrated application of skills, methods, techniques, and tools to effectively manage the processes required to define and complete the project's scope. This requires an understanding of the knowledge areas and processes defined in the Guide to the PMBOK.

Project Management Body of Knowledge (PMBOK®): A term and acronym that covers the totality of knowledge needed to practice the profession of project management. This includes both theory and practice. The body of knowledge is dynamic, requiring academic research and continuing education. It is a practitioner-driven knowledge base supplemented by academic research.

Project Management Professional (PMP®): An experience- and examination-driven certification administered by the Project Management Institute. Maintenance of this credential requires continuing education.

Project management software: Any computer-based software application that helps the project manager and the project manager's organization to plan, execute, and control one or more projects. Typically, the software is focused on schedules, costs, and resources. The term *enterprise* software implies an application that works across multiple cost centers or departments with the functionality to provide performance and portfolio reports typically with data stored on a common server.

Project management team: The members of the project manager's team that influence or perform the work needed to complete the project

Project manager or Porject Management (PM): The individual empowered to lead and manage the work required to complete the project's scope. Responsible for managing a project or program.

Project phase: One part of the project life cycle. A project phase may end with either a deliverable or a milestone.

Project plan: A group of documented and approved planning elements required to execute and control the completion of a project. The number of elements is a function of the project's complexity.

Project plan development: Typically begins with a scope analysis and work breakdown structure (WBS), and includes the development of other project plan elements such as a risk management plan, project budget, project schedule, and may also include a Responsibility Assignment Matrix (RAM), organization breakdown structure, a project quality plan, a project communications plan, a project procurement plan, and ties them all together into an integrated planning document.

Project planning: The development, execution, and ongoing management of the project plan including its constituent elements.

Project procurement management: An element of the project plan that is focused on the procurement processes when goods and services are externally secured. The procurement processes include planning, solicitation, source selection, contract administration, and contract closeout. In some organizations, the contract takes the form of a purchase order.

Project quality management: An element of the project plan that includes quality planning, quality assurance, and quality control. In some companies, the project quality plan is supplemented by a quality management system that covers all projects.

Project risk management: An element of the project plan that identifies and responds to risks. Risk planning and management includes the following processes: identification, qualification, quantification, response planning, and risk monitoring and control. Risk identification may require root cause analysis. Risk responses include acceptance, avoidance, transference (deflection), or mitigation.

Project schedule: Typically drawn up after the development of a work breakdown structure and activity sequence diagram. It includes determination of the activity relationships and defines specific dates for the completion of deliverables and associated milestones.

Project scope management: An element of the project plan that includes scope planning, definition, validation, verification, and control. The control element includes the definition of a scope change management process, that is, part of a larger integrated change management process that links the scope change to all the corresponding elements of the project plan.

Projectized organization: A term that designates an organization that understands the efficiencies of project management and empowers the project manager. This empowerment includes the prioritization and management of resource regardless of the resource's originating functional department.

Q

Quality assurance (QA): The ongoing process of assessing project performance to assure conformance with quality standards. In some cases, this includes external project audits. In this context, "external" refers to a department that does not provide project managers or project team resources.

Quality control (QC): The ongoing process of evaluating the results of project activities and their application to related quality standards. Quality control includes root cause analysis and preventative and corrective actions. In some companies, quality control is a responsibility shared by the project manager and the manager of the organization's quality management system.

Quality management system (QMS): A comprehensive approach to ensure quality. A QMS may be compatible with approaches such as ISO, Six Sigma, and TQM.

Quality planning: In the context of project management, it is the development of a project quality plan that correlates to the quality standards applicable to the managed project and facilitates the project team's conformance to those standards.

R

Request for information (RFI): Formal interrogatory when responding to either a bid, an RFP, or RFQ. Typically, RFIs from multiple sources are combined and shared with all respondents.

Request for proposal (RFP): This is a mechanism whereby the buying entity asks the selling entity to submit a proposal, typically with cost information, as to how a project will be planned or how a problem or situation will be addressed. To facilitate uniformity of responses, the buying entity usually determines the format of the responses they will accept.

Request for qualification (RFQ): A tool to screen potential bidders or RFP responders. RFQs typically require firms to submit documentation to prove that they meet the criteria to subsequently bid or respond to a planned RFP.

Resource leveling: If the workload or availability of resources is a concern and the strategy to address this is by adjusting the schedule, the project manager is said to be leveling resources. Typically, an activity network analysis precedes any schedule changes.

Resource planning: As part of the project planning effort, the project manager determines the human and material resources needed to complete the project. This determination is referred to as *resource planning.*

Resources: They may be human or material. Human resources include project team members and supporting staff. Material resources include hardware, software, equipment, and supplies.

Responsibility Assignment Matrix (RAM): The result of a correlation between the project's organization breakdown structure (OBS) and the work breakdown structure (WBS). In lay terms, the RAM determines *who* will complete *what.*

Risk event: An occurrence that may affect the project or the project plan.

Risk identification: The process of determining potential events that may affect the project or project plan. Skilled project managers, when appropriate, employ root cause analysis to correctly identify the risk issue.

Risk qualification: A high-level assessment of the potential impact of a risk issue. For example, high, medium, or low impact.

Risk quantification: This has two elements: (1) It is the process by which the probability of the event's occurrence is calculated and (2) the process by which the impact, such as the dollar or time value, is calculated or evaluated.

Risk response control: This represents *how* risk events are managed inclusive of changes to the project plan.

Risk response development: Determining what activities and tasks can manage positive risk issues or help mitigate negative risk.

S

S-curve: A graphical display in which the *x*-axis represents time and the *y*-axis represents a value or quantity (such as project costs) against that time line. The S-curve occurs when a project starts slowly, accelerates, and then tails off.

Schedule control: The process by which the schedule is monitored and, when appropriate, revised. The schedule control process always attempts to align or realign the schedule to baseline.

Schedule development: An analysis of activities, taking into account their durations and relationships, with the intent of developing the most time and cost-effective sequence. In this context, the term *relationships* refers to SF (Start to Finish), FS (Finish to Start), SS (Start to Start), and FF (Finish to Finish).

Schedule performance index (SPI): The ratio of work performed to work scheduled. See Table A.2.

Schedule variance (SV): The difference (when it exists) between what has been scheduled (such as the completion of an activity) and the actual state. See Table A.2.

Scope: The totality of the project's deliverables and services with, when appropriate, their performance criteria that must be produced or completed.

Scope change: Any change to the project scope. Remember the Triangle of Truth—a change in scope almost always requires a change to the project's cost and schedule.

Scope change control: The process by which changes are managed. In other words, the process by which changes in scope are addressed in the remaining elements of the project plan.

Scope definition: Decomposing the deliverables into smaller components. Typically accomplished via a work breakdown structure.

Scope verification: The process by which the project manager confirms the completion of the project deliverables. Typically, as specified in a contract, the specification may include performance criteria.

Six Sigma: An approach to quality that may become part of a more comprehensive quality management system. Six Sigma relies on statistical and measurable results.

Slack: A term that is interchangeable with "float."

Statement of Work (SOW): A document that, among other things, describes the deliverables, products, and services that comprise the scope of work. See section titled "Statement of Work" (SOW) in Chapter 2.

T

Total Quality Management (TQM): An approach to ensure quality that focuses on the processes of an organization.

U

Unit-price contracts: Typically, the part of a contract. Unit prices specify the dollar value of specific deliverables. For example, the price to be paid for every server is handed over to the customer. In a service, it might be, for example, the billable hourly rate of a Project Management Professional or a Certified Associate Project Manager.

W

Work breakdown structure (WBS): A powerful tool that is almost always an essential part of the project planning process. As per the Guide to the PMBOK®, "A deliverable-oriented grouping of project elements that organizes and defines the total scope of the project. Each descending level represents an increasingly detailed definition of a project component. Project components may be products or services." See section titled "Work Breakdown Structures" in Chapter 2.

Work package: A deliverable at the lowest level of the work breakdown structure. The more defined the work package the easier it is to estimate the time and resources needed to complete the deliverable. Work packages can be further decomposed into activities and activities into tasks.

Workaround: The activities that respond to an unplanned risk event.

Technical ISP (Internet Service Provider) and Internetworking Terms

A

Access control: This element of a security policy determines access (as well as levels of access) to a server or network. Firewalls can be used to control such access.

Ad server: A component of an architecture that manages Web-based advertisements.

Address spoofing: This happens when a hacker discovers an Internet Protocol (IP) address and then uses it to simulate that location. This simulation may result in the hacker obtaining confidential information input by users who have been fooled into thinking they are in a real site. This is also known as *phishing*.

Application: Typically describes software. For example, MS Project may be called an application.

Application gateway firewall: Software known as a proxy on a firewall. The proxy receives Internet client requests and if consistent with its protocol will direct the transmission to an internal server. Telnet, FTP, and HTTP are examples of proxies.

Application layer firewall: A firewall designed to protect a network from a "masquerade" intrusion. Packet-filtering firewalls, in contrast, cannot protect it.

Audit: Represents a documented record of events or transactions. Some ISPs will keep records, such as traffic, for customers. Often, the audit is based on bastion host traffic.

Authentication: Verification that the entity attempting to communicate with a server, notebook, or desktop computer is the entity it claims to be. Username combined with password is an example of authentication.

Authorization: The process by which the access level of a user is determined. For example, one user may have access to public Web pages, and a different user may have access to internal Web pages along with the public ones. Authorization follows authentication effectively making this a two-step process.

B

B1 rating: A security rating from the trusted computing base. The B1 firewall is a sophisticated, compartmentalized arrangement that functions as follows: There are three software compartments. One communicates with the Internet, the second communicates with the business, and the third is a gateway that manages communication between compartments one and two. This arrangement effectively protects the network from intrusion from the Internet.

B2B commerce: A term that essentially means that the electronic Web-based traffic is between two businesses (business-to-business). Typically, this includes procurement and billing functions.

B2C commerce: This term represents electronic Web-based transactions between a business and a consumer. The purchase of a quality book, such as "*The Internet Project Manager: Practitioners Desk Reference*," on Amazon is an example of this.

Bastion host firewall: A type of "traffic cop" that addresses security and network communications. The bastion host manages authorization and authentication in order to manage traffic.

Bandwidth: A term used to describe how much information is being transmitted or received, or both. High bandwidth represents a high or large quantity of information.

Blind links: This is a link that intentionally leads you to a location different than the link you clicked on. More often than not, the redirect is done to advertise products and services. Some blind links connect you to sites that will attempt to automatically download an application to your computer.

C

Centralized authorization: A single entity that manages a database for the express purpose of controlling access to a server or network.

Certification authority (CA): This is an entity to authenticate users. This is done via a digital certificate that indicates that the user is, in fact, who he or she claims to be. There are organizations whose business is the issuance of digital certificates. Root certificate authority is the highest type available.

Channel service unit/data service unit (CSU/DSU): A piece of equipment that is essentially a digital modem that is needed for a network to communicate over telephone lines. It is typically located at single entry and exit points in the architecture.

Choke hub: Similar to a funnel that acts as the point of entry to a network. It can be useful as it can stop traffic when needed. This machine can intentionally shut down a bastion host, which effectively stops traffic. It is typically activated when site security is at risk.

Choke point: A location in the architecture that all traffic must pass through. It can serve as a monitoring or security point.

Committed information rate (CIR): A term that represents the data transmission rate within a frame relay connection.

Cookie: A kind of file written on the user's hard drive. It contains information about the user such as name and address that facilitates communication to a Web site. Users usually have the ability to accept or reject cookies. Some sites, nevertheless, may require cookies.

Credential: A credential is like an ID with a predetermined expiration date. A digital certificate is a type of ID that can last for months or x amount of years. Tickets are a different kind of ID with a substantially smaller life time. Ticket life may be measured in hours. In traffic between networks, each party may have to exchange credentials to enable duplex communication.

Customer network: This is simply the local area network (LAN) of a customer.

Customer premises equipment (CPE): Hardware that is located at a customer site. It may be simple modems or CSU/DSU modems. Architectures that include CPE, from a project management perspective, represent schedule dependencies.

Cyber cash: A term that describes an electronic payment such as the use of a credit card to pay for a product or service.

Cyber trust: An essential security tool that ensures the validity of transmitted information. It is also known as a Secure Socket Layer (SSL).

D

Data integrity: The assurance that the data transmitted between two points has not been corrupted or changed.

Data privacy: This addresses information confidentiality concerns between two points.

Denial-of-service attacks: A favorite of hackers wishing to intentionally damage a Web site. It is nothing more than the creation of overwhelming fake traffic that dramatically slows or shuts down a server's ability to respond to real traffic.

Dialer: A simple program that can dial a number from a computer.

Digital certificate: An electronic document that vouches for the originator of a message or transaction. It is similar to an ID card that verifies you are the person sending a message or request to a network.

Digital signature: Another way to authenticate the identity of the person sending data to a network. The digital signature is attached to a message. In some parts of the United States, documents such as contracts can be electronically signed, thus obviating the need for physical paper.

Domain name: The name of a Web site that matches a specific IP address.

Domain name hijacking: This is how hackers wreak havoc by redirecting traffic. Traffic that is intended to a domain's IP address is instead directed to a different site. Instead of, for example, connecting to IBM, you are redirected to Apple.

Domain Name Service (DNS): It provides an IP address that corresponds to a host/domain name.

E

Eavesdropping: As the term implies, individuals listen to transmissions that are not intended for them. The defense most used is the encryption and decryption of data. Encryption and decryption may be effected via software or embedded in hardware chips.

E-commerce: This is a term used to indicate the procurement of goods and services over the Internet.

E-mail: Electronic mail that has become ubiquitous. An advantage of e-mail is that it can be set to document communications. A disadvantage is that if not used correctly, it can become a source of miscommunication.

E-mail bombing: Similar to a denial-of-service attack. Hackers will overwhelm individual users or mail servers, which results in true messages getting lost and the e-mail server crashing.

Encryption: It is like sending information in a secret code. Only those that can decode the message are able to read it. Encryption is the coding of a message; decryption is the decoding of a message. This coding and decoding is done by using a "key."

End-to-end encryption: This is maintaining the encryption of messages as they pass through pipes and networks that are public in nature.

EquSant: An Internet service provider entity that facilitates access to POPs and helpdesks.

F

Fault-tolerant design: An architecture that has been designed to ensure continuity. It involves the creation of alternate routes and failover equipment and sites. This is done to minimize the impact on the users of a network.

File Transfer Protocol (FTP): A set of rules that facilitates the transfer of files from one location to another.

Filtering router: This is a router filtering Internet traffic between networks or specific hosts. Some firewalls are simply a screening router between your network and the Internet.

Firewall: A virtual wall that protects a network from unwanted intrusion. It can manage inbound traffic and protect individual users or corporate local area networks.

Frame Relay: A shared network connection to the Internet as contrasted with a private line.

Fraudulent purchases: This occurs when one individual uses the authorization of another to procure goods and services.

H

Human factors attack: When an individual is fooled into giving another person's authorization information such as a username or password. This is typically the result of a fraudulent telephone call.

I

Internet backbone: A fiber-optic or copper cable on which Internet transmissions flow. Internet service providers typically own this cable. The cable is frequently referred to as a *pipe* or *pipeline.*

Internet service provider (ISP): A company that provides access to the Internet. There are large ISP firms such as AOL and smaller ones such as Webjogger, both with the ability to provide high-quality service ISPs that typically offer associated products and services such as firewalls, load balancing, edge caching, Voice-over-IP (VoIP), virtual private networks (VPNs), and more.

Internetworking: As the name implies, this term refers to communications between networks or between a network and an individual user via the Internet.

Intranet: While the Internet is a *public* network, the intranet is a *private* one. It is different from other internal local area networks in that it uses a TCP/IP protocol.

Intrusion: An unwanted entry to a network, individual computer, or computing device.

IP address: A set of numbers that represent a location on the Internet.

K

Key: A program that can encrypt or decrypt a message. Keys can be public or private.

L

Local access: This refers to a *local* connection between an individual user and company to the Internet. We are using the term *local* in a telephony context: a telephone connection in or near your area code. This type of connection substantially reduces the cost of communicating over the Internet.

Local area network (LAN): A network composed of connections between computers and computing devices. It is used mostly by large organizations but can be employed by individual users. The communication through the connections between computers and computing devices is facilitated by protocols.

Local exchange carrier (LEC): A telecommunications industry term representing a local telephone company.

M

Masquerade: This occurs when a hacker enters a network or computing device via the Internet by pretending to be an authorized user. Once in the network the hacker can damage files, corrupt data, or install programs that can literally steal information and confidential data.

Modem: A physical device that enables communication between computers or computing devices to a network through a telephone connection.

V.90 56K modems: Modems can communicate at different speeds. 56 kilobits per second (kbps) is the fastest speed on a set of copper telephone wires. "V.90" is the name of a protocol that facilitates communication between 56 kbps transmissions or receptions using a 56K Flex protocol and the transmission or reception using a 56K X2 protocol.

N

Network administrator: An individual who is given specific responsibilities associated with a network. This may include one or more of the following: management of usernames and passwords, network configuration management, hardware repairs, software repairs, and security.

Network operations center (NOC): A facility that continually monitors a network with the capability to respond to problems. Typically, an operations center is staffed 7 × 24 (7 days a week, 24 h a day).

Network protocol: A set of rules coded in a software program that manages network communications.

Network spoofing: This term is equivalent to "masquerade" and means that an individual breaks through a firewall to cause damage or steal confidential information.

Nonrepudiation: An assurance that a user was the person initiating a transmission.

NT: An operating system (OS) created and sold by Microsoft for servers.

O

Operating system (OS): This is a primary application that the typical person uses. Other applications, such as MS Office, are installed on top of the OS. There are many operating systems manufactured by different companies.

Outlook: A software application to send or receive e-mail. This application is typically bundled in either MS Office or Windows.

Outlook rules: The Outlook application contains an interface that allows the user to determine how e-mails are managed. For example, if the e-mail is spam, the user can create a rule that automatically deletes e-mail from the person or company that sent you the unwanted e-mail.

P

Packet filter: A firewall designed to capture and review information packets based on set rules. The rules determine if the packets can pass through the firewall. This type of filter can work with other applications designed to secure a network.

Packets: This is a term used when measuring the amount of information being transmitted or received.

Password cracking: A program designed to steal a password. The stolen password is then used to penetrate a network.

Password sniffing: Another term for "password cracking" (see previous entry).

Peering point: Represents a location used by Internet service providers to cross-connect.

Perimeter security: Like a fence around property, it protects a network from unwanted intrusion. Perimeter security involves a combination of elements such as a choke hub with a firewall. Well-designed perimeter security allows authorized traffic to pass through, and stops unauthorized traffic from entering the network.

Permanent virtual circuit (PVC): A connection that a customer can use through a frame relay network.

Phisher: This term is equivalent to "Web spoofing." Web phishing is done by the creation of a fake Web site that mimics a real Web site when the public, attempting to go to a real Web site, enters a fake one. The person phishering can steal confidential information such as names, addresses, telephone numbers, social security numbers, passwords, and credit card numbers. Protection against phishering requires, at minimum, security authenticating software.

Ping of death: This occurs when a ping transmission carries too much information. This will cause a network to shut down or reboot. Routers can be programmed to stop some, but not all, oversized pings.

Point of presence (POP): A physical location within which Internet data is communicated to access lines or POPs that, in turn, allow communication from the Internet to the transmission's intended recipient.

Pop up: This is a type of forced advertisement that appears on Web pages. Blocking software exists to reduce this.

Pretty Good Privacy (PGP): A term used for an application that contains private keys that protect users from eavesdropping a transmission or penetrating a private file.

Principal: Entities employing a security system. "Entity" is defined, in this context, as either a user or a client–server application.

Protocol: Protocols have two elements: one is a written explanation of how messages should be formatted and the rules needed for devices to communicate, and the second element is the translation of the written protocol into software. The software enables communication between computers, computing devices, networks, and peripherals.

Proxy applications: A software program that is typically integrated into a firewall. A proxy represents a user that is attempting to communicate between his or her local area network and the Internet. This creates a type of barrier between the two systems. The Internet client, therefore, does not penetrate the user's network. Proxy applications typically operate from a server called a *proxy server.*

Public Key Infrastructure (PKI): This represents a security entity that contains a public and private key. This entity can, additionally, contain the following elements: digital certificates, authorized user lists, certificate authorities, and other security-related protocols.

R

Remote Access Dial-In User Service (RADIUS) Server: Typically, a set of servers that check each other's username and password. It operates as follows: a user logs in and the server on his or her end performs a database inquiry to see if the user has access rights; if so, a signal is sent to another RADIUS server, the receiving server performs a database inquiry to validate the incoming transmission access rights. After the user's access rights are confirmed in both RADIUS servers, a communication link is established. If either of the two servers determines that access is not authorized, the transmission is severed.

Root CA: The Root CA has the ability to issue digital certificates to non-Root Certification Authorities. A Root CA is viewed as a trusted source.

Router: This is a device that manages Internet traffic. It literally routes traffic to its proper location. A router may contain security elements. Additionally, routers can serve as a choke point, becoming *the* point of entry to a network.

Run book: A run book is a customer-specific document that contains contact information and technical documents such as the customer's architecture, security policy, and more that facilitate upgrades, maintenance, changes, and emergency repairs.

S

Screening router: This is a router filtering Internet traffic between networks or specific hosts. Some firewalls are simply a screening router between your network and the Internet.

Secure ID: A device that continually generates a random set of numbers. In addition to a user employing a password or PIN, he or she is than asked to input the numbers displayed on the Secure ID device. This protocol adds an additional security layer to a system. The random set of numbers is also known as a *token*.

Security perimeter: A security term that represents a security layer to protect a network from unwanted intrusion.

Security policy: This should represent a well-thought-out document that determines the following: who has access and to what elements of the network, how access is determined, which devices and applications will be installed, and how they will be configured. The security policy influences the architecture design and software protocols. A security policy should be determined prior to the installation of security measures.

Server: It is a kind of dedicated computer that can manage processes and procedures for a network. Servers are configured to perform functions such as file sharing, file transfers, bastion hosting, e-mail, and more, depending on the applications that are loaded.

Site server: This is a server configured to host Web sites and manage the transactions associated with the Web site.

SLA (service level agreement): An SLA is a contractual document that defines acceptable performance. An example of acceptable performance is a Web site that should be able to handle x amount of traffic or be available xy percent of time. Some SLAs contain financial penalties, for example, each time the site is down for more than 4 h, the monthly bill will be reduced by 10%. The better an SLA is, the more costly the service.

Smart card: This is simply a plastic credit card with a built-in computing chip.

Spam: Spam is unwanted e-mail that is usually designed to sell a product or service.

Streaming audio or video: There are two ways available to users if they wish to view or hear audio or video. One way is to access the file that has been downloaded on the user's machine. A second way is to view or hear the video as the file is being received from another server or the Internet. The second way is called *streaming audio or video*.

Super POPs: A physical facility managed by an Internet service provider. The purpose of the facility is to link to POPs that are located outside of the ISP's home country and connect them to their network.

System administrator: This position is similar to a network administrator except that it refers to a system within a network. An individual who is given specific responsibilities associated with a system. This may include one or more of the following: management of usernames and passwords, network configuration management, hardware repairs, software repairs, and security items such as firewalls.

T

T1: It is one of the many types of high-speed Internet connections. Other types are T3, which is faster; ISDN, which is slower; and cable model with a speed similar to T1.

TCP/IP: An essential Internet protocol.

Telecommuting: It is the ability of an employee to work from a remote location, be it home or a hotel room. The user connects to the network as if he or she was actually in the office. There are applications that facilitate the connection. Some of the applications are coupled with security measures.

Transaction pipeline: Connected to a commerce site server, a dedicated pipe that is used for public purchasing transactions such as buying a book from Barnes & Noble through the Internet.

Trojan horse: Analogous to the historical Trojan horse, this is a program that appears to be useful but actually causes harm.

Trusted gateway: This describes a high-security level firewall in a secure environment. To be called a *trusted gateway*, the system needs to receive a rating of B1 or higher. The B1 rating is based on the criteria of the trusted computing base.

U

Uninterruptible power supply (UPS): This is a piece of electrical equipment designed to ensure the continuity of power when the facility's incoming electrical feeder fails or its circuit breaker opens. Feeder circuits open when the circuit breaker trips. Trips can be caused by any of the following events: a voltage level that is above or below the nominal value or a current value that is above or below the nominal value. The out-of-nominal condition can have many causes, the ones that the UPS was primarily designed to address (in this ISP context) are brownouts and blackouts. The UPS stores electricity in batteries and, when the power fails, it continues to supply electricity from the batteries. The amperage hour rating of the UPS batteries determines how long it can continue to provide power. Some UPSs will only provide enough power to enable an orderly shutdown, whereas others can continue to provide power for a much longer period of time. In data centers, this time period is based on the failover time needed to initiate a generator that will continue to supply power until the feeder is restored. High-end UPSs are also used to condition power.

"Conditioning"* is done by routing the incoming feeder to the UPS, which then outputs electricity with consistent voltage and current levels. The conditioning prevents equipment damage due to spikes and sags. Data centers typically house high-end UPSs that conditions power and continues to provide power until a generator is in operation. The generator effectively replaces the electrical feed from the local utility. The importance of UPS can be appreciated when it is viewed in the context of the ISP's service level agreements. Like server banks, UPSs need to be installed in a location where the environmental envelope can be controlled. Typically, the environment is controlled to ensure low-temperature and low-humidity settings. The low temperature extends the life of electronic components and can improve their performance. The low-humidity setting protects the electronic components, both integrated and discrete from damage due to moisture.

UNIX: One of the operating systems that can be installed on servers.

V

Virtual private network (VPN): A VPN is an internal and private network that can operate within an external and public network. In other words, it is a network within a business that can only be used and accessed by authorized employees. What differentiates a VPN from a typical LAN is the use of the Internet. The VPN is created by placing devices at each end of a communication. The data that flows between the devices is secured by encryption.

---

* The circuitry of a UPS typically includes two types of conversion: converting AC (alternating current) to DC (direct current) and the reverse DC to AC. The former allows the device to receive AC power and store it as DC battery power; the latter allows the DC batteries to output AC power. During the conversion process, the UPS circuitry can filter out unwanted voltage or current fluctuations, thus providing clean power. Clean power avoids component damage due to spikes and sags.

Virus: A virus is a damaging program that can corrupt operating systems, files, or applications. In addition to damaging software, it can be designed to spread to other computers or servers. The spreading can be effected in many ways. These include accessing mailing lists and sending the virus to all the recipients or getting copied onto disks and CDs. When the disk or CD is opened on another machine, the virus is released and enters that machine. Viruses are more often than not transmitted as attachments to e-mails. Antivirus programs require maintenance. Maintenance takes the form of regularly downloading and installing new virus definitions. Additionally, some applications' security is maintained by downloading and installing patches written to enhance the application's security.

W

Web-filtering: Filtering is essentially restricting access to specified Web sites. An example of this is a business that will not allow employees to access public entertainment Web pages. Filtering can be done in two ways: one way is simply documenting and promulgating a policy that prohibits access to certain types of sites. The second way is by installing gating software. Some gating applications can also monitor and audit compliance of the policy.

Web spoofing: This is particularly malicious. Web spoofing is done by the creation of a fake Web site that mimics a real Web site. When the public, attempting to go to a real Web site enter a fake one, the person spoofing can steal confidential information such as names, addresses, telephone numbers, social security numbers, passwords, and credit card numbers. Protection against spoofing requires, at minimum, security authenticating software. This is also known as *phishing*.

Wide area network (WAN): A WAN is a network composed of smaller local area networks. WANs are created to facilitate communications between networks when the distance between them is great.

Wiretap: An Internet tap, similar to a telephone tap. In both cases, an unauthorized person is able to hear the communications taking place on the line. The monitored communications can be analyzed to provide intelligence on the network, and in some cases, the business using the network. In some cases, wiretapping is not passive and can actually enter the network and corrupt data.

Voice-over-IP (VoIP)/Telephony Terms

Table A.3 contains a glossary of VoIP and telephony terms.

Table A.3 VoIP/Telephony Terms

Term	Definition
Busy hour traffic	The time period during the day in which a telephone system handles the most calls.
Centrex	Centrex services closely approximate the features offered on a private branch exchange (PBX) and are sold on a fee basis by service providers and serviced from a local CO. Traditional Centrex services are based on Class 5 switches and require one physical telephone line per user telephone. With Centrex, there is no telephone system on the customer premise because the telephone company acts as the phone system.
Circuit switching	A switching system, used heavily in the telephone company network, in which a dedicated physical circuit path must exist between sender and receiver for the duration of the "call."
CLEC	Competitive local exchange carrier—CLECs are carriers, formed after the local communications market was deregulated, that provide telecommunications services in direct competition with ILECs. CLECs may provide a variety of services ranging from local, long-distance, and international telephone services to Internet access, cable TV, and video on demand.
CO	Central office—A CO is a telephone company facility within which all local telephone lines terminate and contains the equipment required to switch customer telecommunications traffic. It also connects customers to Internet service providers (ISPs) and long-distance services.
CODEC	Abbreviation for COmpression/DECompression and/or COding/DECoding. In terms of VoIP traffic, this refers to how packets carrying voice traffic are compressed for transport. CODECs include G.711, G.729, etc. G.711 is uncompressed voice traffic. As compression increases, throughput increases, but quality decreases.

(continued on next page)

Table A.3 (continued)   VoIP/Telephony Terms

Term	Definition
CoMIT	Configuration and Management for Internet Telephony—Developed by ISP to enable management of all network elements from a single device, which streamlines IOS upgrades, troubleshoots problems, and simplifies the changing of network elements at any time. CoMIT reduces the risk of configuration issues when ISP updates its network—interoperability is ensured. CoMIT enables ISP to deliver a scaleable service and contributes to the quality of network management.
CoS	Class of service—CoS is a methodology for delivering QoS. It is based on low-latency queuing through routers. ISP uses CoS to deliver QoS. MPLS is another method to deliver QoS.
CPE	Customer premise equipment—Equipment that resides on the customer's premises.
Delay	Delays in delivery of packets result from various factors, including network congestion, call setup, coding and decoding, buffering, translating, compression, and others. Postdial delay refers to the period of time after dialing and before a ringtone commences.
DID	Direct Inward Dial (also referred to as Foreign Exchange). To illustrate DID, consider this example: a bank with a call center in Iowa has customers in New York. To make it more convenient for customers to contact the call center, the bank has several New York numbers where customers dial a local exchange, which then routes the call to the call center in Iowa. The bank may have DIDs in many cities.
DTMF	Dual tone multifrequency—Tones generated when a button is pressed on a telephone, primarily used in the United States and Canada.

Table A.3 (continued)   VoIP/Telephony Terms

Term	Definition
E.164	ITU-T recommendation for an international public telecommunication numbering plan. Provides the number structure and functionality for the three categories of numbers used for international public telecommunication (national telephone services, global telephone services, and international networks). For each of the categories, it details the components of the numbering structure and the digit analysis required to successfully route the calls.
Erlang B	An Erlang is a unit of telecommunications traffic measurement. Strictly speaking, an Erlang represents the continuous use of one voice path. In practice, it is used to describe the total traffic volume of 1 h. Erlang B is the most commonly used traffic model, and is used to work out how many lines are required if the traffic figure (in Erlangs) during the busiest hour is known. The model assumes that all blocked calls are immediately cleared.
Failover	Failover occurs when a gateway determines that calls cannot be completed over the Internet Protocol (IP) connection and the PBX is instructed to send calls through the PSTN.
Gatekeeper	In the ISP VoIP network, gatekeepers provide the intelligence that manages routing of voice traffic. They also house and manage the dial plan. ISP's architecture is set up for least-cost routing. More generally, gatekeepers are components that provide address translation and control access for terminals and gateways, and also provide other services such as bandwidth management and locating gateways. A gatekeeper maintains a registry of devices in the network. The devices register with the gatekeeper at startup, and request admission to a call from the gatekeeper. Gatekeepers are located in the IP cloud at every point of termination to the PSTN or IXC.

(continued on next page)

Table A.3 (continued) VoIP/Telephony Terms

Term	Definition
Gateway	A special-purpose device that performs an application-layer conversion of information from one protocol stack to another. Gateways translate a TDM signal to an IP packet. Relative to the "intelligent" gatekeepers, gateways are "dumb," simply providing translation. Note that there are two types of gateways associated with voice service: CPE gateways and gateways located in the cloud. CPE gateways translate TDM to IP. Cloud gateways terminate calls to the PSTN/IXCs and also provide translation.
H.323	H.323 allows dissimilar communication devices to communicate with each other by using a standardized communication protocol. H.323 defines a common set of CODECs, call setup and negotiating procedures, and basic data transport methods. H.323 is the only standard in use and is proven for a wide range of IP telephony products. Most server-based gateways and existing gatekeeper devices, for example, are based on this standard.
ILC	Acronym for intra-LATA call.
ILEC	Incumbent local exchange carrier—ILECs are the Bell operating companies and independent telephone companies that had the exclusive right to provide local transmission and switching services prior to the Telecommunications Act of 1996. Due to deregulation of the local telephone market, ILECs now face competition from CLECs.
Inter-LATA call	Call that originates in one local access transport area (LATA) and terminates in another. This type of traffic used to be handled only by IXCs; however, the Telecommunications Act of 1996 opened the door for regional Bell operating companies (RBOCs) to terminate inter-LATA traffic once they met the 14 points outlined in the legislation.
Internet Telephony	Internet telephony is the real-time transmission of voice signals using IP over the public Internet.

Table A.3 (continued)   VoIP/Telephony Terms

Term	Definition
Intra-LATA call	Call that originates and terminates within the same LATA. It may be either a local call (originating and terminating within the same local calling area) or an intra-LATA toll call (within the same LATA yet requiring a long distance charge).
Jitter	Jitter is interpacket delay variance. It occurs as the result of VoIP packets arriving at inconsistent time intervals. Jitter is an important QoS metric for voice and video applications. It can be reduced by introducing a jitter buffer at the point of arrival as packets are translated back into analog. A jitter buffer essentially delays packet delivery slightly, allowing time for subsequent packets to arrive. Significantly delayed packets, beyond the time provided by the jitter buffer, are then dropped.
Landline	Terrestrial circuits, such as wire, fiber, or microwave, constitute landline technology.
LATA	Local access transport area—A LATA is a geographic region defined in the AT&T Modified Final Judgment. The United States is divided into 196 LATAs. After the AT&T divestiture, LATAs helped define the markets that LECs and IXCs were allowed to serve. LECs were allowed to terminate intra-LATA traffic, or traffic within a LATA, while IXCs terminated inter-LATA calls, or calls made from one LATA to another.
Latency	This average, in milliseconds (ms), of the time taken for a packet to cross a network can be thought of as the aggregate of delay. Network latency is the delay introduced when a packet is momentarily stored, analyzed, and then forwarded. Latency is increased when compression is applied to the data stream. Typical delay for a PSTN connection is 50 ms.
Leased line	Telephone line between two or more sites of a private network. Companies that rent leased lines pay a fixed monthly fee for leased lines that are available exclusively to the organization that leases them. Leased lines can be used to transmit voice, data, or video. They are also called *private* or *dedicated lines*.

(continued on next page)

Table A.3 (continued)   VoIP/Telephony Terms

Term	Definition
LEC	Local exchange carrier—Also known as ILECs, LECs formerly had the exclusive right to provide local transmission and switching services within their designated regions.
LNP	Local number portability—LNP refers to a customer's ability to keep the same telephone number when changing service providers, type of service, or location. Mandated by the Telecommunications Act of 1996, implementation of service provider portability was required in the top 100 metropolitan area networks (MANs) by the end of 1998.
MOU	Minutes of use—Voice telecommunications traffic is measured in terms of MOUs.
MPLS	Multiprotocol label switching—MPLS is a method of delivering QoS. It is a frame-based IETF-encapsulating protocol that facilitates the transport of different protocols, with a label that is swapped at different points in the network layer. This process enables quality of service (QoS) because it allows routers to assign network paths by class of traffic. MPLS bridges the area between switching and routing. CoS is another method of delivering QoS. Qwest uses MPLS to deliver QoS, while ISP uses CoS.
Off-net traffic	Voice traffic between two locations—one of which has Black Rocket Voice service, and one that does not.
On-net traffic	Voice traffic between two enterprise sites, both of which are enabled with Black Rocket Voice service.
Packet loss	The discarding of data packets in a network when a device (switch, router, etc.) is overloaded and cannot accept any incoming data at a given moment.
PBX	Public branch exchange—an in-house telephone switching system that interconnects telephone extensions to each other, as well as to the outside telephone network.
POTS	Plain old telephone service—POTS is a standard phone line like the one in a home, usually with DTMF or rotary dialing.

Table A.3 (continued)   VoIP/Telephony Terms

Term	Definition
Protocol	Formal description of a set of rules and conventions that govern how devices on a network exchange information. VoIP protocols include SIP and H.323.
PSTN	Public Switched Telephone Network—PSTN is the regular, ubiquitous telephone network.
QoS	Quality of service—prioritizes voice traffic over standard data traffic to minimize quality impairments, such as packet loss, latency, and jitter. CoS with low-latency queuing through routers is what ISP does to deliver QoS. CoS is a router-to-router method. Another method for delivering QoS is MPLS. MPLS is a network-based method. Qwest uses MPLS.
Quality impairments	Quality impairments include loss of payload, excessive delay, and jitter. These impairments can be minimized by providing preferential treatment to voice payload over other types of traffic, thus leading to a QoS for the voice traffic.
SIP	Session Initiation Protocol—SIP is a standard promoted by Columbia University and a number of vendors, including MCI WorldCom. SIP allows the softswitch to communicate with application servers and other softswitches. It can also be used for communication with a client-end device. SIP is compatible with MGCP and H.248 but is competitive with many aspects of H.323.
SMDS	Switched Multimegabit Data Service—a high-speed switched data communications service offered by the local telephone companies for interconnecting LANs in different locations. It was introduced in 1992 and became generally available nationwide by 1995. Data is framed for transmission using the SMDS Interface or initiation Protocol (SIP), which packages data as Level 3 Protocol Data Units (L3_PDU).

(continued on next page)

Table A.3 (continued)   VoIP/Telephony Terms

Term	Definition
Softswitch	A softswitch is a device, often embedded within a carrier gateway switch, that provides call control and routing functions for network voice and data traffic. It can also serve as a platform for service creation capability and must have carrier-class features such as scalability, support for multiple applications, and SS7 capability. Softswitches are sometimes referred to as *media gateway controllers* or *call agents*.
SS7	Signaling System 7—an addressing protocol that speeds up call processing by operating out of band. SS7 provides capabilities such as fraud detection, caller ID, store and forward, ringback, concurrent data, and so on.
TDM	Time division multiplexing—TDM is used in PSTN. It is a technique in which information from multiple channels can be allocated bandwidth on a single wire based on preassigned time slots. Bandwidth is allocated to each channel regardless of whether the station has data to transmit.
Telecommunications Act of 1996	This legislation, passed by Congress, sought to increase competition in the telecommunications market. The act encouraged LECs to further compete in their local markets in exchange for the opportunity to provide long-distance service. It outlined 14 points that LECs had to meet to prove that their local markets were open to competition. Once these points were met, they could begin to offer long-distance service within their regions. The legislation also required local providers to implement local number portability in large metropolitan regions.
Unified messaging	Unified messaging functionality allows users to access e-mail, voicemail, and fax messages through single mailboxes, either through the telephone or through a Web interface. Users can listen to their e-mail over the phone using TTS technology, as well as send voice and fax messages over the phone as attachments to e-mails. The Web interface typically enables subscribers to check all types of messages; sort, copy, send, and save them; initiate calls; and manage other aspects of their accounts.

Table A.3 (continued)   VoIP/Telephony Terms

Term	Definition
VAD	Voice activity detection—When enabled on a voice port or a dial peer, silence is not transmitted over the network, only audible speech is. When VAD is enabled, the sound quality is slightly degraded, but the connection monopolizes much less bandwidth.
VoIP	An acronym for Voice-over-IP. Using an Internet connection for voice communication.

Index